Practical Guide
to Garden Design

The TIME LIFE
Complete ☀ Gardener

Practical Guide
to Garden Design

By the Editors of Time-Life Books
ALEXANDRIA, VIRGINIA

The Consultants

Yunghi Choi Epstein is co-owner and design director of Lawson Carter Landscape Design in Washington, D.C., which specializes in residential garden design and the preservation of historic gardens. She has directed over 50 projects in Texas, Maryland, Virginia, and Washington, D.C., and provides consultation on garden renovation and maintenance. She holds an M.A. in landscape architecture from Harvard University Graduate School of Design, and has taught landscape architecture and garden design at George Washington University.

Nan Booth Simpson practices residential landscape design in Portland, Oregon, serving clients throughout the West. She is the author of *Great Garden Sources of the Pacific Northwest* (1994) and is at work on a similar book for Texas. She was contributing editor of *Southern Accents* (1985-1993) and associate garden design editor for *Southern Living* (1981-1983), and a contributor to *Garden Design* and *Landscape Architecture* (1989-1994). She has served on landscape advisory boards in Virginia, Texas, Washington, and Oregon.

Library of Congress Cataloging in Publication Data
Practical guide to garden design / by the editors of Time-Life Books.
p. cm.—(The Time-Life complete gardener)
Includes bibliographical references (p.) and index.
ISBN 0-7835-4111-2
1. Gardens—Design. 2. Landscape gardening. 3. Plants, Ornamental.
I. Time-Life Books. II. Series
SB473.G285   1996   712'.6—dc20   96-157   CIP
© 1996 Time Life Inc. All rights reserved.

First printing. Printed in U.S.A.
Published simultaneously in Canada.
School and library distribution by Time-Life Education, P.O. Box 85026, Richmond, Virginia 23285-5026.

TIME-LIFE is a trademark of Time Warner Inc. U.S.A.

This volume is one of a series of comprehensive gardening books that cover garden design, choosing plants for the garden, planting and propagating, and planting diagrams.

Time-Life Books is a division of **TIME LIFE INC.**

PRESIDENT and CEO: John M. Fahey Jr.

TIME-LIFE BOOKS

Managing Editor: Roberta Conlan

Director of Design: Michael Hentges
Editorial Production Manager: Ellen Robling
Director of Operations: Eileen Bradley
Director of Photography and Research:
John Conrad Weiser
Senior Editors: Russell B. Adams Jr., Janet Cave, Lee Hassig, Robert Somerville, Henry Woodhead
Library: Louise D. Forstall

PRESIDENT: John D. Hall

Vice President, Director of New Product Development:
Neil Kagan
Associate Director, New Product Development:
Quentin S. McAndrew
Marketing Director: James A. Gillespie
Vice President, Book Production: Marjann Caldwell
Production Manager: Marlene Zack
Quality Assurance Manager: Miriam Newton

THE TIME-LIFE COMPLETE GARDENER

Editorial Staff for *Practical Guide to Garden Design*

SERIES EDITOR: Janet Cave
Deputy Editors: Sarah Brash, Jane Jordan
Administrative Editor: Roxie France-Nuriddin
Art Director: Kathleen D. Mallow
Picture Editor: Jane A. Martin
Text Editor: Paul Mathless
Associate Editors/Research-Writing: Sharon Kurtz, Mary-Sherman Willis
Technical Art Assistant: Sue Pratt
Senior Copyeditor: Anne Farr
Picture Coordinator: David A. Herod
Editorial Assistant: Donna Fountain
Special Contributors: Cyndi Bemel, Jennifer Clark, Susan Gregory Thomas (research); Catriona Tudor Erler, Rosanne C. Scott, Olwen Woodier (research-writing); Marie Hofer, Ann Perry, Margaret Stevens (writing); Lynn Yorke (editing); John Drummond (art); Lina B. Burton (index).

Correspondents: Christine Hinze (London), Christina Lieberman (New York).

Cover: Apricot roses, golden barberry, and soldierly spires of foxgloves are among the plants that flank a grassy path through this rural Maryland garden. The wooden gate at the path's end beckons toward further delights. **End papers:** *From every seat on this North Carolina patio visitors can enjoy plantings that include rudbeckia, daylily, purple coneflower, purple smokebush, hydrangea, and viburnum. Rocks edging the beds echo the stone wall surrounding the patio.* **Title page:** *Lush plantings of azalea, bougainvillea, lacefern, and southern sword fern, fronted by pink and white impatiens, create a screen of privacy for this California terrace.*

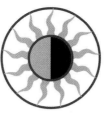

Designing Your Garden

Because gardens are made up primarily of living things, they are places of constant change. The daily patterns of sun and shadow, the plants' seasonal burgeoning and receding, and their steady growth over the years make for an ever shifting vista of shapes, textures, and colors.

Designing a garden with these variables in mind while also fulfilling your aesthetic vision can be a challenge. And when you factor in such practical considerations as how you intend to use the garden and any difficulties presented by the contours of the land, a carefully conceived plan becomes a necessity. In the Maryland garden at right, for example, a problematic slope has been transformed into a patio garden. Besides providing a lovely spot for entertaining and relaxing, the garden links the house with a meadow in the background through the use of ornamental grasses and other plants with relaxed habits. On the following pages you will learn how to design a garden that will suit your needs and desires even as it enriches your life and increases the value of your property.

The key lists each plant type and the number of plants needed to replicate the garden shown. The letters and numbers above refer to the type of plant and the number sited in an area.

A. *Euphorbia palustris (3)*
B. *Polygonum virginianum 'Painter's Palette' (20)*
C. *Maackia amurensis (1)*
D. *Sinarundinaria nitida (1)*
E. *Elaeagnus umbellata (1)*
F. *Miscanthus sinensis (1)*
G. *Yucca filamentosa (10)*
H. *Magnolia virginiana 'Hicksii' (10)*
I. *Liriope spicata (1)*
J. *Begonia grandis (1)*
K. *Sedum x 'Autumn Joy' (30)*
L. *Iris sibirica (10)*
M. *Geranium macrorrhizum 'Spessart' (5)*
N. *Euonymus kiautschovica 'Manhattan' (20)*
O. *Typha angustifolia (1)*
P. *Thalia dealbata (1) and Marsilea drummondii (5) mixed*

Planning for Outdoor Living

Your garden should make as important a contribution to your home life as your house, and its design deserves the same careful attention given your interior decor. Like your house, the garden can be a source of pleasure and relaxation. It can express your interests and tastes. And by projecting beauty and interest to the passing public, it can be an asset to your community.

To design such a space successfully, follow the steps that landscape architects do. First, ask yourself some questions to determine your wants and expectations for a garden. Next, take a discerning look at your property. Then, assess the potential for improvement—what can be upgraded, what should be replaced, what is fine just as it is. Finally, decide on a style *(pages 18-21)*. At that point you are ready to plan—first the hardscape (terraces, walkways, and the like), then the plant choices and the planting arrangement.

Executing a good garden design takes time. A garden will evolve as it matures, changing character as plants grow taller and broader. While this is going on, your needs and interests may change as well. At some point you may have to hire a professional for difficult jobs such as earth grading or tree removal. You might also need to implement your design in stages so you don't break your budget. Fortunately, the design process does not have to be rushed. You can give yourself plenty of time to make the right choices. Begin by asking a basic question:

What Is a Garden?

A garden is fundamentally a humanized outdoor space, an idealized form of the natural landscape. The term *garden* can sometimes mean a discrete planting, such as a perennial border or a vegetable patch. At other times it can refer to an entire property as the object of a comprehensive garden design.

A garden can occupy various locations in relation to the house. It can be on a remote part of the property, as might be typical of a vegetable or cutting garden. Or it can be adjacent to the house—a kind of outdoor room. And, of course, it can encompass all the grounds, including the house itself.

In practice, most properties are made up of more than one garden, each in its own space, according to its use. The individual gardens are then linked into a whole by a unifying network of pathways and sightlines.

Rewards of a Good Design

By linking all parts of your property with the house, a well-designed garden will increase your living space. Various areas will become cherished parts of daily life as places to entertain, play, or relax in comfort and safety. The sense of security afforded you by your house will extend to the surrounding property.

The character of your neighborhood can be a starting point for design decisions. You may want to block a sightline to a neighbor's property or frame a distant view. The style of your house and the history of your area are other possible cues. To complement a 19th-century southern farmhouse, for example, a dooryard flower garden surrounded by a white picket fence, with a stone path leading from fence to door, might be just right. Or you may be influenced by the local ecology, choosing plants to either attract or repel wildlife.

But your garden could also be designed to satisfy less tangible impulses—to create a mood, conjure up memories, or express certain ideals. You might be inspired by the soft feel of pine needles underfoot or the fluttering of swarms of butterflies on a butterfly bush. Such ideas can be the beginning of a highly satisfying garden plan.

Deciding What You Want

Your first step is to assemble a wish list of attributes for your garden. For most people, the top priority is year-round interest. It is a good idea to study your site first in winter to get the clearest idea of its structural framework—the hardscape, made up of imposed features such as walks and fences; and the softscape, composed of trees, shrubs, and ornamental grasses. Another important criterion for most gardeners is conservation—of energy, money, and natural resources. This means devising a plan that minimizes mow-

A DESIGN FOR SUMMER COLOR, WINTER FORM
In summer, a climbing rose scrambles up an arched trellis gateway in this Connecticut garden, drawing the eye also to the tall stand of globe thistles and deep orange Asiatic lilies surrounded by a sweep of English lavender. The fine foliage of Artemisia and Dianthus adds texture and cooling shades of green to the scene. In winter (inset), the underlying plant framework of the garden emerges, including the hedge of evergreen eastern hemlocks that marks the border.

ing, watering, fertilizing, weeding, and pruning, and choosing plants that have proved themselves.

Although the design of your house will directly affect the design of your garden, you should also consider the garden's effect on the house. Shade trees, for example, can reduce the cost of cooling your house. On the other hand, some plants can be destructive and should be grown away from the house. A wisteria vine, for example, can pull down your gutters. And tree limbs overhanging your roof can come crashing down in a storm.

Consult the other members of the family who will be using the garden. What kind of play area will the children want? Do you want a cook's garden with fruits, vegetables, and herbs? Also con-

sider the kinds of pets you have and what their impact may be on a garden.

If you have particular horticultural interests, look for suitable places to realize them—a stony slope for a rock garden, a soggy area for a bog garden, a south- or east-facing wall for an attached greenhouse. The site itself will suggest intriguing possibilities to add to your wish list.

Assessing Your Property

The next step is to make an informal survey of your property. Eventually, you will need to make detailed sketches and keep a record of your ob-

servations *(pages 30-35),* but at this stage you should only be taking an overall look at the site.

Start beyond its boundaries. From here you will see the public face of your property. Walk or drive past and try to look at the site with the eyes of someone encountering it for the first time. Is the house open to view or shrouded by trees? Is the entryway welcoming or obscured by shrubs? What kind of impression does the garden make, and is it harmonious with the architecture of the house?

Ask your neighbors for permission to walk your boundary line from their side, and look at your house from their point of view. From here you'll see what privacy screening you may want or need. Then go inside your house and look out each window and door. From this vantage you'll see opportunities to feature certain sightlines. Inspecting the grounds from upstairs windows is particularly revealing of patterns that are not otherwise apparent. Areas visible from important viewpoints such as a picture window in the living room or the window over the kitchen sink are obvious spots for a garden.

The view from a door might reveal a destination—an inviting, sun-dappled bench, for example—and the passage toward it should begin with a comfortable transition space to the outdoors, such as a wide landing with a pathway leading to a patio or to another part of the garden. You might decide that it is worth enlarging a window or replacing a small door with wider French doors to give the house better views to the garden.

Developing Focal Points

As you explore the views on your property, you will discover eye-catching spots you may wish to feature. These will be the focal points on which to base your garden design.

Focal points occur wherever sightlines intersect. They usually lie within the property but sometimes occur beyond it. In the front of the house, for instance, the focal point is the entranceway, where the strong vertical lines of the front door meet the horizontal of the threshold. In a landscape, a focal point will exist where the curve of a path disappears around a row of shrubs or the corner of a house. It could also be an imposing feature beyond your boundaries—a graceful tree or a pond, perhaps.

The sightline leading to a focal point is known as an axis, and your garden may have more than one. An axis creates movement in the garden, inviting the eye to follow it to the focal point. Together, axes unify the design by linking the viewer

A TERRACE ENCLOSURE IN BRICK
The metal wall sculpture at the rear of this elegant circular terrace garden in New Orleans provides a dramatic focal point that beckons a visitor. Twin pillars topped with geraniums, as well as the potted palms at the entrance, frame the view and strengthen the axis.

to all its parts. These links can be strengthened in several ways. First, a focal point itself will become more prominent if an object or a plant is placed there, or if it is framed or enclosed. Also, an axis will be accentuated if a pathway is built along it and the line enhanced with plantings. For instance, the focal point of a view from a patio might be a small flower bed. Adding a flagstone walk from the patio to the bed and framing the view with a pair of vertical shrubs or an arched trellis will create a unified arrangement.

Moving through the Garden

Just as you surveyed your property from the vantage points of the street and the house, you should also stroll through the garden itself to find existing or potential focal points. These will become destinations, and the axes leading to them will become pathways rich with a sense of anticipation.

You can best create this delightful effect by establishing a series of spaces, or rooms, that are either open or closed, beginning with the enclosed space of the house, moving away from the house, and then back again. For example, a network of axes might start from the living room, conveying the visitor through sliding glass doors to the deck, then across a lawn to an intimate shade garden with a hammock under a tree, then over to a sunny, open vegetable garden, and finally back to an herb garden beside the kitchen door.

A garden subdivided into such separate rooms, each with its own character, is both inherently interesting and functional. As in a house, each space has its own purpose: A sunny corner near a hedge might be a retreat; the open lawn, a playing field; the patio, a place for dining alfresco.

Traffic circulation through the garden is important not only in practical terms but also as it affects your experience of the garden. You can manipulate the speed of circulation by the way you design pathways, stopping places, and landmarks. For instance, a walk along a narrow, winding path bordered with interesting flowers is likely to be slower than one along a straight, wide path crossing a lawn. Gates at transition points and steps built into a sloping path also affect the pace of your walk, forcing you to slow down and take in the scene.

Finally, it is the stopping places—a deck, patio, walled courtyard, clearing, or shady bench overlooking a view—that lend a garden a feeling of shelter and restfulness. Be sure to have several such stops on your garden journey, and keep them separate and discreet so that they are a pleasure to rediscover each time you arrive.

The Principles of Design

Historically, gardeners have relied on certain widely accepted conventions of design to organize the landscape around them. These visual "rules" convert the landscape to human proportions, producing a feeling of security and purpose in what might otherwise seem an ungovernable wilderness. Properly applied, they bring the garden space together, knitting the parts into a harmonious whole and maintaining interest by juxtaposing contrasting elements. Professional landscape designers base their work on these concepts, but they also take inspiration from natural forms, acknowledging that the garden they create is a partnership with nature.

Unity

The first governing principle of garden design is unity—the perception that all the elements of the garden have coalesced into a coherent composition. These elements include the materials and plants used to build a garden and their positions relative to each other.

You can achieve unity in several ways. First, the house and the garden should complement each other in style. For example, a Federal house typically would be surrounded by a formal garden *(pages 18-19)*. Further, the materials of the house and the garden should be similar. If a house is built of brick, unity is furthered when the garden walls are also brick. By the same token, a rustic wooden house is enhanced by a wooden fence.

The materials you use should also be compatible with the land itself. In a seaside garden on a granite shore, for example, you might use a similar rough stone for the retaining walls. You might even incorporate some large stones into the design of a flower border.

Another approach to establishing unity is to repeat an existing line, form, texture, or color in

HOUSE AND GARDEN UNIFIED BY STYLE
The cottagelike feel of this house in southern California, painted Colonial blue with white shutters, is matched by the plain picket fence and backyard border of 'Heritage' climbing roses, pinks, pansies, and Mexican bush sage. A path of irregular paving stones and a venerable shade tree complete the picture.

your design. You could mirror the curve of a dramatically arched doorway in the contour of a flower bed or the rounded edge of a patio. Repeating a foliage or flower color is a familiar device to tie together the design of a border. Such visual rhythms, as with musical rhythms, carry you from one point to another in a composition.

And, of course, you strengthen the unity of your design by providing strong focal points to orient the parts of your garden to one another.

Simplicity

Although choosing between simplicity and intricacy may seem a matter of taste, simplicity has proved to be not merely a design approach but a fundamental virtue. Human beings have a need for a certain amount of order and clarity, and by keeping your design simple and straightforward you answer that need. Too much ornamentation, too many focal points, too great a variety of plants and other materials can create an impression of restlessness and confusion. Even if you're design-

ing a garden that is meant to perform many functions for many people, try to keep it simple. You can isolate each function from the others with screening plants and provide a clear circulation pattern so that visitors easily understand how to get from one part of the garden to another.

Proportion and Scale

Proportion is the size relationship among parts of a whole—the dimensions of one tree, for example, seen against the size of a grove of trees. Scale is the measurement of one object or space in relation to another. In a garden, we relate the size of objects and spaces primarily to the size of our own bodies. By that measure, the plants in a rock garden are tiny and a redwood tree is huge.

Designers understand that the principles of proportion contribute to the mood of a garden. For example, if the height of the largest vertical element in a garden, such as a wall or a fence, is more than half the width of the garden itself, the space will feel oppressively constraining. There

WORKING WITH LIGHT AND DARK
The contrast between the bright openness of the lawn and the darkness of the shady patch under the river birch adds weight and dimension to the streamside plantings in this Charlottesville, Virginia, garden. Cheerful splashes of yellow 'Hyperion' daylilies glow next to the dark Hosta sieboldiana 'Elegans'. The stream itself cuts through the greensward like a shiny black ribbon.

13

fore, in a small city garden surrounded by apartment buildings,
it would be wise to plant small
trees and shrubs that are in proportion to the garden's dimensions to counteract the looming
effect of the tall buildings. On the
other hand, if your garden reaches out in a vast
expanse from your house, then a space enclosed
within vertical human-scale elements—a trellised
wall or a hedge—provides a welcome sense of
intimacy and security.

Human scale is not the only measuring stick in
matters of proportion. Every garden composition
will consist of objects related to one other by size.
The flowers in a border are usually arranged by

height, for example, with the tallest in the back
and the shortest in the front; a widely accepted design principle is that the tallest should be no taller
than half the depth of the border. Your house is an
important determinant of scale; the trees and
structural elements around it should neither over-
power it nor be diminished by it.

The size of an object is also relative over distance. This can be a useful tool for manipulating
space. The farther an object is from the viewer, the
larger it must be to be seen clearly. For a flower
garden to make an impact at a distance, for example, it should be at least half as wide as the distance between the viewer and the garden.

Study the relative size of every object and plant
in your garden to find a balance that pleases you.

You will notice that the combinations you like will tend to be harmonious—composed of related forms, textures, and colors.

Harmony and Contrast

When the elements of your garden are similar to one another they are harmonious. Closely related colors, comparable textures and forms, and similar qualities of line "sound" together like the musical tones that make a chord. If two objects or plants are too much alike, however, they are unable to create harmony; they blend and lose their separate identity or perceptibility. Thus, the garden designer faces a paradox: For elements to be

The Delights of Water

A water feature such as a pool, a fountain, or a stream adds much to a garden and can be a mesmerizing focal point. The quiet music of trickling and burbling masks unwanted background noises and creates a touch of the countryside even in the middle of the city.

If you don't have a natural water feature on your property, it is relatively easy to build one *(pages 71-73)*. You can simulate a stream or a waterfall by using a simple recirculating pump to draw water from a pool to a higher point where it will run down in a rivulet. The pool below, in Missouri, is built to look like a stream flowing and splashing through a rock outcrop at a meadow's edge. Dotting the rocks are colorful native plants such as yellow Ozark sundrops and rosy poppy mallow. Pink prairie phlox and lance coreopsis, behind the phlox, also do well in the fast-draining rocky soil.

This pool's irregular shape, rough materials, and native plants harmonize with the naturalistic design of the garden. In a more formal design, water's refractiveness can create a further symmetry within the geometry of the garden. A formal rectilinear, round, or oblong pool uncluttered by anything but the simplest arrangement of water lilies or a central fountain can act like a glimmering mirror. If you lack the space for such a pool, try a wall fountain that trickles a stream of water into a basin.

harmonious, they must contrast with each other in some way. An all-white flower garden, for instance, can only be harmonious when it is composed of different flower forms or textures that contrast with one another.

In garden design, try to achieve a balance between harmony and contrast. Too much contrast becomes chaotic; too much harmony becomes bland. Begin by juxtaposing open and enclosed areas. Think of your garden as space, and the structures and blocks of plantings as the solid elements within that space. Balance the proportion of empty and solid spaces and carefully plan how they will flow together and connect.

Similarly, the alternations of light and shade in the garden create an interesting contrast. They can be used to subdivide the space into discrete areas, each with its own purpose, such as a shady deck for reading and relaxing, a sunny area for a

swimming pool, a dappled woodland for strolling. At night, skillfully arranged artificial lighting can carve out still other spaces in the garden.

Harmony and contrast also figure in the selection and arrangement of plants *(pages 78-95)*. Most important for the purposes of design is a plant's form, or habit. Most plants are round, prostrate (or carpeting), vase shaped, arching, conical, or columnar. Each shape produces a different effect in combination with other plants to make a coherent design. Planting arrangements draw the eye from place to place, emphasizing axes and focal points and reinforcing the overall design.

But don't omit the other senses from your planning. The contrast between the feel of grass and that of moss along a woodland path, the sudden pungency of a rosebush in bloom, and the gentle sound of a burbling fountain help enrich the garden experience.

Natural Patterns

With gardens that are ornamental versions of the natural landscape, it is logical to look to nature for basic shapes when designing them. One of these shapes is the meandering stream. This is a sweeping curve that repeats itself and often includes clusters of vegetation on the outward side of each arc or on an island within the stream. In a garden, such a shape could be used for pathways, beds, and even a deck or patio, mimicking the place in nature where a blockage in a stream has widened it into a pool.

There are rarely any hard edges or boundaries in the natural world. Areas of contrasting texture are more likely to merge into each other. You might think of this principle when you blend the edge of a patio into a lawn, perhaps by using sections of flagstone matching those of the patio to begin a pathway

PLANTS IN SCALE TO SUIT THE SITE
In this San Francisco terrace garden attached to a one-story house, a eucalyptus tree provides midsummer shade. The white 'Alister Stella Gray' rose will reach only to the roof, and the musk rose 'Ballerina', between the chairs, grows just high enough to waft its fragrance to anyone seated there.

Visual Devices for an Illusion of Space

To create the illusion that a small garden is larger than it really is, designers use optical tricks. They manipulate the scale of the plants and objects along the axis to a focal point and reshape the spaces within the garden. If you have a small or awkwardly shaped lot, one or more of these devices might work for you:

• Place large objects in the foreground and small ones at a distance. For example, front your patio with large planters and place smaller pots at a focal point at the back. Decrease the size of paving blocks as they recede to the rear.

• Group plants by size and texture. Position those with large leaves up close, those with finer foliage at the back. As a rule, decrease the leaf size by half for each planting along the axis to a focal point.

• Simulate the perception that parallel lines converge toward a focal point by slightly tapering a pathway, lawn, or pool so that it narrows at the far end.

• Place repetitive vertical elements along the axis to a focal point, shortening the intervals between them as they approach the focal point.

• Use a hedge, trellis, or bed to partially block the view to a focal point.

• Subdivide your garden and make strong transitions from one space to another.

AN ARCHWAY TO NOWHERE
Several visual tricks in this Massachusetts garden—bright colors and large foliage up front, a mirroring symmetry to strengthen the archway focal point, and a tapering lawn—suggest a large plot leading into the woods. In fact, it ends just behind the row of hemlocks.

onto the lawn. Or, at a transition to a woodland, you could plant a small grove of trees just at the edge of the woodland to welcome you in.

In nature, plants and rocks tend to cluster. Do the same with your arrangements, whether you have a group of trees at a focal point, perennials in a bed, rocks in a rock garden, or bulbs naturalized in a lawn. The clusters will eventually merge into drifts and come into contact with one another.

Finally, plants in nature grow at different levels. This establishes a layered pattern that you can mimic in your garden. Tall trees will create a top layer or canopy. Under this canopy, you can plant smaller shade-tolerant trees and shrubs typical of a shady understory. At the lowest level will be flowers and ground covers. Such a design is inherently unified and harmonious.

The Elements of Style

A garden may have a certain character or style, just as houses do. Styles have historical associations, but they are also influenced by regional cultures and growing conditions. Your first consideration should be to keep the style of your garden in harmony with that of your house. Next, take into account climate, soil, and the lay of the land. In fact, many popular garden styles have developed over the years specifically to address regional environmental conditions.

But the style you choose should not be the result of practical considerations alone. Your taste, your sense of beauty, and your ideals are the stylistic influences that will make a garden distinctively yours. Thus you might juxtapose different styles in your garden to appeal to facets of your personality and your interests and to create stimulating contrasts. The style designations that follow are only an indication of the range of possibilities.

Formal and Informal Gardens

A house with a strong classical design calls for the strong axes and crisply defined focal points of a formal garden. Building materials such as brick or stone block look appropriate in a formal setting.

Formal gardens are boldly geometric in structure. Straight lines, simple curves, precise angles, and clean edges all contribute to a formal feeling. The plants in these gardens are arranged and cultivated with a certain artifice and theatricality. Straight lines and rows, symmetrical pairings mirroring each other and framing a central feature, carpet planting of a single type of plant, and ornate pruning are all elements of a formal design.

Despite this rigidity, formal gardens come in great variety and include rose and herb gardens, flower beds arranged like mosaics, water gardens that reflect the sky in yet another kind of symmetry, and walled vegetable gardens called potagers. Their strong ground plans are easy to read, and they retain a presence even in winter's landscape.

If you like the formal look but only up to a point, you can soften the formal geometry with a cascade of wisteria or a climbing rose on a wall or with a naturalistic planting of herbaceous perennials that billows over a border's straight edge. This softening of the formal style became the basis for the classic English cottage garden, typically a charming, informal tangle of annual and perennial blooms set within a well-defined space.

During Colonial times, American houses had cottage or dooryard gardens that were similar to their English-cottage counterparts, with a profusion of flowering plants blooming in beguiling disarray on either side of the front door and along the front of the house. Today, a more structured version of the dooryard garden has become the most popular American landscape style—an informal garden with a somewhat loose, natural appearance featuring irregular or compound curves. But this is not laissez faire gardening. The style calls for crisply defined beds forming a strong ground pattern. Planting arrangements, though not usually symmetrical, are carefully balanced. Brick, stone, and concrete effects borrowed from the house are built into paths and walls.

The axes and focal points in an informal garden are subtler and the patterns less regular than in a formal arrangement. They may exist naturally on your land, needing only a little emphasis from you to bring them out. Or a focal point might be implied by making a clearing in a line of trees, and the axis leading to it may be no more than an irregularly spaced line of shrubs.

In addition, the mechanism for framing a focal point by bracketing it will be more naturalistic than in a formal garden. For example, rather than balancing two identical clipped shrubs on either side of a focal point, you might achieve an informal balance with a small conifer and a clump of soft foliage to one side and a large rock on the other. The two masses may be equivalent in visual weight, but their textures and forms are quite different.

Japanese-Inspired Gardens

Blending some of the rigors of formality with the asymmetry of informality is the Japanese style. In this style, natural forms are controlled to achieve an exquisite effect—a rock is placed just so, a tree is pruned to display a delicate balance over a fish-filled pool, the sinuous motion of a stream is captured in the flowing bends of a path.

The plants and building materials in a Japanese garden reflect a fine attention to detail and are generally kept to a small scale. The emphasis is on the texture and form of plant foliage, rock, and wood, with occasional splashes of flower color.

A BACKYARD PARTERRE
Enclosed by a low hedge of Japanese holly, this Atlanta, Georgia, parterre—four rectilinear beds laid out in a carpetlike pattern—lends a formal accent to the stone steps leading up to the back garden. Wall germander outlines the central beds, which are filled with red wax begonias surrounding a pot of trained ivy.

Regional Gardens

Regional garden designs reflect local climate and growing conditions. They incorporate native plants best suited to that environment and include structural elements, such as walls and water features, that temper the effects of the weather.

Desert gardens thrive in extremes of drought and heat. A desert is not hot all year round, but it is dry, with annual rainfall of less than 10 inches. Plants grow low to the ground, and trees are spaced widely to conserve water. A desert garden follows that model, using plants like prickly pear, ocotillo, and spiky yucca. Trees such as carob, acacia, and common olive have deep taproots to reach underground water, and cast cooling shade. High courtyard walls and sun-screening trellises help moderate the heat and glare.

Mediterranean gardens are a variation on the desert garden. Originating in the arid climate of Spain, North Africa, and the eastern Mediterranean, they have transplanted easily to California and the American Southwest. Suited to contemporary, stucco, or Spanish-style houses, these gardens nestle in the shelter of a courtyard or atrium. The plantings can be lush, featuring exotically colored and scented tropical trees such as citrus, banana, and palm, all surrounding a central fountain. Vines such as jasmine and bougainvillea climb the garden's walls, and ferns, hibiscus, oleander, and bird-of-paradise grow in pots and raised beds.

Landscape Plants for Specific Styles

FORMAL

TREES
Acer
(maple)
Cedrus
(cedar)
Cupressus sempervirens
(Italian cypress)
Fagus sylvatica
(European beech)
Magnolia
(magnolia)
Picea
(spruce)
Quercus
(oak)

SHRUBS
Berberis thunbergii
(Japanese barberry)
Ilex crenata
(Japanese holly)
Ilex vomitoria
(yaupon)
Prunus laurocerasus
(cherry laurel)
Rosa hybrids
(hybrid roses)
Taxus baccata
(English yew)

VINES
Rosa
(climbing hybrid rose)
Wisteria
(wisteria)

GROUND COVERS
Calluna vulgaris
(heather)
Hosta
(plantain lily)

INFORMAL

TREES
Acer rubrum
(red maple)
Acer saccharum
(sugar maple)

SHRUBS
Euonymus alata
(winged spindle tree)
Lagerstroemia indica
(crape myrtle)
Rhododendron
(rhododendron)
Rosa rugosa
(rugosa rose)
Syringa
(lilac)

JAPANESE

TREES
Acer palmatum
(Japanese maple)
Malus floribunda
(Japanese flowering
crab apple)
Pinus densiflora
(Japanese red pine)

SHRUBS
Chaenomeles
(flowering quince)
Juniperus
(juniper)
Pieris japonica
(lily-of-the-valley bush)
Pinus mugo
(dwarf mountain pine)

VINES
Wisteria floribunda
(Japanese wisteria)

GROUND COVERS
Liriope muscari
(big blue lilyturf)

Acer rubrum
(red maple)

Woodland Gardens

Wherever it might appear, a woodland garden consists of the same two elements: a number of large trees to create an overhead canopy, and a succession of underlayers—smaller trees, shrubs, and ground-level plants like wildflowers, ferns, and mosses. To create a successful design, reduce the natural abundance of a woodland to a few simple elements. Build in a clearing to let in light for the less shade-tolerant plants and to bring about a contrast of light and dark. But make sure a few saplings are interspersed among the older trees to ensure successive generations of shade trees. Then make a path through the garden to take you from place to place and to keep visitors from trampling delicate plants. If you choose plants that produce berries and flowers to create a habitat for wildlife, after a time you will develop a self-sustaining environment that requires little further effort.

Meadow and Prairie Gardens

While woodland gardens provide a shady oasis, wildflower meadow and prairie gardens are open, sunny, and alive with color and texture. They also are more precarious, requiring periodic mowing to prevent unwanted saplings from taking over and to allow desirable seedlings to become established. These gardens work especially well as transition areas between the more structured part of the garden and the openness of the surrounding countryside. Plant mixtures for meadows and prairies will vary according to soil and rainfall, but all will require full sun. You can purchase seed mixes suited to your area from seed companies. These mixes will include annual and perennial wildflowers, such as daisies, sundrops, butterfly weed, and Texas bluebonnet. The annuals should reseed themselves after the first year. Also included will be native bunch grasses like switch grass, big bluestem, and little bluestem. Bulbs planted in broad swaths also naturalize well in a wild meadow.

EAST MEETS WEST
A North Carolina garden sets the simplicity of the Japanese style within a Western border and lawn. Plants indigenous to Japan, such as red laceleaf Japanese maple, multicolored Houttuynia cordata, and two varieties of Japanese cedar, are in concordance: The shape of the pyramidal rock, for example, is echoed in the smaller cedar 'Bandai-Sugi'.

Entrances and Exits

The journey through your garden should be punctuated by entrances and exits that not only provide access to its spaces but also organize them. As points of arrival and departure between house and garden and within the garden itself, they will unite the separate parts of your property and set the stage as you move from one area to the next.

use appropriate materials and scale. But don't forget the practicalities. The front door should be visible and the path direct. Look closely to find natural traffic patterns: People and pets will instinctively take the shortest route to a destination, crossing over lawns and even through hedges to get there (for more on pathways, see pages 24-25).

The Front Entry

Because your front door is the first destination for visitors, the passage to it should allow clear access from the front sidewalk without sacrificing privacy. Paradoxically, this passageway can seem more inviting if it is fronted by a hedge or a fence. An enclosure around the front of your property conveys a sense of shelter from the outside world. A gate or a trellised archway will frame the view to the house and help direct visitors to the front door.

For the shape and dimensions of your front pathway, look to the style of your house and the contours of your land. Keep the design simple, and

From House to Garden

When guests walk out of your house on their way to the garden, whether through a front, side, or rear door, the area outside the door should give them the impression of linking the interior with the exterior. This space can be as small as a doorstep or as large as a patio or deck. It can incorporate elements that are extensions of the house—lighting, furniture, even an awning or a roof. At the same time, it can introduce elements of the garden, such as a small pool, a climbing rose, or clusters of plants, even a tree, in containers.

The transition from one space to another with-

A GARDEN IN A SIDEWALK STRIP *Extending an entranceway welcome almost to curbside, a Los Angeles garden fills the strip of earth between the sidewalk and the road with Tulbaghia violacea (society garlic), Geranium incanum, and a red-flowered Leptospermum scoparium (New Zealand tea tree). In many garden, such island beds are the only locations in full sun. Before planning a sidewalk garden, find out if your municipality has height restrictions on sidewalk plantings.*

in the garden can be marked or signaled in several ways. The subtlest is a change in the materials underfoot. For example, the transition from lawn to a woodchip path can mark the entrance to a woodland. A gravel walkway that becomes a concrete sidewalk may indicate an exit from the garden to the driveway. More obvious are the portals created by open or gated passages, standing free or as part of a hedge or fence. The simplest is a passage between two shrubs at either side of a pathway. More elaborate would be an arch or the trellised tunnel of a pergola. A picket or wrought-iron gate will give the visitor a glimpse of the space beyond, whereas one of solid wood, if tall enough, will block the view and make the entrance a surprise.

AN INFORMAL ENTRANCEWAY
A picket gate mounted on rough-hewn posts has been embellished by a rustic archway of interwoven boughs. The style fits in with the informal pebbled path leading to the utility area of this southern California garden. Wild lilac, snakebeard, and 'Bonica' shrub roses edge the pathway.

Choosing Openness or Privacy

The impression made by the entrance to your house can be altered with a few simple landscaping changes, depending on the design of the house. A dramatic front door or a handsome roofline may call for an arrangement that boldly displays them. On the other hand, you may want more screening if, for example, you have large windows that look out on the street.

The house below is fronted by an open expanse of lawn, its foundation softened by a line of shrubbery. Vertical accent shrubs flank the entranceway and strengthen it as a focal point. To a visitor, such an exposed design may seem imposing, if not slightly forbidding. Curtains or shutters in the windows are needed to maintain a sense of privacy.

Planting a screen of trees and a hedge creates a sheltering enclosure in front of this house. The trees block upper-window sightlines from the street. Indoors, the house is bright because curtains can be left open. Outdoors, the hedge-enclosed space feels more intimate and inviting to a visitor than an open space would.

The Importance of Paths

Paths and walkways look best when they are consistent with the style of the house and of the garden itself. For example, a path through a formal garden may be built of brick or flagstone. An informal path, by contrast, may be as simple as a clearing between beds with grass underfoot.

The width of a walkway should be determined by how much traffic it bears and by its location. Thus, a main path that leads from the house to the garden should be wide enough to allow two people to stroll comfortably side by side, while paths between beds need only provide room for the gardener to move about while tending plants. As a rule, allow 2 to 4 feet of width per person.

Materials for lining walkways include brick, flagstone, concrete, asphalt, grass, and gravel. Concrete or brick—durable, low-maintenance materials—are ideal for heavily trafficked areas near the house. For other pathways, consider materials prevalent in your region, such as oyster shells near the ocean or pine needles in wooded uplands.

Edging is also an important consideration in the creation of a garden path. Paths with brick or stone edging are viewed as more formal than those without such sharp definition. A carefully dug edge that establishes a boundary between a bed or border and a path can be an equally successful and less costly treatment.

Negotiating Levels

The contours of your property may include changes in grade steep enough to require steps. Even if this is not the case, minor rises can be highlighted through the use of steps. Steps not only provide access to hard-to-reach areas, they also serve as an interesting design component in their own right. Like walkways, steps can be built from many different materials for varied effects. Brick, stone, concrete, and railroad ties are several of the choices that can be used alone or in combination.

Safety is a special consideration in determining the size of a step. A good minimum width for stair-

Defining the Path with Plants

Plantings along a pathway can elicit different feelings or moods depending on the plants used. For example, parallel rows of dwarf fruit trees along a path would create a formal processional way, whereas tall, dense evergreen shrubs might, in time, produce a tunnel-like effect.

Plants define and reinforce the garden structure. Think of your garden layout as a road map, with paths the roadways and plants the attractions along the route. Important elements to consider when choosing plants for pathways are height, width, and growth habit. Whether your choices are subtle or dramatic, you can orchestrate the experiences throughout the garden.

*A **uniform border of low shrubs or perennials along a curved path,** as shown here, mimics the vegetation lining a fast-running stream and reinforces linear movement along the pathway. A colonnade of trees or tall shrubs along the same path would give the illusion of enclosing the path with a physical barrier and thus even more strongly direct the eye along its length to a destination in the distance.*

To deemphasize a pathway— say, a driveway—you can counteract its linear flow with plantings that intersect it laterally. You can further diffuse its linearity by widening the path and installing beds of plants at that point, making a stopping place in the path. Trees or shrubs clustered in the bends of a curved path, like the pooling of water in the bend of a stream, also create lateral emphasis along the length of the path.

ways in the home garden is about 42 inches. Depending on how easy you want the climb to be; treads might be 12 to 18 inches deep, and risers might be between 3 and 6 inches high. The treads should have a slight downward pitch from the center to the outer edges for good drainage.

Outdoor steps, which are built to accommodate the random and unpredictable topographic changes found in nature, should be generous in size and proportion to give the visitor more warning of grade changes. When putting in steps along a walkway, use at least three—anything less will be hard to spot.

Driveways

Driveways present a particular design challenge. A driveway, because it is also a pathway, should be connected to the path system for the house and garden, yet its width puts it out of proportion to the other walkways. You can reduce some of its impact by installing plants along its edge. But keep the views from the driveway to the doors of the house clear—that way, if a small child or a pet should dash out toward the car, you'll see it earlier and have more time to react.

Framing the Garden View

Other pathways to consider in your garden design are the visual pathways, or sightlines. You can orchestrate views within the garden—as well as from inside the house to the garden and beyond—through the use of axes and cleared vistas that lead to focal points. Sightlines can also be designed using an important technique in Japanese gardens called borrowed scenery, where views from adjacent property are captured and framed.

A PATHWAY TO A DAPPLED WOOD *Winding up a woodland hill, a path of steppingstones in this Virginia garden takes a visitor on a journey past an array of shade plants. The transition from lawn to woodland is marked by bamboo-like native wild oats and pale green 'Honeybells' hosta. White dogwood and royal blue alpine columbine brighten the path as it wends its way upward.*

Places for Stopping and Viewing

Whether you seek a cozy spot to rest after an afternoon of planting and pruning or a vantage point from which to admire the perennials in bloom, your garden must include places to stop, rest, and reflect. Benches are probably the most popular kind of stopping place, but you can create a number of other arrangements for comfortably appreciating the garden that will add both individuality and appeal to your site.

Patios and decks are something of a middle ground between the house and the garden. They allow a comfortable transition between indoors and outdoors, and can be treated as an extra "room" in which to relax and entertain. Because of its proximity to the house, a patio should be built of materials that either are consistent with the house treatment or complement it, thus unifying the house with its surroundings. A brick house might have a brick or colored concrete patio, for example, and a clapboard house a patio surface of flagstone or terra-cotta tile.

Decks extend out over the property and can be used to deal with difficult gradients, such as a site too steep for walking or even for steps. With their elevated vantage point, they also offer a unique view of the garden. And the materials typically used to construct decks—pressure-treated pine, redwood, and cedar—work well aesthetically with the design and building materials of most houses.

Planting Arrangements

Your garden design can include beds of spectacular plantings arranged to be stopping places at the ends of pathways or along their length—espe-

cially when the spot is equipped with a bench for restful viewing. With plantings calculated to provide interest through a long season of growth, these stopping places will maintain their appeal for much of the year.

An Elevated Perspective

If an overlook, such as a balcony or an accessible rooftop, is part of your property, it can become the visitor's ultimate destination. From there, an appealing view of your garden or of a distant vista can be a delightful surprise.

Roof gardens and balcony plantings can be part of your overall garden design. If the view from your overlook is less than captivating, you can minimize it by creating a focal point within the roof garden or screen offending views with a simple garden structure such as a latticework trellis.

Designing a roof garden is always a challenge. Your plants will generally grow in large containers or planters, which must be designed to allow for adequate drainage. The drain water must, in turn, be effectively channeled off the roof. Also keep in mind that the soil mix must be light enough to be supported by the roof once the plants are in place. One technique to ensure safety is to position heavy plantings directly over the supporting pillars of the structure.

Balconies are interesting places to experiment with container gardening. Make sure you take note of the growing conditions before you make plans—sun angles and the direction and strength of the wind will affect your plant choices.

Depending on the size of your balcony, you may be able to grow climbing vines against the building walls for green cover as well as have annual and perennial plantings for seasonal interest. Before you move any containers onto the balcony, however, find out how much weight it can safely support.

A ROSY BOWER ON A GINKGO FRAME
An arbor made of ginkgo trees supports the fragrant weight of a climbing white Rosa soulieana. Such a sheltered stopping place provides shade and seclusion and even some protection from a light summer rain in this East Hampton, New York, garden. The white-edged leaves of the variegated hostas thriving in its corners pick up the white of the blossoms.

CHAPTER TWO

Developing Your Plan

It's essential to know as much as possible about your property before you begin your garden design. You must consider not only the existing plantings and structures on your land but also the type of soil you have, the contours of the land, how much sun or shade it receives, and the views outward from your yard. All will affect your design decision making.

Doing such an assessment on the Maine garden at right, for example, would involve taking note of the gentle slope leading up to the guesthouse, the structure itself, and the stone stairs and pathway. Important plantings to consider would include the large lilac just to the left of the guesthouse and the long flower beds filled with daylilies and the occasional purple spires of lilyleaf ladybells.

This chapter will show you how to document the key features of your property on a garden map. By doing so you will gain the information necessary to create a design that makes the most of your property while fulfilling your fondest dreams for a garden.

A. *Syringa vulgaris (3)*
B. *Hemerocallis lilioasphodelus (many)* **C.** *Adenophora liliifolia (2)* **D.** *Macleaya cordata (1)* **E.** *Potentilla (1)*
F. *Nicotiana alata 'Lime Green' (6)* **G.** *Helichrysum petiolatum 'Roundabout' (2)* **H.** *Artemisia stellerana 'Silver Brocade' (2)*
I. *Astilbe sp. (6)* **J.** *Amsonia tabernaemontana (1)*

The key lists each plant type and the number of plants needed to replicate the garden shown. The letters and numbers above refer to the type of plant and the number sited in an area.

Mapping Your Site

Whether you work with a landscaping professional or do the job yourself, the first step in the garden design process is to take stock of your property, record all aspects that relate to the garden, and put that information on a base map. You could commission a professional to do the mapping *(page 36),* but if you tackle it yourself, you will acquire an understanding of your property that will prove invaluable as you care for your garden through the years.

Professionals call this property inventory a site analysis. Although the term may sound daunting, the process isn't. You can complete a site analysis in just a few hours if you record only the information that doesn't change with the seasons—the location of trees, shrubs, fences, patios, and walks, for example. A more thorough inventory—one that includes seasonal features—will take you several months, even a year, to complete. You'll want to note such items as the location of spring- and fall-blooming bulbs, the spot where a sharp winter wind cuts through the property, or the depth of the shade created in summer by a tall tree or a dense shrub.

Start with a Base Map

To record the information you collect from your site analysis, you'll need a base map that shows your lot boundaries drawn to scale. It should also have an accurate outline, or "footprint," of the house and any other permanent structures on the property. You can create the base map from scratch, but you'll save time if you start with the official plat of your property drawn up by professional surveyors. Most homeowners receive a copy of their plat along with the other documents that accompany the purchase of a home. If you can't find your plat, call your tax assessor's office. It will sometimes provide a copy free of charge.

A plat typically includes a notation about the scale of the drawing. A scale of 1:20 means that 1 inch on the drawing represents 20 feet. If the scale isn't shown, work it out by measuring a distance on the plat in inches and correlating it with the actual distance on your property.

Most plats are printed on standard 8½-by-11-inch paper. To give yourself enough space to record all the pertinent facts about your property, take the plat to a good blueprint company. They can blow it up into a much larger map that is easier to work with and convert the original scale into a larger one that you can use as you add features to the map. You may want to have four or five copies made so you will have extras on which to record the subsequent stages of your design.

What Information to Record

The more information you gather and record about your property, the better equipped you'll be to make design decisions. The items presented below should give you a good body of information. If you want a sharper focus to your analysis, you might start with an overall goal or purpose for your garden and then assess the property against that goal. In addition to recording physical factors, mark down aesthetic features, such as the best location for watching the sunset.

Lot size and shape. The plat will include the boundaries of your property, so you'll have a clear

Mapping Shade Patterns

The patterns of light and shade in your garden will change throughout the day and with the seasons. Although a sunny site will collect the most light at noon in midsummer, when the sun is at its zenith, a property with many deciduous trees will actually be sunnier in winter, after all the leaves have dropped.

Shadows will be longest when the sun is low in the sky in winter. Shadows also extend westward in early morning and eastward in the evening, creating larger patches of shade at those times of the day.

Take note of the amount and intensity of shade in your garden. A north-facing wall will cast dense shade for most of the day, making the space unsuitable for any but the most shade-tolerant plants. By contrast, a tree with a light canopy will cast a patchy, variable shadow ideal for the wide range of plants that thrive in dappled or partial shade.

The illustrations at right show a garden map with the shade patterns drawn for noon in midsummer *(above, right)* and midwinter *(right)*. Use this map as a guide as you observe and record the shade in your garden. If you have complex shade patterns, indicate them on your own map, differentiating areas of deep shade from brighter shady areas and noting the location and length of the shadows in the morning, noon, and afternoon as well as in each season.

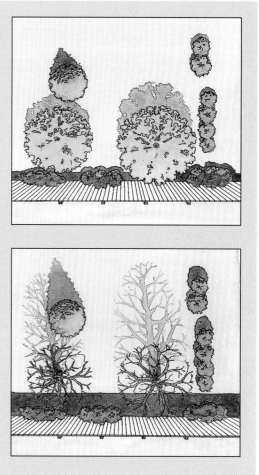

idea of the lot shape. Think about how you can use that shape to best advantage. At first glance, a level, rectangular plot may seem ideal, but in its unaltered form such a layout is in fact relatively devoid of visual interest. You may want to consider breaking up the space so that the entire garden cannot be seen at once; intriguing glimpses from one space into another will beckon the viewer to move through the garden with pleased anticipation. By the same token, you can turn an awkward shape such as a wedge or a long, narrow plot to advantage with a clever design. You might turn a narrow strip at the side of your house into a meandering stone "stream," for example, complete with shrubs and perennials along its edges.

The house. Sketch in a rough diagram of the ground floor of your house, including the location of windows. Note outside doors and whether they open in or out. Define traffic patterns from the house to the garden; a frequent problem in older homes with only front and rear or side doors is difficult or uninviting access between the house and the garden. For example, if your only access to a backyard garden leads you around the side of the house, you might want to create a small garden by the door with a pretty path leading to the main part of the garden.

Measure the distance from the ground to the sills of first-floor windows. This information will alert you to potential views into the garden from key rooms in the house and let you determine which plants will fit under the windows when fully grown. Take note of any rooms that get too hot in the summer and might benefit from a nearby shade tree, or any that are too dark because of trees with dense, leafy canopies.

Utilities and easements. A county plat should indicate any easements—strips of your property that are subject to limited public use for pass-throughs of major utility lines, public pathways, and the like—and any buried electric, gas, water, telephone, and television cable lines for your own house. If your garden design will call for digging deep planting holes for trees or excavating for terracing or other projects, you will need to know not only the location but also the depth of these installations. Check with the utility company for this information. Also, record the location and height of any overhead wires.

If a sprinkler system is already installed on your

HIGHLIGHTING A PROPERTY'S STRENGTHS AND WEAKNESSES

On a property-survey plat serving as a base map, the homeowner has used red ink to indicate existing plantings and record notes on topography, views to emphasize or screen, and possible drainage problems. The assessment reveals minimum landscaping but plenty of scope for an outstanding garden on this property, which covers nearly an acre. Two obvious problems demand attention: The overgrown woods to the south and west take up considerable space and loom over the house to such an extent that it is not even necessary to mark the oppressive shade they cast. Another target for major redesign is the steep slope in the eastern corner, planted with randomly scattered trees.

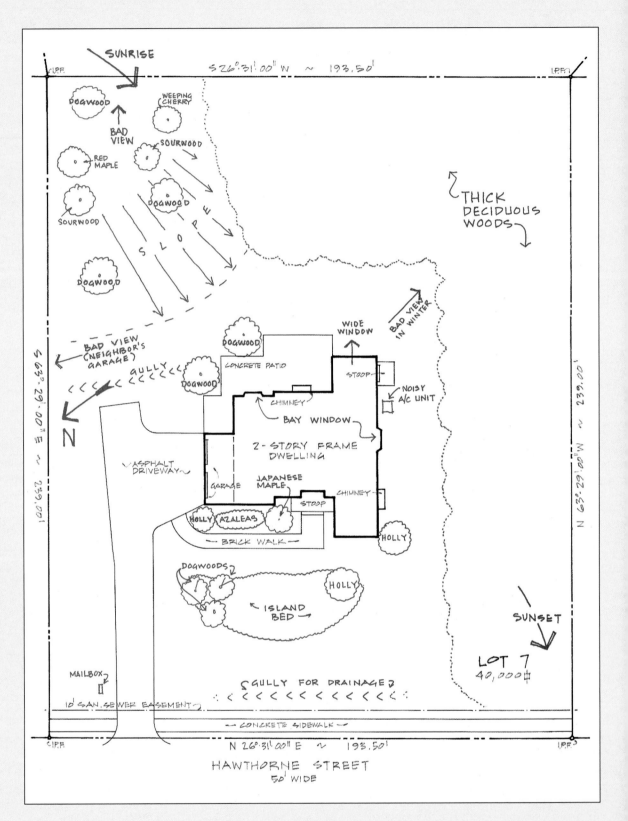

SUNRISE

S 26° 31' 00" W ~ 193.50'

I.P.F.

DOGWOOD

WEEPING CHERRY

BAD VIEW

SOURWOOD

RED MAPLE

SOURWOOD

DOGWOOD

SLOPE

DOGWOOD

THICK DECIDUOUS WOODS

BAD VIEW (NEIGHBOR'S GARAGE)

GULLY

N

S 63° 29' 00" E ~ 239.00'

DOGWOOD

DOGWOOD

CONCRETE PATIO

WIDE WINDOW

BAD VIEW IN WINTER

STOOP

NOISY A/C UNIT

CHIMNEY

BAY WINDOW

2-STORY FRAME DWELLING

N 63° 29' 00" W ~ 239.00'

ASPHALT DRIVEWAY

GARAGE

JAPANESE MAPLE

STOOP

CHIMNEY

HOLLY AZALEAS

BRICK WALK

HOLLY

DOGWOODS

ISLAND BED

HOLLY

SUNSET

LOT 7 40,000#

MAILBOX

GULLY FOR DRAINAGE

10' SAN. SEWER EASEMENT

CONCRETE SIDEWALK

C.I.P.F.

N 26° 31' 00" E ~ 193.50'

I.P.F.

HAWTHORNE STREET
50' WIDE

34

property, mark the location of water lines and sprinkler heads on your base map.

Indicate where air-conditioning units and utility meters are located so you can make plans to screen them. Keep in mind the noise an air conditioner makes when you plan the location of outdoor seating areas and other entertainment spaces.

Sunny spots and shade. The amount and quality of natural light in your garden will affect plant choices as well as the placement of a seating or dining area or a pool or other water feature. You may find it useful to track the position of the sun and the movement of shade throughout the day and with the seasons *(page 31)*.

Prevailing winds and microclimates. A gentle summer breeze that blows across your front porch on a hot day is an asset for garden and gardener alike. But a winter wind ripping through your property can damage even the hardiest plants. And if you live on a seacoast, salt-laden air will continually buffet your garden. In these situations, you will need to choose plants that can tolerate such conditions, or erect a windbreak.

Likewise, microclimates—those areas where the contours of the land or the structures on it slightly alter the prevailing temperatures—will affect your garden design. For example, for the north side of a house, where the soil can take weeks longer than other areas to thaw in spring, or for low-lying areas prone to frost, you would select different plants than you would for a protected, south-facing spot. Record such climatic factors on your map to help you make informed decisions about how to take advantage of a microclimate.

Topography and drainage. Indicate any changes in elevation. Steep slopes are readily apparent and present their own design challenges and opportunities, but even a slight gradient or low-lying spot may present drainage problems.

Note the location of downspouts and drains and where the runoff goes. Wait for a heavy rain, then check the efficiency of the drainage system. Mark the location of any areas that stay damp because of clay soil or poor grading, and areas that are eroding. Also indicate any sections of the garden that are particularly dry.

Soil. The nature of your soil will be critical in deciding what type of garden to design. Not only will your choice of plants be driven by the type of soil you have, but your soil assessment may impel you to pave large areas, create raised beds, or embark on a major soil-amendment project.

Test your soil for pH and nutrient composition with a kit available at nurseries or garden centers, or have it tested by your local Cooperative Extension Service. Gather soil samples from various places on your property, making sure to take samples from a depth of 3 to 6 inches.

Existing vegetation. Trees have the most impact on a garden visually, spatially, and horticulturally, so carefully record the trees on your grounds, indicating the approximate diameter of the crown of each tree with a circle drawn to scale. Sketch in all shrubs similarly. If you know the genera, species, and cultivars, note them. Indicate plants that are in poor condition, and note the locations of established beds and specialty gardens, such as those devoted to vegetables, roses, or herbs.

Consider the aesthetic effect created by your plants. Does a given plant seem too big for its space? Does a tree provide shade at a crucial place? Most large shrubs and small trees can be transplanted successfully, so view any healthy plant as an asset, even if it isn't growing quite where you want it. This inventory will help you decide which plants are worth keeping and which aren't.

Structures and pavings. Draw to scale any structures not shown on the plat, such as a storage shed, playhouse, arbor, pergola, gazebo, or guesthouse. Draw in patios, terraces, and decks; fences, walls, and hedges; ponds and pools; and children's play areas, sandboxes, and basketball hoops. Indicate the driveway, sidewalks, and garden paths, and note the paving material.

If cars have damaged lawn or plantings adjacent to the driveway, or if people continually cut across the lawn rather than staying on a path, note these problem spots. Jot down details such as whether steppingstones are spaced a comfortable distance apart or if paths are wide enough.

Lights. Mark outdoor lights on your map, and if possible indicate where the wiring is buried. If you intend to install lights in your garden, plan for them in the early stages of your design. New low-voltage lighting systems are much easier to install than older types, but if you are going to bury the wire, do the digging before the garden is well established *(pages 74-76)*.

Views, noise, and odors. Views can be enjoyable or unsightly, sounds can soothe or jangle the nerves, smells can be pleasant or unpleasant. Take note of all of these on your property so that you will be in a position to showcase, mute, or keep clear of them in your new design.

Legal considerations. Building codes, covenants, and permit regulations vary from community to community. Check with your local authorities about permit requirements and restrictions on items such as fence heights and design, decks, spotlights, pools, extensive grading, electric work, and structures. Note any property-boundary setback regulations or rights of way on your map.

Beginning to Design

The very process of assessing and mapping your site is likely to give you a lot of ideas for developing your landscape. Now is the time to put these concepts down on paper. To get all points of view, gather your family together and find out what each member would like to have in the garden.

At this early stage, no notion should be considered too outrageous or too expensive. Write them all down. Of course, a lot of ideas will eventually be rejected for one reason or another, but you may be pleasantly surprised to find elements of many suggestions incorporated into your final plan.

Be sure your initial thoughts take into account the way you live and your family's needs. If you enjoy entertaining, plan an area suitable for tables and chairs for outdoor parties. If you have small children, think about setting aside space for a play structure and a plot of grass where they can romp. Adults and children alike enjoy outdoor sports and games; consider allotting space for them.

You may also want to set aside room for an herb or vegetable patch or some other kind of specialty garden. Do you need a space tucked out of sight where you can put in a nursery bed or work on your potting and seed starting? What about storage for tools, mowers, spreaders, pots, bags of fertilizer, and all the other garden paraphernalia?

Be realistic about the amount of time you want—or have—to spend working in the garden. The bountiful herbaceous borders pictured in so many garden books are a joy to behold, but they can take an enormous amount of upkeep. Unless

A RETREAT FROM LIFE'S STRESSES *In this Virginia garden, woods enclose a garden room with a cobblestone floor, providing the owner with a place to relax. The soft yellow-green foliage of a Robinia pseudoacacia 'Frisia' (black locust) tree planted next to the lounge chair is echoed by the yellow needles of Picea orientalis 'Skylands' (Oriental spruce) in the raised bed.*

Finding Professional Help

If you feel overwhelmed by all the design possibilities and plant choices, you may want to turn to a professional to help you design your garden. Within the field of garden design are landscape designers and landscape architects. Landscape designers are knowledgeable about plant materials and design principles, with their know-how sometimes based more on experience than on formal training. They are often employed by nurseries or landscape contractors.

A landscape architect must have graduated from a program in landscape architecture that focuses on elements of engineering, horticulture, and architectural design. Some states require landscape architects to obtain a license by passing the United National Examination, which tests knowledge of grading and drainage, landscape construction, landscape design and history, and professional ethics.

For large-scale or complex construction or significant landform reconfiguration you will probably need a landscape architect to draw up the plans and a landscape contractor to implement them. However, a landscape designer will be cheaper for a design based primarily on plantings and small-scale hardscape installations.

To find the person you'll be happiest with, ask friends for recommendations, or find out who did the design for a garden you admire. Consider taking a landscape design course. You'll hear about the local people who are respected in the field, and you'll also learn a lot that will help you work with the professional you ultimately choose.

When interviewing a designer or architect, ask to see his or her portfolio, then go to view one or two of the gardens. Request the names of several former clients and ask them whether the project kept to budget and was completed on time. Most important, choose someone who will encourage you to become actively involved in the design, who will spark your creativity and listen to your ideas.

you can give many hours a week to weeding, dead-heading, fertilizing, and watering, you're better off with a scheme that requires less maintenance. You'll enjoy your garden more if you aren't overwhelmed with time-consuming chores.

On the other hand, some avid gardeners with plenty of time to devote to their favorite pursuit delight in giving over most of the yard to flower beds. If you fit this description, then you can design the kind of garden where meticulous care will produce spectacular results.

Style Preferences

When settling on the garden style you'd most like to have, remember that the garden and its various structures will be seen within the context of the house and the neighborhood. A picket fence with a clematis twining through it may be charming with a traditional house, but it might look silly next door to a modern home featuring unexpected elevations and angles. Choose a style you like, but also be sensitive to the overall surroundings.

Once you've decided on a style, however, you need not be a slave to it. You should feel free to indulge in wide-ranging interpretation. Often, for example, structural elements of a formal garden, such as a straight path or a clipped hedge, can be combined with informal plantings to achieve an elegant effect. The best gardens reflect the unique character and personality of the homeowner rather than adhering unwaveringly to "rules."

Getting Ideas from Books and Magazines

Garden publications chock-full of color photographs are a great source of inspiration as you look for ideas for your landscape plan. Page through as many as you can lay your hands on and

TURNING GARDEN PROBLEMS INTO ASSETS

Problem	Solution
Poor soil	• Amend soil with organic materials • Construct raised beds • Use extensive paving and containers
Unsightly view/lack of privacy	• Plant trees, shrubs, tall ornamental grasses, or hedges for screening • Grow vines on walls, trellises, or chain-link fences • Build a trellis to create an "invisible wall"
Hot sun	• Create filtered shade with lath-covered structures • Install a pond or fountain to create a cool microclimate • Plant shade trees • Mulch to conserve moisture and cool plants' roots
Poor drainage/flooding	• Install a drainage system, such as French drains • Contour the surface and construct berms to direct water • Create a water or bog garden • Construct raised beds
High wind	• Plant trees or shrubs as windbreaks • Build a fence or wall to block the wind
Noise	• Build a fence or wall to cut noise • Mask traffic sounds with falling water • Plant a dense screen of shrubs to absorb noise
Steep slope	• Build terraces with connecting steps • Create steps and paths with steppingstones in a switchback pattern across the hillside • Plant the slope with a low-maintenance ground cover
Cramped space	• Use small-scale plants, including trees • Plant in layers, with tall plants in back, short ones in front • Use tricks of perspective to create a sense of depth, such as shortening the length of patio bricks as they move away from the house or narrowing a path as it recedes from the main viewing point

MAKING THE MOST OF A GARDEN'S ASSETS

Asset	How to Maximize
Good view	• Emphasize by framing the view with a pair of trees, an arbor, or a pair of statues • If the view is distant, use paths or other landscape elements to draw the eye to it • Create a seating area where you can enjoy the view
Windows looking into the garden	• Create garden rooms or vignettes designed to be seen from indoors • Plant sweet-smelling foliage and flowers under the window • Install garden lights to enhance the scene at night
Summer breeze	• Build a patio or terrace and furnish with comfortable chairs and tables so you can enjoy the cooler air • Install fragrant shrubs and herbaceous plants that will waft sweet smells toward the house or seating area
Mature trees and shrubs/special specimen plants	• Prune and thin mature plants to appropriate form and scale • Design the garden to make a chosen specimen the focal point

mark the gardens you like. Also take note of particular plants and plant combinations that appeal to you, as well as garden accents such as containers, sculptures, benches, and paving materials.

Don't write off an appealing garden approach just because the example you're looking at is much bigger and grander than anything you might aspire to. At this point you shouldn't be worried about what's realistic for your property. You may discover an aspect of the large garden that can be translated to your own. In addition, you can often tailor a grand effect to a much smaller space by scaling down the number and size of plants.

As you mark pictures, you'll probably notice a pattern emerging—specific plants, design features, and garden styles may appear over and over in your favorite examples. That's a good indication of what you really like. If you are working with a professional, this process will be invaluable for communicating your natural preferences.

Looking through garden photographs is also an excellent way to find ideas for solving tricky landscape problems. Often you'll see a problem situation in a picture that is very much like one you're coping with—except that the problem has been solved. If you like the solution, incorporate it into your own garden plans.

Garden Design Programs for Home Computers

Computer-generated garden designs are an accommodating alternative to the hand-drawn base plan. Landscape design programs allow you to manipulate garden schemes so that you can try various plants in combination and move them around without even having to erase lines on paper.

Programs for the home user come equipped with drawing tools, such as lines, rectangles, polygons, arcs, curves, and ellipses. Also included are predrawn mapping symbols for trees, shrubs, ground-cover plants, and hardscape items such as decks, pools, mulches, and even outdoor furniture. Some programs contain libraries of specific plants, including photographs and profiles of their life span, bloom season, and color; cultural information such as soil, water, and light requirements; and even an audio track that gives you the correct pronunciation of their botanical names.

As the demand for these programs increases, more sophisticated versions are being introduced. Soon you'll be able to scan a photograph of your house into the computer and, with the click of a button, superimpose botanically correct images of plants onto the picture so you can see exactly how the design will look. These programs also will be able to show how the same design will look in different seasons and in subsequent years as the plants grow and change.

Working within a Budget

Even a small property can eat up large amounts of money if you're putting in a swimming pool, lots of paving, and expensive specimen plants—and paying landscape architect fees and garden construction labor costs to boot. Fortunately, it's possible to create a lovely garden within a reasonable budget, if you're willing to do a lot of the work yourself. In addition, there are inexpensive alternatives to expensive looks you may want to achieve. For example, brick is a beautiful, but pricey, paving material. You can cut costs by paving your path or patio with poured concrete that's colored and molded to look like tile or brick. Flagstone is another less expensive option.

The least expensive surface to install is a lawn sown from seed, but don't forget upkeep. Over the years, the expense of fertilizing, liming, dethatching, watering, and other maintenance chores can exceed the costs of paving.

Another way to save money on landscaping is to buy smaller plants—those in 1-gallon containers rather than larger sizes. Although initially the garden will look a bit skimpy, smaller plants are actually a wise choice from a cultural as well as an economic point of view. They will settle into their new environment more quickly than larger, older specimens, and in some cases small plants put in at the same time as large ones will catch up in size in just a few years. Whatever your budget, don't skimp on such crucial elements as good-quality soil and, in dry climates, a proper irrigation system. Spending money on such items is not as emotionally satisfying as buying beautiful plants, but if you've invested in a plant, you'd better invest as well in creating an environment where it can thrive.

If money is short, draw up a plan to implement your design project in stages as your budget allows. Although you may have to make adjustments to the plan as you get new ideas or reevaluate it as results take shape, at least you can count on being able to work steadily toward your ultimate goal.

Using a Camera to Help Visualize Your New Design

A camera can be one of your most useful garden design tools. If you have difficulty picturing from drawings what a garden plan will actually look like, you can enlist the aid of familiar reality in the form of a photograph of your house and grounds. By superimposing your proposed garden design onto a photo, you can see clearly exactly how the final product will look. Plus, it's easy to make adjustments at this stage if something is not quite right.

The steps are simple. Photograph your house and garden from vantage points that give you a good perspective of the property. You may want to climb a ladder to get above large shrubs and to give a slight overview. If you can't fit an entire scene into one shot, buy a disposable panoramic camera, or take multiple photographs that can be taped together. Have the photos printed in 4-by-6-inch format so that they photocopy more clearly. Copy the image on a good-quality photocopier, enlarging the picture to either 8½ by 11 inches or, if you want lots of room to draw, 11 by 17 inches. A black-and-white reproduction should be adequate, but you can have a color photocopy for a few extra dollars.

Tape a sheet of tracing paper over the enlarged photocopy and outline the major features of your house, including walls, windows, doors, and roofline. Also trace any existing plantings that you plan to keep. Then draw in your planned design and see what you think. (Don't worry about artistic skill; an outline of the basic plant shape will be sufficient for your purposes.) Keep the plan to scale as much as possible, and draw plants at their mature size so you know how many you'll need. If you're not satisfied with the design, simply start again on a new sheet of tracing paper.

A Garden of One's Own

The gardens you see in books or magazines are rarely textbook designs. They may evoke a certain style or theme and follow accepted design principles, but invariably something of the designer's personality comes through that makes the garden uniquely his or her own.

No matter what type of garden you desire—a shady retreat, a splashy showcase of color, a focus on foliage in every shade of green—you can leave your personal imprint on it. This can be as simple as choosing plants that evoke fond memories of a particular region of the world or of the garden of a favorite aunt. Or you might take elements of one garden style and marry them with compatible elements of another, as some of the gardeners have done in the examples presented here. For a planting guide to each garden, see pages 50-53.

MARRYING THE FORMAL AND THE INFORMAL
The owner of this stone cottage near Philadelphia opted for a formal design yet filled the beds with plants that evoke a colorful cottage garden—lilies, delphiniums, summer phlox, and astilbe.

MEDITERRANEAN INFLUENCE

A love of the Provence region of France was the inspiration behind this northern California garden. Cool grays and greens were purposely selected to suggest a sunny Mediterranean landscape; mounds of French and English lavender and sprays of deep pink Erysimum (wallflower) provide harmonious waves of color. Reflecting the undulating rhythm of the border planting, a stepped pathway of rounded Colorado River-washed stones leads to the back entrance of the house, which is flanked by olive trees. The massive Plectostachys at the entrance to the path (lower left) began as a small 1-gallon container plant; it owes its healthy growth both to careful pruning and to the addition of turkey manure to this garden's sandy loam.

43

**A WELCOMING
DISPLAY**

*Reminiscent of an Early
American dooryard
planting, this delightful
Maine garden of herbs,
vegetables, and flowers
combines such tradi-
tional elements as a
straight path—leading
here to a bench instead
of a door—a profusion
of plants, and a fence
enclosure with an un-
usual location: The gar-
den is installed on the
site of an abandoned
clay tennis court. The
plants were carefully
chosen and arranged
to maximize color, tex-
ture, and fragrance
and to provide a boun-
ty for the kitchen as
well. Tall Phlox panicu-
lata in striking pink
welcomes a visitor en-
tering the path, which is
lined with 'Lemon Gem'
marigolds. Feathery
yellow-headed dill off to
the left of the walkway
fronts raspberry bram-
bles, while purplish blue
bellflowers and lilies in
pale pink and yellow
create a pleasing com-
bination on the right.*

44

A TRANQUIL REFUGE
The owners of this verdant Japanese-inspired garden near Boston wanted a peaceful spot to which to retreat from the stresses of city life. Perfect for quiet reflection and restoration of the spirit, the garden borrows some elements of a traditional rock-and-water planting: A stream, defined by well-placed fieldstone, encircles an island bed dominated by a simple, evocative ornament. But rather than rely on a few strategically placed and perfectly manicured plants, the gardeners have indulged their desire for lush flowers and foliage, including in the mix Spiraea japonica 'Little Princess' (foreground), Geranium endressii, and a variety of ferns, along with colorful splashes of azalea and iris, a magnolia, and a Japanese maple.

**A MEADOW,
DESERT STYLE**
*Swimmers in this pool
in Phoenix, Arizona,
might think themselves
afloat in the midst of a
prairie meadow—ex-
cept that this planting is
composed of wildflowers
native to the desert.
Scarlet flax, purple
arroyo lupine, and yel-
low California poppies
combine with Indian
fig, prickly pear, and
saguaro to rim the edge
of a man-made oasis,
providing privacy for
sunbathers as well as
sanctuary for the quails,
doves, hummingbirds,
owls, hawks, and
butterflies that flock to
this inviting, low-
maintenance garden.*

MARRYING THE FORMAL AND THE INFORMAL

pages 40-41

A. *Lilium 'Luxor'* (lily) (many)
B. *Paeonia officinalis* (peony) (3)
C. *Filipendula ulmaria* (queen-of-the-meadow) (3)
D. *Lilium speciosum 'Rubrum'* (showy Japanese lily) (3)
E. *Hosta fortunei 'Francee'* (plantain lily) (2)
F. *Buxus sempervirens 'Suffruticosa'* (edging boxwood) (many)
G. *Buxus sempervirens 'Arborescens'* (boxwood) (1)

H. *Monarda didyma* (bee balm) (3)
I. *Delphinium elatum 'Pacific Giants'* (candle larkspur) (4)
J. *Astilbe thunbergii 'Straussenfeder'* (astilbe) (5)
K. *Astilbe chinensis var. taquetii 'Superba'* (astilbe) (3)
L. *Achillea filipendulina 'Gold Plate'* (fern-leaf yarrow) (many)
M. *Liatris spicata 'Kobold Rose'* (button snakewort) (many)
N. *Lilium tigrinum* (tiger lily) (9)

O. *Hedera helix* (English ivy) (1)
P. *Wisteria sinensis* (Chinese wisteria) (1)
Q. *Castanea dentata* (American chestnut) (1)
R. *Phlox paniculata* (summer phlox) (1)
S. *Lilium 'Apollo'* (lily) (5)
T. *Iris ensata* (sword-leaved iris) (3)
U. *Hosta fortunei 'Aoki'* (plantain lily) (1)

**MEDITERRANEAN
INFLUENCE**

pages 42-43

A. *Plectostachys serphyllifolia* (1)
B. *Erysimum* (wallflower) (2)
C. *Digitalis* (foxglove) (3)
D. *Chamaerops humilis*
(European fan palm) (1)
E. *Olea europaea*
(common olive) (2)

F. *Solanum jasminoides*
(potato vine) (1)
G. *Lavandula angustifolia*
(English lavender) (1)
H. *Lavandula dentata*
(French lavender) (3)
I. *Salvia leucantha*

(Mexican bush sage) (3)
J. *Erigeron karvinskianus*
(fleabane) (1)
K. *Verbascum bombyciferum*
(mullein) (1)

*NOTE: The key lists each plant type and the total quantity needed to replicate the garden shown.
The diagram's letters and numbers refer to the type of plant and the number sited in an area.*

A WELCOMING DISPLAY

pages 44-45

A. *Phlox paniculata* (summer phlox) (4)
B. *Anethum graveolens* (dill) (many)
C. *Antirrhinum majus 'Rocket Mix'* (snapdragon) (24)
D. *Delphinium* (larkspur) (1)
E. *Digitalis purpurea 'Foxy Hybrids'* (common foxglove) (12)

F. *Tagetes 'Lemon Gem'* (marigold) (60)
G. *Rubus sp.* (raspberry) (21)
H. *Lathyrus odoratus* (sweet pea) (20)
I. *Campanula lactiflora* (milky bellflower) (3)
J. *Lilium Asiatic hybrids* (lily) (15)

K. *Papaver sp.* (poppy) (12)
L. *Lilium x aurelianense 'Golden Splendor'* (aurelian lily) (15)
M. *Pinus strobus* (white pine) (1)
N. *Prunus pensylvanica* (wild red cherry) (1)

D(1)

E(1)

C(1)

F(2)

I(3)

H(4)

G(6) D(1)

K(4)

J(2)

G(1)

M(3)

B(2)

A(1)

A(1)

L(2)

A TRANQUIL REFUGE

pages 46-47

A. *Spiraea japonica*
'Little Princess' (spirea) (2)
B. *Geranium endressii*
(Pyrenean cranesbill) (2)
C. *Magnolia stellata*
(star magnolia) (1)
D. *Acer palmatum 'Bloodgood'*

(Japanese maple) (1)
E. *Cedrus atlantica* (Atlas cedar) (1)
F. *Pieris japonica*
(lily-of-the-valley bush) (2)
G. *Rhododendron 'Hinodegiri'*
(azalea) (7)
H. *Rhododendron 'Polar Bear'* (4)

I. *Rhododendron 'Hinocrimson'* (3)
J. *Athyrium filix-femina*
(lady fern) (2)
K. *Iris ensata* (sword-leaved iris) (4)
L. *Athyrium goeringianum*
(Japanese fern) (2)
M. *Iris cristata* (crested iris) (3)

E(1)

E(1)

E(1)

G(1)

F(1)

J(5)

H(1)

I(1)

B

A

D(1)

C

C

D(1)

A

B

C

A MEADOW, DESERT STYLE

pages 48-49

A. *Lupinus succulentus*
(arroyo lupine) (many)
B. *Linum grandiflorum*
'Rubrum' (scarlet flax) (many)
C. *Eschscholzia californica*
(California poppy) (many)
D. *Larrea tridentata*

(creosote bush) (2)
E. *Olneya tesota*
(desert ironwood) (3)
F. *Acacia farnesiana*
(sweet acacia) (1)
G. *Carnegiea gigantea*
(saguaro) (1)

H. *Lycium fremontii*
(wolfberry) (1)
I. *Opuntia violacea*
var.santa-rita
(purple prickly pear) (1)
J. *Opuntia ficus-indica*
(Indian fig) (5)

NOTE: The key lists each plant type and the total quantity needed to replicate the garden shown.
The diagram's letters and numbers refer to the type of plant and the number sited in an area.

CHAPTER THREE

Furnishing the Landscape

Once you've settled on your garden style, but before you choose any plants, it's time to decide which landscape elements—walks, benches, sundials, terraces, pools, and the like—will best meet your practical needs while carrying forward your aesthetic intent.

The Berkeley, California, garden at left strikes a fine balance between style and practicality, demonstrating how landscape elements can work with plants to create a cohesive design. The wood trellis functions as both a garden boundary and a backdrop for lush plantings of vegetables and ornamental plants, while the gate contributes a break in the design and offers a glimpse of what's beyond. And in the foreground a sundial provides a focal point as an attractive garden accent.

Now it's your turn to decide where to place paths or walkways, what objects to install as focal points or dividers, how to add vertical interest, and whether to put in a water feature or garden lighting.

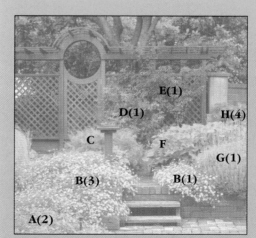

A. *Geranium x 'Mavis Simpson' (2)*
B. *Erigeron 'Moerheimii' (4)*
C. *Daucus carota (many)*
D. *Rosa 'Iceberg' (1)*
E. *Prunus 'Santa Rosa' (1)*
F. *Phaseolus vulgaris (many)*
G. *Lavandula x intermedia 'Dutch' (1)*
H. *Tropaeolum majus (4)*

The key lists each plant type and the number of plants needed to replicate the garden shown. The letters and numbers above refer to the type of plant and the number sited in an area.

Pathways and Pavings

The path in this New Hampshire garden is paved with long rectangular stones set in a zigzag pattern; within the frame they create are multicolored cobblestones and round and diamond-shaped concrete slabs. Simple plantings, including a compact Rhododendron 'Ramapo' and an arborvitae hedge, line one side of the path; yellow shrubby cinquefoil spills in from the other.

Paths and walkways create physical links between one place and another. In working them into your garden plans, keep in mind that no matter where they go or what they are made of, walkways should be compatible with the style of your house and with your landscape.

Start by deciding where you want the walkways to begin and end. Stroll around your property, examining its dimensions and contours. Do your design ideas lend themselves to pathways that follow a straight line, as in a formal garden? Or are meandering routes more appropriate, paths that induce the visitor to stop here and there along the way?

Take plenty of time in your exploratory walk through the garden, following natural routes from place to place. Once you've chosen the likeliest lines for your paths to follow, wait for a good heavy rain to come along, and then go out and check drainage patterns along and adjacent to these lines. Improperly positioned walkways can act like dams, exacerbating drainage problems.

In general, heavily traveled walkways, such as those leading to the house from the front sidewalk or the driveway, should be formal in design and constructed from hard, durable materials like concrete, brick, unglazed tile, or stone. They should follow straight lines and right angles or simple curves, and their edges should be well defined. For safety's sake, all walkways should present smooth but nonslick surfaces, and, ideally, they should be wide enough—4 to 5 feet across—for two people to walk abreast comfortably.

Informal Paths

Informal styles are usually chosen for less traveled paths, such as those leading into and through the garden, and can be constructed with softer paving materials. Such paths often have a meandering quality, but they can take any form you want them to. Merely setting out stone slabs in an irregular pattern through your garden will create a simple walkway and add visual interest. A winding gravel path with wood rounds set into the gravel at intervals would not only be aesthetically pleasing

but would also encourage a leisurely stroll. Informal paths are usually narrower than main walkways—from 2½ to 3 feet wide—but should still be wide enough for you to traverse comfortably with garden equipment. For an even more informal look, you can soften the effect of paving materials by letting plantings spill over onto them. Place small mound-forming plants like moss, thyme, or alyssum around paving stones to add texture, beauty, and softness to the surface.

Selecting Pavement Styles

The mood a hardscape material contributes to your overall design is a major consideration in choosing it. But equally important are such practical matters as cost and ease of installation and maintenance. If you don't have a lot of time to devote to plant care, you may want to invest in an intricate paving pattern or a mosaic tile that will act as a focal point, and then put in plants and ground covers that virtually look after themselves. If, on the other hand, you have considerable time for gardening, select a simple garden paving material and offset it with glorious flower borders.

Weather is another practical matter to consider. Some paving materials are more susceptible than others to damage by frost or hot, baking sun. And some, such as smooth concrete, tile, wood, brick, and stone, can be slippery when wet.

When you've worked out the practical questions, it's time to consider aesthetics. First look at the style and colors of your house and at the colors and textures of your present plantings. Decide how you want your pathways to fit in with them.

CUTTING A SWATH AMONG LUSH PLANTINGS
The gray stones of this Berkeley, California, pathway take a backseat to the Dianthus 'Rose Bowl', thrift, and Dalmatian bellflower that grow between them. Geraniums and Santa Barbara daisies offer a profusion of blooms, while spotted dead nettle, lamb's ears, and Siberian iris add texture and lushness.

Making a Natural Fieldstone Pathway

Using only a shovel, you can build an informal pathway of natural fieldstone. This material, an unquarried stone, fits in well with rustic, naturalistic landscape designs. The one drawback is that the stones are heavy, so it's best to have your local stone yard or quarry deliver them and deposit them beside the site of the pathway.

Choose randomly sized stones that are flat on top and large enough to tread upon comfortably. Then experiment with different arrangements, mapping out a route that is underlain by firm soil. Working along the route, but before you have begun digging, set the larger stones in place to get the general shape of the path. Then fill in the gaps with smaller stones. Leave a natural stepping distance between large stones laid in a line—about 18 inches. If your path is curved, set a large stone at the points where the path bends, to serve as stopping areas. Vary the size of the stones, and try to match shapes of adjoining stones so that their sides align fairly well.

To set a steppingstone path of large, widely spaced stones, dig a hole for each stone, add a little builder's sand or stone dust (available where you buy the fieldstone), and position the stone in the hole. Adjust the material underneath the stone and replace the soil around it until the stone is firm and stable. For a path of closely set stones, follow the directions below for laying the stones in a trench.

1. Before you dig your trench, *do a practice run by laying the stones down in a pattern that's both comfortable to walk on and aesthetically pleasing. Once you have settled on a workable path, dig a trench 5 to 6 inches deep and spread a 3-inch-deep bed of builder's sand or stone dust over it. Then lay the stones in place, aligning their irregular sides as much as possible.*

2. When the stones are set in the trench, *fill the spaces between them with soil. To keep the stones from tilting or wobbling, make sure at least two-thirds of the thickness of each is encased firmly in the soil. Then wet the soil with a fine spray of water. If the soil settles, add more. The surface of the stones should stand slightly higher than ground level. Plant grass or a ground cover between the stones or sweep builder's sand between them (left).*

Paving Materials

The possibilities for paving are almost limitless. Your choices range from such hard materials as brick, concrete, flagstone, fieldstone, granite, tile, and wood to softer materials, including loose aggregates such as gravel, cobbles, crushed rock, woodchips, or bark chips. And, of course, you can combine hard and soft materials very successfully.

Stone works especially well in naturalistic settings; you can find it in many sizes and in both regular and random shapes. In making a choice, remember that different types of stone vary in durability, slipperiness, and resistance to frost damage. Tiles—both terra-cotta and the more durable high-fired types—though relatively expensive are highly decorative, conveying a feeling of elegance. Tile is a poor choice, however, in climates where cycles of freezing and thawing occur, because wide cold-weather temperature fluctuations can cause it to crack. Remember, too, that in the rain, glazed tiles are slipperier than unglazed types.

Wood is a versatile paving material and conveys a warmth difficult to achieve with a harder material such as concrete. Woods that can be left to weather naturally, such as red cedar, cypress, and redwood, can be especially attractive. Although easy to install and fairly inexpensive, wood pavings will eventually decompose. You can extend their life somewhat by installing them in a way that allows for ventilation on the underside.

Loose Aggregates

Gravel is a popular choice among loose-aggregate paving materials. Inexpensive and easy to install, it is especially useful in spots where a less porous paving might create or exacerbate a drainage problem. Some maintenance is required, however. You'll need to rake gravel periodically, because it gets squeezed out of place when walked on. Your pathway will also require an edging to keep the migrating gravel from spilling over onto plantings.

Gravel tends to refract and absorb light, which can help soften the appearance of the entire garden. Remember, though, that gravel may look a bit boring when used exclusively, so plan to interrupt the line of a simple gravel path by introducing other paving materials at random, such as stone pavers or wood rounds.

The same holds true for other visually neutral materials, such as woodchips. It is best to combine them with other, more intricate-looking pavers. And no matter what type of loose-aggregate material you use, be sure to place layers of newspaper under it to help control weeds.

Patterns and Textures

As you plan your walkways, consider the roles that color, pattern, and texture play in the appearance of your garden. Simple, neutral paving works best with complex planting schemes. If your garden is filled with flowers, for example, brick might clash with red, pink, or orange blooms. Consider using gravel or flagstone and save brick for areas where the focus is on evergreens or foliage.

You can use pattern and texture in paving to convey various moods. Woodchips used together with steps created from landscape timbers, for example, lend a quiet, woodland feel. Wood planks set in a base of gravel give a more dynamic feeling—the mixture of textures, patterns, and materials keeps the eye moving.

Straight lines that run away from a particular viewpoint intensify a sense of direction and depth, whereas lines that cross the field of vision create a sense of breadth. Patterns that have a static quality—regular, symmetrical shapes such as squares, circles, and hexagons, for example—can help create a restful effect. Use them in places where you might want guests to linger. If you do choose a static arrangement, pay attention to the size of your paving units. A broad expanse of small units can create a fussy or dull appearance.

Edgings

There are several good reasons for bordering your pathways with some sort of hard edging. First, if you pave a path with a soft material such as gravel, bark, or woodchips, you will need some sort of edging to contain the material and prevent it from spreading out onto the surrounding ground and thinning out on the path until bare earth shows through. Second, if the path traverses the lawn, edging will serve the dual purpose of keeping the turf grass within bounds and providing a hard surface for the wheels of your lawn mower as you mow the edge of the lawn.

You will find a variety of edgings at home stores. Brick can be set on edge or on end, for example. You can also buy stone or concrete pavers or concrete sections designed to be set end to end. For rustic or woodsy landscapes, pressure-treated 4-by-4 or 6-by-6 timbers and uncut stone work well.

Paving with Brick

Brick comes in many colors, shapes, and textures, and adds warmth and interest to virtually any landscape. It can be arranged in a variety of different patterns and looks equally appropriate in formal and informal settings. It is also durable and easy to work with.

In selecting a specific brick, first consider your climate. Where frost occurs, look for brick designated SX, which means it will resist the effects of freezing and thawing. Then select a brick texture: Some have smooth, sleek surfaces and sharp edges, whereas others are more porous, with rounded edges.

The way in which you lay the brick can create moods. A running pattern—used alone, as shown below, or in combination with a stacked bond pattern—conveys fluidity and movement. By contrast, a basket-weave pattern gives a feeling of containment.

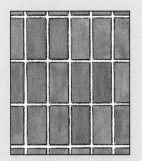

STACKED BOND

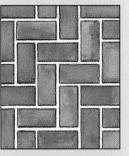

HERRINGBONE

RUNNING AND STACKED BOND

BASKET WEAVE　　**DIAGONAL HERRINGBONE**

Enclosing the Garden

The fences, walls, and gates you place around the outskirts of your property and at the boundaries of its internal "rooms" should act like picture frames, defining and showcasing the space within. But these elements must be useful as well as beautiful. On the practical side, walls and fences enclose your property, provide protection and privacy, act as windbreaks, help contain pets and small children, and muffle street sounds. Walls generally make more formidable barriers than fences because they are usually made of such weighty, permanent materials as poured concrete, stone, or brick. Fences can be solid structures, too, but they are typically constructed of wood in decorative, open patterns. They offer less privacy but let in more light and air.

Walls and fences play a major role in garden design because of the strong vertical dimension they impose. They also provide wonderful planting opportunities. A wall might double as a support for a

raised bed; a fence might serve as a trellis for climbing flowers or vines.

You can also use walls and fences to espalier shrubs and ornamental trees: The patterns created by flowers, fruit, and seasonal foliage color will ornament the structure as well as enliven the garden. Even the simplest of planting strategies—for example, just setting a few containers of flowers at its base—will add interest to an expanse of wall or fence.

An important focal point in either a wall or a fence is its gateway. An attractive or unusual garden gate serves not only as a passageway but also as an accent in its own right, framing a view within or beyond the garden. Gates can add ornamental interest, focus the eye, and break up the solid line of a garden boundary.

By their bulk, weight, and strength, walls contribute a sense of stability and permanence to your landscape. The commonest building materi-

A BACKDROP FOR EXOTIC PLANTINGS
Bright red bougainvillea crests a concrete wall in this garden in Rancho Santa Fe, California (left). Echoing the tawny hues of the surrounding desert, the wall also serves as a backdrop for a profusion of native plantings, including Agave, Sedum, Aconitum, and Euphorbia.

Living Garden Boundaries

Hedges are a lovely natural alternative to walls and fences. But remember that some trees and shrubs can take 10 years to grow to a useful height for a hedge. One tree that is ideal for this purpose is x *Cupressocyparis leylandii*, a handsome, fast-growing tree with a columnar habit. In cool, temperate climates, choose from such evergreens as *Viburnum tinus* 'Spring Bouquet', *Prunus caroliniana* 'Bright 'n' Tight', *Rhododendron* 'Fragrantissimum', *Euonymus japonica*, *Pieris, Taxus, Buxus, Pyracantha, Thuja, Spiraea, Ilex crenata*, and *Prunus lusitanica*. For tropical gardens, *Griselinia* and *Olearia* perform well, as does a ficus hedge like the one at right.

If you prefer a flowering hedge, forsythia is inexpensive and easy to grow. And if you want roses, both *Rosa rugosa* and *R. eglanteria* make beautiful informal hedges that produce not only blooms but also bright rose hips in the fall.

A Gallery of Wooden Fences

Wooden fences can range from the simple to the ornate. Slats can be diagonal, horizontal, or vertical; picket fences can have various intervals between pickets and tops that are pointed or rounded, spearheaded, or double- or triple-saw-toothed. The look of the fence will also be affected by the finish. Unfinished wood creates a rustic appearance as it ages. Or, if you prefer, you can stain the wood or paint it.

Pressure-treated pine is the least expensive fence wood that offers resistance to insects and decay. But typical pressure-treated pine fencing will often be poorly cured and subject to warping, and it will have knots, holes, and splits. Furthermore, it will be considerably darker than untreated pine and may have a greenish cast from its chemical treatment. Thus, it will not weather handsomely if it is left unfinished. If the design of your fence will be intricate, opt for redwood, cypress, or cedar, which are more expensive but are better choices when fine workmanship is required and appearance is a priority.

CONCAVE-TOPPED DOUBLE PICKET

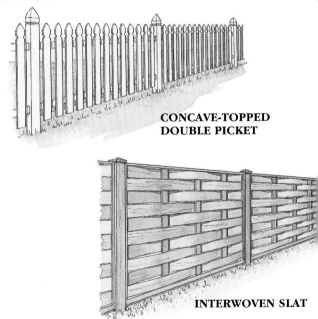

INTERWOVEN SLAT

als for walls are concrete block, poured concrete, brick, and stone. If you decide on a stone wall, select a stone that will help merge the style of your house with the landscape. Keep in mind that stone can be either dry-laid or mortared in place. If you choose brick or concrete block, you have the further option of building with pierced brick or block, which will make your wall a bit more like a screen, allowing for a limited pass-through of air and light.

To decide on a building material, you must first consider the purpose of the wall, which will, in turn, help you select its location, height, and length. If, say, you want a barrier to prevent children and small dogs from wandering into the street, you may need a wall only 3 feet high. If you want to keep out intruders or large animals, you'll need a wall at least 6 feet high.

Remember that a wall will become a prominent feature in your garden. The strong line it introduces might not necessarily fit best along the property line, so experiment with various possible positions.

Doing It Yourself or Contracting Out

Some walls have heavier work to do than merely enclosing the perimeter of your property. For these, you will have further choices to make.

If you want to build a retaining wall, for example, you may need to consult a professional about materials, siting, and design before tackling the job. Something so relatively uncomplicated as a dry-laid retaining wall made of stone—or even broken chunks of sidewalk—can be an efficient way to control erosion on a slope or to change grade. But you must be sure your wall will withstand the downhill pressure of soil and water.

In a few locales a retaining wall as low as 18 inches is subject to building regulations concerning construction methods and form—although in most jurisdictions the code doesn't apply unless the wall is at least 3 feet tall. It's best to hire a contractor if the wall you want will be tall enough to come under the local code. And if you are planning a wall with a height of 6 or more feet, or one that will run near the property line, make sure you're clear on local height and setback restrictions.

Adorning a Wall with Plants

The right plantings, of course, can provide the perfect finishing touch for a stone wall. Consider installing succulents or rock plants such as alyssum or campanula in the crevices to help soften the look of the wall. Espaliered apple or pear trees can lend year-round interest and interrupt the unbroken expanse of a high wall. Vines with long, supple branches can do the same for a long, low wall. Good choices include *Euonymus fortunei* (winter creeper) and *Campanula poscharskyana* (Serbian bellflower).

To support vines or espaliered limbs, drill holes in the wall at mortar intersections, hammer in expandable steel plugs, and screw in steel eyes.

PRIVACY—
WITH A VIEW
Prominent wooden posts interrupt the expanse of latticework fencing that encloses this Long Island, New York, garden. The open design of the fence allows air to circulate and affords a sense of privacy that is enhanced by the plants— sage, strawberries, phlox, and hibiscus— growing in borders and containers alongside it. Red 'Queen Elizabeth' roses and the pale pink blooms of the climbing rose 'Compassion' spill over the top of the fence at intervals, breaking its horizontal line.

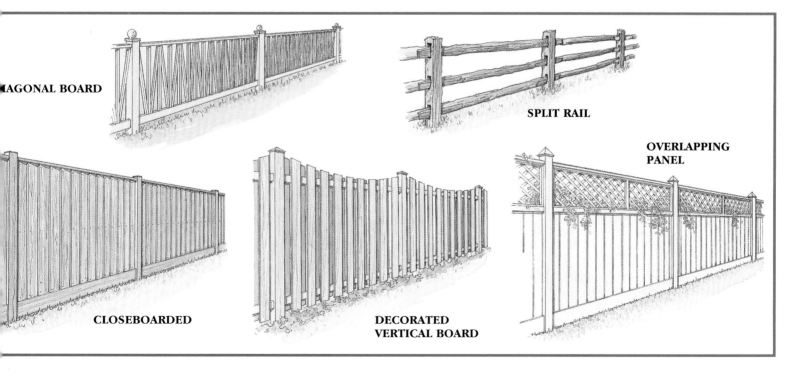

DIAGONAL BOARD

SPLIT RAIL

OVERLAPPING PANEL

CLOSEBOARDED

DECORATED VERTICAL BOARD

Then string braided metal wires through the eyes in any pattern you like, and attach the growing stems to the wires with plastic ties.

Fences

Fences, like walls, should serve as far more than boundary markers. They offer almost limitless opportunities for introducing pattern and texture as well as vertical and horizontal interest.

Fences are generally less imposing, easier to install, and less expensive than walls. And they can, like walls, lend unity to your landscape if you use construction materials that harmonize with the overall style of your house and complement your garden. The more formal the look of the garden, the more architectural the fence should be.

Choosing a Fence Design

Decide in the planning stages how much privacy you want. Depending on style and design, fences may offer substantial privacy or virtually none at all. Fences of interwoven slats or louvered wood, for example, let in limited light and air, leaving you quite enclosed within your garden. A louvered fence is a good choice for encircling a patio, as it offers a degree of ventilation, filters sunlight, and softens wind. You can paint a louvered fence, stain it, or allow it to age naturally.

Open fence styles like lattice and wrought iron are more for decoration than privacy, although they can serve as effective psychological barriers against casual intrusions. They also make wonderful mounting surfaces for a variety of plantings and allow good ventilation. Lattices made of vinyl look good, last longer than wooden ones, and are available in several colors. Wrought iron has a quiet, distinguished look that is particularly suited to urban areas. And a split-rail fence, often made from untreated wood, is so open that it merges your property with the surrounding landscape.

Picket fences blend easily with a variety of house styles, and can look just right in the city or in rural and suburban settings. When painted white, they are bright and cheerful additions to the landscape. But white fences look their best when freshly painted, so keep time and maintenance requirements in mind when you choose a finish. If you don't want the obligation of repeated upkeep, consider a dark stain for your picket fence—it will give a more formal appearance with far less maintenance.

Before you install a fence, find out about local regulations regarding allowable fence heights. In many places the height limit is 42 inches for front-yard fences and 6 feet for backyard fences. If you are not sure of the exact location of the property line, contact a surveyor when building a fence on a boundary. You may want to position the fence a few inches inside the line to be sure of avoiding legal entanglements with touchy neighbors.

Gates

Gates can be plain and sturdy or highly detailed and ornamental. They can be either traditional or contemporary in style but work best, of course, when the design and materials of the gate are coordinated with the dominant architecture of the property. Because a gate is the focal point of a wall or fence—or even of a dense hedge—it can communicate a certain style or feeling. A solid wooden gate with a lattice design on top, for example, suggests openness without sacrificing privacy. A white wooden gate placed midway along a brick wall and decorated with climbing roses lends color and charm. And a wrought-iron gate looks elegantly formal at the entrance to a Victorian-style home. Whatever type of gate you choose, you can add ornamental interest with catches, hinges, and locks that enhance the overall effect.

Anchoring Wooden Fence Posts

To delay rot, set fence posts in concrete. First dig a posthole deep enough to set one-third the total length of the post belowground. Then place a flat-topped stone in the hole to act as a base. Insert the post, then pour in and tamp down 4 to 6 inches of gravel. Fill the hole with concrete 2 to 3 inches at a time, tamping it in as you go and using a level to make sure the post is vertical. To allow for expansion, cut two pieces of plywood into wedges that are several inches long, as wide as the post, and about an inch thick; coat them with motor oil, then position them on either side of the post as you pour the concrete. Remove them after the concrete dries and fill the spaces with sand or tar.

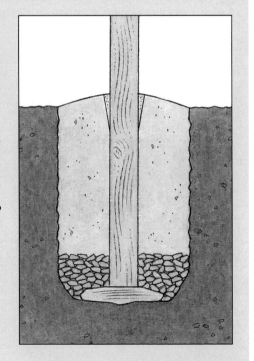

Decorative Garden Objects: from Casual to Classic

CONTAINERS ON PARADE
Culinary plantings of thyme, oregano, fennel, sage, tarragon, and mint share space with ornamental daisies, pinks, heliotrope, and alyssum in a trio of terra-cotta containers at the edge of a brick patio.

Decorative elements such as containers, statuary, benches, and sundials can help you create a garden that's more than just a pretty collection of plants. Thoughtfully selected and placed, outdoor decorative pieces can create a focal point, complement foliage and flowers, define boundaries, provide smooth transitions between plantings, and increase the space available for cultivation. Before you select your garden decorations, make sure you know your garden well, and let its size, style, and purpose guide you. Classical statues look appropriately imposing in a formal garden with well-defined beds; a stone frog hiding under some parsley sprigs might better suit a kitchen garden.

Container Gardening

Containers, a favorite of the city gardener with limited space for cultivation, come in many shapes, sizes, and materials. Filled with annuals or perennials, they can go almost anywhere to brighten an existing plant bed or to extend your growing area on patios, decks, balconies, sidewalks, and even walls. People confined to wheelchairs or those for whom bending and kneeling are difficult may find containers a pleasing gardening alternative to

Making a Log Planter

A fallen tree trunk can be recycled into a distinctive wooden planter that will hold a mixture of perennials and annuals. First, dig out the center of the log to a depth of about a foot, then cut a V-shaped groove from the center opening out to one end of the log; this will provide drainage. Fill the hole with an appropriate soil mix, then plant easy-care varieties such as begonias, hostas, impatiens, or bulbs.

Place one or more logs around a patio or along a garden path; or place your log planter in a less structured setting. Set several small boulders around the log to stabilize it and help it blend with its setting.

working in the ground. Containers can also become garden focal points or accents if they have sufficient presence.

Be sure to choose containers that will suit their contents. If you want to highlight your plantings, simple containers are best. If, on the other hand, you wish to feature a lovely pot, choose a simpler plant. And if an outdoor container is to hold perennials, be sure it is large enough to keep freezing temperatures from reaching the roots.

Choosing Containers

Pick a container that is the correct size and weight for your plant and your purposes. If you are hanging plants from a ceiling or wall, lightweight plastic planters or a wire-and-moss arrangement may be best. Heavier trees and shrubs need to be based in sturdy tubs or barrels so that they are not blown over by a strong wind. And always locate your containers where they're not too difficult to reach for watering.

Anything from a wheelbarrow to an old sink can be turned into a container for plants. Most of the containers available commercially are made of terra cotta, wood, plastic, cast stone, or concrete or fiberglass molded to look like stone.

Terra cotta works well in both formal and informal settings, and its neutral color harmonizes with almost any color of flower or foliage. But it may not stand up to repeated freezing and thawing, and glazed terra cotta is even less resistant to fluctuating hot and cold temperatures.

Wood containers, such as barrels or tubs, are unaffected by frost and can be treated to resist rot. They look better in casual settings and, because they are available in large sizes, are often used for permanent plantings such as ornamental fruit trees, juniper trees, and some varieties of cypress, azalea, and rhododendron. Small wooden boxes are attractive underneath windows, on porch or deck railings, or along the perimeter of a patio. You can paint them for added visual interest.

Because plastic and composite containers start to look shabby relatively quickly, it's best to limit their use to annuals. Petunias, impatiens, geraniums, and snapdragons will flourish in a plastic container hung from the porch ceiling. Plastic is

A CORE OF PRECISION IN A SHIMMERING BED
Vinca 'Little Bright Eyes', Cleome 'Royal Queen', Zinnia elegans 'Bouquet White', and Artemisia schmidtiana 'Silver Dust' surround this New Jersey garden's sundial in summer. In winter, the absence of flowers will bring out its elegant form even more strongly.

available in a variety of colors. Green and other neutral colors are a safe bet with any planting; white containers quickly show scratches and dirt.

Cast stone and concrete containers are appropriate for both formal and informal gardens. They resist damage from rain, snow, and freezing temperatures. Plan the placement of a large stone container carefully—once it is filled it will be difficult to move. Some fiberglass containers look like stone but are much lighter.

Decorative Details

Garden ornaments can make a garden uniquely your own. Adornments help set a garden's tone, be it whimsical, understated, formal, practical, or sentimental. An ornament might be a focal point, or you might tuck one in an out-of-the-way corner to be come upon unexpectedly.

Heavy stone objects like urns look best in a formal garden with well-defined paths. In this sort of setting you might use an obelisk or a sundial on a pedestal as a centerpiece. A fragrant herb garden would be a prime location for a conical beehive shape; small stone sculptures of dogs, cats, frogs, rabbits, turtles, or gnomes are popular additions to a woodland garden.

Ornaments of all sorts are available in gardening stores and through catalogs, but if you're creative, you can turn almost anything into a garden decoration. Birdbaths and old birdcages lend a piquant air. Or if an old weather vane or lantern appeals to you, try it out. After all, it's your garden.

Seating

Before you choose seating for your garden, consider these questions: Will a seat at a given location serve as a brief rest spot, an afternoon lounging retreat, or a vantage point from which to view a certain portion of the landscape? Will the seating be permanent, or will you want to shift it as the sunlight fades and the seasons change?

A bench or chair for the garden is more than just a place to sit; it can be used as a decoration as well. Various kinds of seats are available in a range of sizes, materials, and colors. The challenge is to make sure that your seat, bench, or swing harmonizes with its surroundings. A formal scrolled-iron bench, for example, may look out of place among plant containers created from rusted milk pails and weathered wine cases.

In formal gardens, stone benches might be used to define boundaries between cultivated

beds; they can also work in tandem with such stone ornaments as statues, vases, and urns to contribute to the stately tone of such gardens.

You might also place a bench at the end of a path, grass alley, or arbor to provide a visual focal point and a convenient resting place after a stroll in the garden. Cast-iron furniture looks at home in a formal setting, while rustic twig furniture adds a homey touch to a more informal garden. Wicker and rattan contribute an exotic flavor to many settings; they will survive longer if they are somewhat protected from the elements.

Traditionally, garden furniture has been green, white, or black. White contrasts most sharply with the surrounding foliage; green blends more smoothly with the varied tints of leaves, bushes, and grasses; and black is the most stately. But many colorful alternatives are now available.

A NATURAL SEATING AREA IN A CASUAL GARDEN
The owner of this Los Angeles garden, not Mother Nature, provided the large flat-topped stone on which to sit and enjoy the scenery. Set atop flagstones among plumes of rose fountain grass, feather grass, and drifts of sweet alyssum, the stone seat also provides a visual transition between the two plant groupings.

Vertical Garden Structures

Vertical elements—trellises, arbors, pergolas, lath houses, and gazebos—can be the most interesting and decorative structures in your garden. They create design interest in the landscape by leading the eye upward. And, like the walls or fences that enclose your garden, they strengthen its sense of composition by framing what lies beyond them.

Whether simple or elaborate, vertical landscape elements perform practical as well as aesthetic functions. They can provide shade for plants and people, sheltered spots for seating, and alcoves or other places for repose. They can serve as focal points. They can provide niches for container plants or act as supports on which to train climbing flowers and vines.

Vertical elements should be aesthetically pleasing, blending with your overall garden design. When planning for such objects, it is important to see in your mind's eye the structure that will underlie the imagined glories of a crown of flowers. For unless it supports an evergreen climber, over the long winter the framework of your arbor or pergola will be clearly visible.

Construction materials used for vertical elements include wood, stone, brick, metal, and wrought iron. You can also fashion appealing rus-

tic structures from willow or grapevines gathered in your own garden or a nearby field *(right)*.

While vertical structures can add greatly to the visual impact of your garden, they are also capable of overpowering it if installed without forethought. One such architectural element goes a long way, so exercise restraint. As with any garden structure, a vertical one should be proportioned to match the scale of the garden and home so that it complements and does not overwhelm the landscape.

Freestanding Structures

Pergolas, arbors, trellises, and gazebos are usually ornamental—even fanciful—elements within the garden. An arch or a pergola can resemble a piece of sculpture, beautiful in its own right and enhanced even further by the adornment you choose for it. Beyond their aesthetic appeal, freestanding garden structures provide shade along with privacy and protection—all without sacrificing light or air. They make wonderful supports for all manner of plantings. A trellised archway draped with wisteria or fragrant roses makes a lovely frame for a garden pathway. One caution: For the larger of these structures, be sure your plantings are vigorous enough to cover it adequately. Small, wispy plants will look skimpy, or even sickly, when strung out on a robust frame. On the other hand, don't be tempted to swamp a small frame with plants. Prune your plantings regularly to control their growth.

Pergolas and Arbors

Pergolas, elongated structures of columns supporting a sturdy overhead gridwork of wood rafters, are bold, linear affairs. Traditionally, they function as covered walkways and should therefore lead somewhere, connecting one area to another or perhaps just ending a garden stroll at a seat or ornament. Plan the location of a pergola with care—it will take up considerable room. You might build one over a patio as an extension of your house, or locate it as a freestanding unit at a distance from the house, creating a garden retreat.

Pergolas originated as frameworks for such climbing plants as grapevines. *Vitis vinifera* 'Purpurea' and the hybrid 'Brant' provide wonderful color on a pergola in the fall. Other climbing vines also do well on pergolas.

Arbors, with their graceful arches and enclosed seats, are generally less imposing than pergolas. An arbor can be used to create a private nook off the beaten path, a quiet spot for resting or reading,

FRAMING A GARDEN ENTRYWAY
An arched trellis laden with pink clematis beckons visitors to pass beneath it and into the Salem, Oregon, garden beyond. Along with the fence, the trellis acts as both a focal point and a garden divider. A border hedge of boxwood lines the walkway, and white hawthorn blooms in front of the fence.

Making a Rustic Trellis

Fashioning your own trellis from flexible grapevines or willow twigs is not difficult and can lend a pleasant rustic touch to an informal garden design. To make a trellis like the one shown below, first construct a rectangular frame of sturdy branches—cedar, maple, walnut, or sycamore—by nailing the pieces of wood together to form posts and crosspieces. Then bend flexible grapevines or willow shoots so that they arch over the frame, and attach them to the supporting pieces with twine or plastic ties.

Wind additional grapevines around the crosspieces for a decorative touch. Then prop your finished trellis against a garden wall or fence and train climbing roses, vines, or even vegetables to scurry up it.

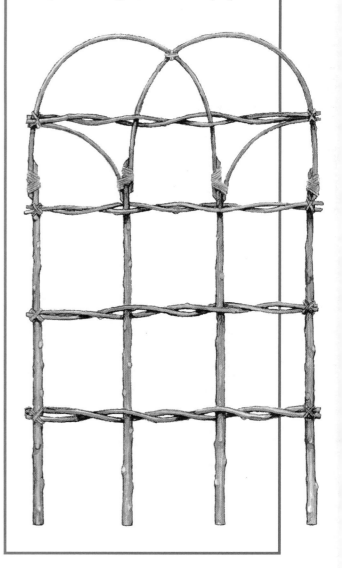

or for just enjoying your garden in solitude. If you design it so that it faces a lovely view in the garden or occupies a particularly warm and sunny spot, you'll be sure to enjoy it to the fullest. Arbors are usually associated with climbing plants—classically, grapes and roses. Train them to climb up the sides of the structure and cascade over the top.

Trellises

A trellis acts like a screen, creating a partial barrier that provides a measure of shade, shelter, and privacy but never completely blocks out air and light. A traditional trellis has panels of wood latticework that can either abut a wall, a fence, or the side of the house, or stand freely. If you incorporate a seating area into your trellis, it can provide a wonderful spot for enjoying tranquillity and repose.

Traditionally, trellis panels are made from a grid of perpendicular wood slats attached to a frame. The design of the trellis can be simple or intricate, incorporating a variety of arches and posts. You can build a trellis from decay-resistant woods such as redwood, cypress, or cedar that weather naturally into a handsome hue over the years. If you

use pine, however, it should be pressure-treated; otherwise, you will have to treat it with a preservative and either stain or paint it to prevent rotting.

Although a trellis primarily serves as a plant support, don't mask the underlying wood pattern with too much vegetation. Take into account the style and intricacy of your trellis design and balance that with the habit and vigor of your climbing and twining plants. If your trellis is of a tightly woven crisscross pattern, for example, it's better to use a light, airy climber like clematis than a larger-leaved climber, which would look too heavy.

Gazebos and Lath Houses

A gazebo is a roofed and often elevated pavilion that serves as a kind of ornate freestanding deck and gives a whimsical focus to the garden. It is usually circular, square, or octagonal, with low latticework sides that often support pretty flowering vines. A lath house is similar to a pergola in form but much more lightly constructed. Its main purpose is to create dappled shade rather than to support climbing plants, though it may well bear light herbaceous vines.

A PERGOLA FOR DINING AND ENTERTAINING *This pergola constructed over a patio in Santa Barbara, California, creates a garden room for outdoor relaxation. The chairs and the table, with its tree-trunk pedestal, echo the natural look of the pergola. Juniper shrubs flank the structure, and Laurentia fluviatilis 'Blue Star Creeper' fills the spaces between the flagstones.*

Rock Gardens and Water Features

Adding rock gardens or water features to your property is not a simple undertaking; it requires thoughtful planning to make the finished elements look as if they belonged in a particular spot. Yet nothing compares with the topographical texture, color, variety, and focus these features bring to a garden, to say nothing of the elegance they impart.

If a rock garden is high on your list of wants, you should first candidly assess whether it will look natural in its setting. Don't try to impose one on a region lacking natural rock formations. And remember that once it is set in place, a rock garden is not easily rearranged, so before you undertake any heavy lifting, prepare carefully. Concentrate first on the overall design for placement of the rocks, as this task will be more demanding than that of drawing up a planting plan.

Begin by sketching a design on paper. If your garden will be larger than a few square yards, work out a schedule for building it—perhaps in stages over several seasons. Good drainage is important,

ROCK ANCHORS FOR BRIGHT COLORS
Fluffy white double arabis tumbles downward through the grade changes in this upstate New York rock garden, finding a foothold in gravelly patches along the way. Composed of native granite stones in various shapes and sizes, the man-made outcrop provides a home for pink phlox, golden Aurinia, and shade-tolerant Ajuga.

so avoid low, wet places. A possible exception to a location with good drainage is a spot on a slope with a drainage problem that might be solved or at least ameliorated by installing a rock garden.

As you create your design, take advantage of existing features—rock formations, a mound or rise, or shrubs that will provide background. If your garden already contains a single large rock or an attractive collection of them, use these as your starting point.

Adding Elevation

If your rock garden will be large, include minor grade changes in your plan—stones and rocks generally look best in layers, just as they occur in nature. Choose stones that are flat and wide and are native to your area.

If you'd like a sloping rather than a vertical rise in elevation, place each succeeding tier of stones

several inches back from the one beneath it. Position each stone to slant downward toward the rear so rainwater will seep back among the stones.

Installing a Water Feature

Planning for a water feature begins with assessing its purpose. Will it be a dominating feature in your landscape or brighten a hidden corner? From what spot on your property would you like to view it? How will it fit into the rest of your garden plan? What wildlife do you expect to attract? Do you want to have fish? If your landscaping style is informal, you might want to simulate a natural pond. Such a free-form basin requires considerable space. If you prefer straight lines and geometric patterns, a formal pool with a fountain or a piece of sculpture might suit you best. Given its shape, a formal pool will most likely require a concrete bottom and sides—and installing these is most likely a job for a contractor.

For the health of your pool, look for a place that receives direct sunlight for at least 3, and preferably 6, hours each day. Containers that hold less than 100 gallons, however, do need shade in the middle of the day to prevent overheating of the water, which could be fatal to fish and plants. Avoid low places where runoff might collect under your pond and damage concrete or masonry during freezes and thaws. If possible, avoid overhanging trees, whose falling leaves could pollute the water.

As you plan your pond, consider the visual effect you want to create. The color of the pond liner—the sheet of waterproof material laid along the bottom and sides to serve as the actual container for the water—is important. A dark liner intensifies reflections and creates a mirrorlike effect; a light liner cuts down reflections and invites the observer to look deeply into the pond.

Building the Pond

If your pond is not of Olympic proportions and does not require concrete, you can probably do the work yourself—or at least oversee it. Lay out the shape of the pond in any design you choose, using a garden hose or a rope. To line an irregularly shaped pond, you will need a strong synthetic-rubber liner at least 45 millimeters thick. Its length and width should be the same as that of your excavation plus twice the maximum depth.

You might wish to plan for both a shallow area in your pond where birds can drink and a deeper one that will provide fish with cool temperatures and security. Depending on the climate, the depth of your pond should vary from a minimum of 4 inches to a maximum of 3½ feet. Dig two or three tiers in your pond, finishing with a shelf around the perimeter to lodge the coping stones that will form the edging of the pond and anchor the lining in place. Line the excavation with sand, carpet padding, or even newspapers to protect your pond liner from being punctured by sharp stones or roots. Lay the liner in the excavation and weight the edges with brick or stone coping.

Fill the pond with water and let it stand at least 1 week to reduce the chlorine levels before you introduce any fish or plants. In a well-balanced pond—one stocked with oxygenating grasses—algae growth will be restrained and the pond will remain reasonably clean. Bog plants and flowering aquatics will thrive along with water lilies submerged in widemouthed pots.

Avoid stocking the pond with more fish than the miniature ecosystem can support. To prevent a buildup of toxic ammonia and solid waste, you will probably need a filtration system. A pond of a capacity of less than 1,000 gallons needs only a small pump to circulate at least half the water every hour through a filter box and up to a fountain that aerates the water. You can purchase effective filtering systems that use either biological, mechanical, or chemical means.

A TRANQUIL HAVEN
The lush textures of a full-blown summer morning are reflected in the dark, velvety waters of this garden pond in Birmingham, Alabama, where bog plants, water lilies, and other aquatics thrive in submerged containers. Potted caladiums and ferns complete the cheerful setting and tie the water garden to the soft lawn beside it.

TIPS FROM THE PROS

Making a Pond Self-Sustaining

A new pond is likely to become cloudy with algae at first, because its natural chemical balance, its microorganisms, and the plant populations you put in need time to establish themselves. To keep unicellular algae—the floating cloudy stuff —under control while that process takes place, you can use a commercial algicide. However, don't try to get rid of all the mosslike algae that clings to the sides of the pond. It may be unsightly, but it is also useful to the health of your water garden. And natural scavengers, especially snails and tadpoles, will graze on it and help keep it in check.

To maintain a good ecological balance in the pond, include the following elements:
• One bunch of submerged plants for each 1 to 2 square feet of pond surface. Small ponds (fewer than 100 square feet in surface area) and those that receive a great deal of sun will need a higher ratio of plant material than larger and shadier ones.
• Floating leaf plants to cover roughly 50 percent of the pond's surface.
• One scavenger fish for each 1 to 2 square feet of pond surface.
• Up to 20 gallons of water for each 4-inch fish.

Lighting Your Garden for Utility and Beauty

Bathing the nighttime landscape with the warm glow of soft light can add an ethereal quality to your garden and extend the hours you spend enjoying it with family and friends. Whether your plans call for ground-level lanterns, lamps set high on posts, recessed lights in walls or steps, or accent lighting, the key is to use very soft lighting so that the effect is subtle, not harsh.

Safety First

You'll need to plan your lighting scheme so that it not only shows off your plantings to best advantage but also helps your guests avoid bumping into objects or tripping on steps or walkways. At a minimum, you should focus the lighting on paved surfaces. Ankle-level lights along the edges of pathways, for example, will deflect light downward, both illuminating the walkway and lending a flattering glow to plants and flowers bordering the path. You should also install lighting in or alongside steps, on walls, or underneath railings to help people see where they are walking, and illuminate pools, decks, and patios for safety as well as for aesthetic reasons.

Advanced Lighting Technology

If you thought you needed an electrician or a landscape architect to install lighting in your garden, think again. The advent of low-voltage outdoor lighting systems has changed all that. Operating at 12 to 24 volts of electricity instead of the 120 volts that household fixtures require, these lighting systems are inexpensive to install, maintain, and use. No permits are required, the cables don't need to be heavily protected and buried, and the only special equipment you need is a step-down transformer to reduce your household current to the correct voltage. Do-it-yourself lighting kits, complete with the transformer, are available at most garden centers. Many of these kits also come with timing devices to turn the lights on and off automatically.

Another advancement in garden lighting has been the introduction of new, smaller bulbs. These bulbs are more energy efficient than older models and can cast light with laserlike accuracy or great subtlety, giving you a choice of design effects not previously available.

Types of Installations to Choose From

Garden lights range in type from freestanding lamps and lanterns to ground-level path lights, recessed step lighting, floodlighting, and accent lighting. In regions that receive plentiful sunlight, small, pagoda-shaped solar-powered walk lights require no wiring and can be placed at any sunny spot in the garden.

Lighting fixtures are made of all types of materials—plastic, cast brass, bronze, copper, steel, aluminum, granite, and stone. As a rule of thumb, outdoor lights should be inconspicuous—it is their effect, not their design, that should have the greatest impact on your garden. Of course, some fixtures are meant to be decorative, such as lampposts at the entrance to a path or lanterns to frame a gate. But ideally, your lighting plan will be designed so that, once installed, the fixtures will be virtually unnoticeable during the day. Placing fixtures high in trees is one way of hiding them while at the same time creating intriguing shadows and diffusing the light (page 76).

Bulbs of clear, white light can be used anywhere in the landscape. Color filters are usually reserved for illuminating water features; overuse of colored lights can create a garish effect. Yellow lights, however, are good for discouraging mosquitoes and other flying insects.

All fittings must be grounded for safety; and cables, above- or belowground, must be weather- and childproof. Of course, installations in wet spots and pools must use submersible fixtures.

Using Lighting to Create an Effect

To achieve the effect you want, think about what parts of the garden you wish to illuminate—not only what must be lit for safety reasons, but which structural accents, trees, or shrubs you want to

MAGICAL GLOW IN AN EVENING GARDEN *Ornamental lanterns, glowing just after twilight, illumine the way along a lush green path in this Asheville, North Carolina, garden. Just peeking over the tops of the plants, the rustic lanterns marry well with the informality of the timber steps and the tumbled plantings of pink phlox, orange 'Berie Ferris' daylilies, and yellow chrysanthemums that spill onto the walkway. A lavender butterfly bush and a pale green pyramidal Cryptomeria japonica 'Sekkan-Sugi' anchor the planting.*

highlight for aesthetic reasons. Take a powerful flashlight outdoors and shine it in various directions, playing up light and shadow to see where lighting will have the best impact. You will most likely have to use trial and error to find the right lighting scheme for your property. A simple change in the location, intensity, angle of beam, or the number of lights you use can dramatically affect the outcome.

For the most natural look, it is better to err on the side of caution; overlighting will give an artificial look to your plants. Instead of installing one or two powerful lights, use five or six low-wattage ones for a softer, warmer glow.

Plants to Light Up the Night

White blooms are particularly lovely at night. Under soft illumination, flowers like *Phlox paniculata* 'Mount Fuji', *Nicotiana alata*, and *Ipomoea alba* appear to float above their dark greenery. Plants with silver or variegated leaves also produce a beautiful effect under night lighting. Since white flowers tend to be more heavily scented than brightly colored ones, planting jasmine or lily of the valley along the edge of a pathway or along steps will send up a wonderful perfume to add to the pleasure of your nighttime garden strolls.

Artful Highlighting

Lights can be positioned to illuminate objects in your garden in dramatic or subtle ways, allowing you to showcase trees, shrubs, and ornaments. Whether you wish to highlight a particular plant feature or perhaps imitate moonlight, you can find a fixture and a mounting position to create the desired effect. Some of the methods shown here require a wall as a backdrop; others rely solely on clever positioning of the lights. Modern lighting fixtures are easily moved, making it simple to change the lighting scheme when desired.

Silhouetting: If a small tree or shrub with attractive symmetry or unusual form is growing in front of a wall, you can feature it by placing a light behind the plant to show it in full relief.

Shadow lighting: Another treatment for a tree or shrub in front of a wall is to aim a light source at the plant from the front. The light will do double duty, both illuminating the plant and casting its form in shadow against the wall.

Downlighting: Mounting soft, diffuse lighting at least 20 feet up in a tree will allow the light to filter down, imitating a gentle moonlight effect. This can also be a particularly subtle and evocative way of illuminating ground cover or a walkway beneath trees.

Uplighting: Placing light sources in front of your trees and angling them upward highlights bark and foliage, accentuating textures and shapes.

Crosslighting: Placing fixtures high in trees so that beams of light cross each other will accentuate depth and texture, highlighting the three-dimensional forms of your plantings and softening shadows falling within the combined beams.

Introducing Landscape Elements into the Design

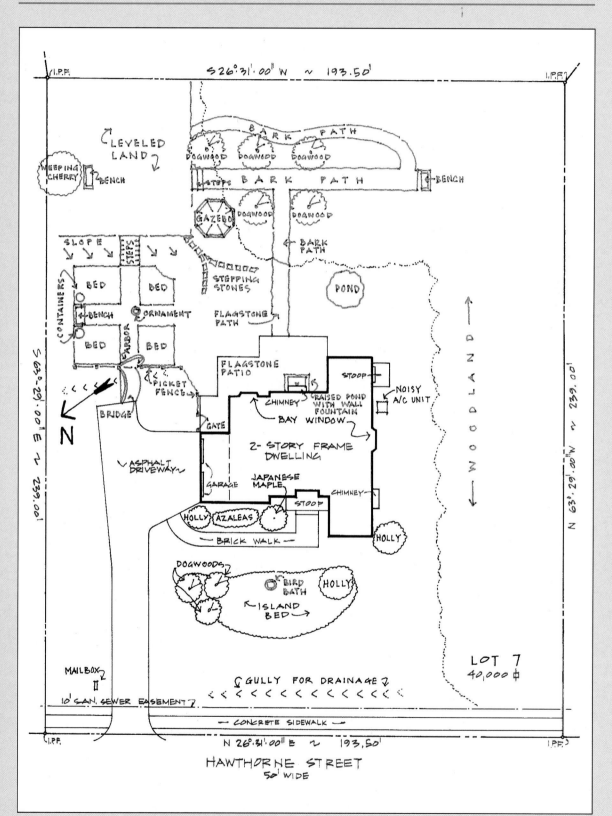

S 26°31'00" W ~ 193.50'

LEVELED LAND

WEEPING CHERRY BENCH

BARK PATH

DOGWOOD DOGWOOD DOGWOOD

STEPS BARK PATH BENCH

GAZEBO DOGWOOD DOGWOOD

BARK PATH

SLOPE STEPS

CONTAINERS BED BED STEPPING STONES

POND

BENCH ORNAMENT

BED BED FLAGSTONE PATH

ARBOR

BRIDGE PICKET FENCE

FLAGSTONE PATIO

STOOP

CHIMNEY RAISED POND WITH WALL FOUNTAIN NOISY A/C UNIT

N GATE BAY WINDOW

2-STORY FRAME DWELLING

ASPHALT DRIVEWAY

JAPANESE MAPLE

GARAGE STOOP CHIMNEY

HOLLY AZALEAS

BRICK WALK HOLLY

DOGWOODS

BIRD BATH HOLLY

ISLAND BED

LOT 7
40,000 ⌀

WOODLAND

S 63°29'00" E ~ 239.00'

N 63°29'00" W ~ 239.00'

MAILBOX

GULLY FOR DRAINAGE

10' SAN. SEWER EASEMENT

CONCRETE SIDEWALK

N 26°31'00" E ~ 193.50'

HAWTHORNE STREET
50' WIDE

BUILDING ON THE OLD TO CREATE THE NEW
The first phase of designing a new garden is to decide on and position the landscape elements, as well as to make any necessary changes in existing landforms, hardscape installations, and vegetation. Here, the homeowner has noted changes and new installations in blue ink over the permanent features on the original property plat (page 34). Some trees have been transplanted and others removed, and the east-corner slope has been regraded into a terrace. The woods have been thinned, and undergrowth has been cleared away. Beds have been laid out. And a scheme of walkways, paths, trellises, benches, gates, and other hardscape elements has been added. The design has now advanced to the point where it is time to draw up a planting plan—which is the business of the next chapter.

Designing with Plants

By the time you sit down to choose the plants for your garden, you will already have a picture in your mind—and a plan on paper—formulated around the style of the garden you want, the purpose behind the design, the size of your property, and those plants already in the ground.

To make that plan a reality, you will need to select and group your plants so that their forms, textures, and colors blend to create the visual effects you desire. In the Ashton, Maryland, garden at left, for example, the homeowner has used a sequence of green tones—with pink roses as a foil—to draw a visitor irresistibly toward the archway and into what she calls a "fairy garden" of silvery foliage beyond.

On the following pages you will learn how to make selections from among the entire panoply of plants—beginning with the garden's most stalwart members, the trees and shrubs. Your choices will bring to a gratifying conclusion the design ideas you have so carefully considered and lovingly put into place.

A. *Rosa 'Aloha' (6)*
B. *Rosa 'Belle de Crécy' (1)*
C. *Berberis thunbergii (10)*

A(6)

C(5)

B(1)

C(5)

The key lists each plant type and the number of plants needed to replicate the garden shown. The letters and numbers above refer to the type of plant and the number sited in an area.

Laying Down the Framework

The architecture of a garden is formed by its trees and shrubs. They serve as visual linchpins that hold the entire planting scheme together. Some may already be growing on your property and are sited just where you want them; others may need transplanting to fit into your design. In addition, you will unquestionably want to put in a number of new shrubs and trees—both deciduous and evergreen. If you select these plants carefully for shape, winter silhouette, and visual density, they will create shade, accent focal points, define spaces, provide backdrops, and screen out unwanted views.

But there is much more to garden design than just these architectural plants. Evergreen ground covers and small areas of lawn, for example, will help balance the design of your garden. Like trees and shrubs, they are permanent elements in the landscape. Vines also have a part to play: They can climb walls and fences or stand in for a shrub in a narrow space. Ornamental grasses, too, can partially fill the role of shrubs. While not as permanent as woody plants, they will provide interest for 10 or 11 months of the year. Tall varieties can be used as focal points, and smaller, weeping specimens are ideal for planting around a patio or a pond.

The most prominent of all these garden inhabitants are the trees that tower over the scene and give your garden its fundamental character. Large trees that flourish in full sun not only bestow generous amounts of shade but also lend an air of solidity to even an immature garden. Because such trees link your property with the surrounding land, it's a good idea to choose species similar to those growing nearby, which are likely to be native or adapted types.

Deciduous trees are the best choice for providing shade next to the house. In summer their leafy canopies block out the sun and naturally cool your

A SHADY OASIS IN SUMMER
This house and garden in Washington, D.C., are shielded from the scorching summer sun by midsize deciduous trees. Twelve river birches and two each of dogwood, redbud, and serviceberry create dappled light and ideal growing conditions for the ivy, sweet woodruff, wild ginger, and other shade-loving plants growing in this formal space.

home's interior; in winter the bare branches allow the sun to brighten and warm the rooms. To create shade for a bed or border, choose deciduous species with fine-textured foliage or an open habit that will cast dappled shade. Avoid trees with shallow roots, such as silver and Norway maples and American sweet gum, because they will outpace the roots of smaller plants in the competition for growing room, moisture, and nutrients. If space is limited, use small varieties of ornamental trees that won't overwhelm the house or the landscape or require constant pruning to restrain their size. Install cultivars of dogwood, Japanese maple, sassafras, birch, and hawthorn in groupings of three or more to screen an area from late afternoon sun.

Keep your intended location in mind when choosing trees. For example, don't plant fruiting types near a deck, patio, or walkway, where the dropping fruits will make a mess underfoot and will stain stonework, decks, or outdoor furniture.

Accent Plants

An easy way to create anchors or focal points is to plant individual accent trees and shrubs—also known as specimens. Some specimen trees and shrubs add color to a planting design with spring or summer flowers or brilliantly hued fall foliage, while others capture interest with such features as textured bark, twisted limbs, or distinctive leaves.

A tree with contorted or sculptural lines will take on a more dramatic appearance if it rises from a ground cover or a sward of green grass. The simplicity of the setting will allow you to focus on the strong lines of a trunk or spreading branches. To maintain this feeling of openness when planting a specimen tree in an island bed, surround it with plants that grow only a few feet tall.

You can also place two specimen plantings in such a way that they call attention to each other. Plant low-growing *Acer palmatum* 'Dissectum Atropurpureum', for example, in the same bed with *Cedrus atlantica* 'Glauca' (Atlas cedar), which raises its silvery blue steeple to dramatic heights. In winter, the weeping leafless branches of the maple will set off the cedar's pale bluish green needles.

An accent tree can also be used as a focal point in front of an evergreen hedge or a fence or to soften a corner of the house. But take care not to overwhelm the scene with an outsize or excessively showy selection. Your accent tree should match the scale of its surroundings.

A DESIGN FOR ALL SEASONS
Flowering Sargent cherries and blue pansies are among the plants that provide springtime color in this Charlottesville, Virginia, garden. Throughout the year the rounded boxwood, the line of the wall, and the ziggurat of the steps make a striking composition.

Recommended Trees and Shrubs

FAST-GROWING SHADE TREES
Acer rubrum
(red maple)
Aesculus glabra
(Ohio buckeye)
Fraxinus americana
(white ash)
Fraxinus pennsylvanica
(red ash)
Gleditsia triacanthos
(honey locust)
Liquidambar styraciflua
(American sweet gum)
Liriodendron tulipifera
(tulip poplar)
Pistacia chinensis
(Chinese pistachio)

SPECIMEN AND ACCENT TREES
Acer palmatum 'Bloodgood'
(Japanese maple)
Acer palmatum 'Dissectum Atropurpureum'
(threadleaf Japanese maple)
Chilopsis linearis
(desert willow)
Cornus kousa
(kousa dogwood)
Cotinus coggygria
(smoke tree)
Euonymus alata 'Compacta'
(winged spindle tree)
Magnolia stellata
(star magnolia)
Prunus subhirtella var. *pendula*
(weeping Higan cherry)
Punica granatum 'Legrellei'
(pomegranate)
Stewartia pseudocamellia
(Japanese stewartia)
Syringa reticulata
(Japanese tree lilac)

EVERGREEN TREES
Cedrus atlantica 'Glauca'
(blue Atlas cedar)
Cedrus deodara
(deodar cedar)
Chamaecyparis obtusa 'Crippsii'
(hinoki false cypress)
Ilex opaca
(American holly)
Ligustrum ovalifolium 'Aureum'
(California golden privet)
Magnolia grandiflora
(bull bay)

81

TREE AND SHRUB SHAPES

Columnar Plants	Type/Growth Pattern	Height	Zones	Weeping/Arching Plants	Type/Growth Pattern	Height	Zones
Acer platanoides 'Columnare' (Norway maple)	fast-growing deciduous tree	40-50 ft.	4-9	*Buddleia alternifolia/ B. davidii* (butterfly bush)	fast-growing deciduous flowering shrub	6-10 ft.	5-9
Acer rubrum 'Columnare' (red maple)	fast-growing deciduous tree	40-50 ft.	3-7	*Fagus sylvatica* 'Pendula' (weeping beech)	moderate-growing deciduous tree	40 ft.	4-7
Ginkgo biloba 'Princeton Sentry' (maidenhair-tree)	slow-growing deciduous tree	50 ft.	4-8	*Forsythia* x *intermedia* 'Spring Glory' (golden-bells)	fast-growing deciduous flowering shrub	6 ft.	5-9
Malus 'Sentinel' (crab apple)	fast-growing deciduous flowering/fruiting tree	15-20 ft.	4-8	*Pyrus salicifolia* 'Pendula' (willow-leaved pear)	moderate-growing deciduous flowering tree	25 ft.	5-7
Pinus sylvestris 'Fastigiata' (Scotch pine)	fast-growing needled evergreen tree	25-40 ft.	2-8	*Tsuga canadensis* 'Pendula' (Canada hemlock)	slow-growing needled evergreen tree	20 ft.	2-8
Rhamnus frangula 'Columnaris' (alder buckthorn)	fast-growing deciduous flowering/fruiting shrub	12 ft.	2-8	**Broad-Spreading Plants**	**Type/Growth Pattern**	**Height**	**Zones**
Pyramidal Plants	**Type/Growth Pattern**	**Height**	**Zones**	*Aesculus parviflora* (bottlebrush buckeye)	fast-growing deciduous flowering shrub	15 ft.	4-8
Oxydendrum arboreum (sourwood)	slow-growing deciduous flowering tree	25-30 ft.	5-9	*Castanea mollissima* (Chinese chestnut)	moderate-growing deciduous tree	30-60 ft.	4-9
Pseudolarix kaempferi (golden larch)	slow-growing needled deciduous conifer	30-50 ft.	6-8	*Cephalotaxus harringtonia* (Japanese plum yew)	slow-growing needled evergreen shrub	20 ft.	6-9
Quercus palustris (pin oak)	fast-growing deciduous tree	50-80 ft.	2-9	*Crataegus* x *mordenensis* 'Toba' (hawthorn)	fast-growing deciduous flowering/fruiting tree	25 ft.	4-9
Sciadopitys verticillata (Japanese umbrella pine)	slow-growing needled evergreen tree	40-80 ft.	4-8	*Photinia* x *fraseri* (Fraser photinia)	fast-growing evergreen flowering/fruiting shrub	10-15 ft.	8-9
Thuja occidentalis 'Pyramidalis' (American arborvitae)	moderate-growing evergreen shrub	10-20 ft.	3-8	**Rounded Plants**	**Type/Growth Pattern**	**Height**	**Zones**
Fan/Vase Plants	**Type/Growth Pattern**	**Height**	**Zones**	*Aesculus* x *carnea* 'Briotii' (red horse chestnut)	slow-growing deciduous tree	40 ft.	3-7
Amelanchier canadensis (shadblow serviceberry)	fast-growing deciduous flowering/fruiting tree	6-20 ft.	4-9	*Amelanchier arborea* (downy serviceberry)	moderate-growing deciduous flowering/ fruiting tree	20 ft.	4-9
Cercis (redbud)	moderate-growing deciduous flowering tree	20-30 ft.	4-9	*Buxus sempervirens* (common boxwood)	slow-growing evergreen shrub	15 ft.	5-8
Magnolia x *soulangiana* (saucer magnolia)	moderate-growing deciduous flowering/ fruiting tree	20-30 ft.	4-9	*Chaenomeles speciosa* (flowering quince)	medium-growing deciduous flowering/ fruiting shrub	2-10 ft.	4-8
Prunus x *blireiana* (blireiana plum)	moderate-growing deciduous flowering tree	25 ft.	5-8	*Malus* 'Coralburst'; *M.* 'Snowdrift' (crab apple)	moderate-growing flowering/fruiting tree	8-20 ft.	3-8
Salix matsudana 'Tortuosa' (dragon-claw willow)	moderate-growing deciduous tree	35 ft.	4-9	*Raphiolepis indica* (Indian hawthorn)	fast-growing evergreen flowering/fruiting shrub	5 ft.	9-10

Plant Features as Accents

When trees with fine and feathery foliage are sited alongside trees bearing large, bold leaves, they create a pleasing contrast, adding variety to massed plantings. Tree foliage comes in many shapes, sizes, and textures, including the heart-shaped leaves of *Cercis canadensis* 'Forest Pansy' (eastern redbud), the fan-shaped leaves of maidenhair-tree, and the large compound leaves of *Aesculus parviflora* (bottlebrush buckeye). For gracefully long leaves look to sourwood. If you want foliage of a finer texture, consider the deeply laciniated and feathery leaves of *Sambucus racemosa* 'Plumosa Aurea' (European red elder), the delicate tracery of threadleaf Japanese maple, and the feathery foliage of evergreens such as *Chamaecyparis* (false cypress) and Atlas cedar.

Flowering and fruiting ornamentals provide double pleasure. In the spring or summer they produce lovely blooms, and in the fall colorful foliage and fruits. Among the best examples are two trees, Washington thorn and *Prunus maackii* (Amur chokecherry), and several shrubs, including shadblow and *Viburnum dilatatum* (linden viburnum). You can get the same effect with a number of plants that may be shaped as either shrubs or small trees: kousa dogwood, *Sorbus alnifolia* (Korean mountain ash), golden rain tree, *Stranvaesia davidiana* (Chinese stranvaesia), pomegranate, and *Prunus* x *blireiana* (blireiana plum).

Shrubs that produce both showy flowers and strikingly colored leaves include *Pieris japonica* 'Red Mill', *Nandina domestica* 'Nana Purpurea', Oregon grape, and witch alder. These plants can be chosen to harmonize or contrast with the house trim or a facade of brick or stained wood siding. If nestled against a backdrop of evergreen plantings, they will stand out even more dramatically.

Some deciduous trees and shrubs continue to provide interest after leaf fall with shaggy, mottled, corky, or richly colored bark or with gnarled, twisted, knotted, or multiple trunks or branches. Those with the most striking bark are 'Heritage' river birch, *Acer palmatum* 'Senkaki' (coral bark maple), Amur chokecherry, *Salix alba* 'Britzensis'

A DESIGN EMBELLISHED BY NATURE
Perfuming the air with their delicate flowers, Lonicera heckrottii (goldflame honeysuckle) and Trachelospermum jasminoides (star jasmine) climb an arbor in Columbia, South Carolina. The jasmines were planted against the adjoining fence—a good 10 feet away on either side of the arbor—and have worked their way onto the support over the years.

Beginning with a box-wood in the left fore-ground, this garden room in Doylestown, Pennsylvania, is en-closed by a display of (clockwise) cherry lau-rel, Japanese barberry, a yew hedge, a star magnolia, and a low-growing azalea. In early summer the dark hedging is punctuated with the bright flowers of the azalea and the star magnolia, as well as with astilbes and rose mallows.

(coral bark willow), *Pinus bungeana* (lace-bark pine), *Platanus occidentalis* (eastern sycamore), and Amur cork tree. The eastern sycamore has an intriguingly shaped trunk, as does *Crataegus* x *mordenensis* 'Toba' (hawthorn). And *Corylus avellana* 'Contorta' (Harry Lauder's walking stick) grows strikingly twisted branches.

Focusing on Evergreens

A planting design that features the shapes, tex-tures, and colors of evergreen trees and shrubs will ensure year-round structural interest. But be careful not to overuse evergreens, which can cre-ate a heavy feel. It's best to strike a balance be-tween the weight of evergreens and the airiness of deciduous ornamentals.

Evergreens range in shape from miniature cones to tall pyramids, from neat mounds to weep-ing giants. Their foliage also varies dramatically: It may be needled or broad-leaved, with needle tex-tures ranging from soft and feathery to coarse and stiff, from glossy and prickly to smooth and silky. Broad-leaved varieties might be long and droop-ing, small and round, or narrow and pointed. Col-ors run the gamut from palest to darkest green, as well as blue-green, blue-gray, silvery blue, or varie-gated yellow and green or cream and green.

Some evergreen shapes and foliage textures are suited to particular landscape styles. For example, the loose, irregular forms of broad-leaved rhodo-dendrons, *Pieris japonica*, and mountain laurel go well in a woodland garden or a shaded formal gar-den. The stiff, pyramidal shape of Colorado blue spruce, the cone-shaped *Sciadopitys verticillata* (Japanese umbrella pine), and the almost perfectly rounded littleleaf boxwood add formality to a de-sign. The rangy shapes of x *Cupressocyparis ley-landii* (Leyland cypress) and deodar cedar are at home in an informal garden, while the irregular but compact hinoki false cypress and Atlas cedar are equally suited to a formal or an informal design.

Dwarf evergreens are good choices for a rock garden, and can give shape and weight to any loose arrangement of foliage and flowers. Good choices include *Ilex cornuta* 'Carissa', *Ilex crenata*, *Picea abies* 'Nidiformis', *Picea glauca* 'Conica', *Rhododendron* 'Moonstone' and *R.* 'Ramapo', and *Taxus baccata* 'Repandens'. For vertical accents, plant taller evergreen varieties such as cedar, English holly, bull bay, Norway spruce, and Douglas fir. They will stand out dramatically when surrounded by low or round shapes.

Plants for Screening

Hedges are the workhorses of the garden. They not only perform as stately backdrops for herbaceous borders, they can also provide privacy, block undesirable views, and muffle street noises. They can direct the flow of traffic in a garden and lead the eye toward a focal point. They can be planted to form intimate, enclosed garden rooms, and they can give structure to a flat, featureless expanse of lawn. A row of shrubs or trees can also act as a windbreak, keeping the house and garden warmer. When planted near a vegetable garden, a windbreak can create a warmer microclimate, shielding tender young plants and extending the growing season.

When you buy trees and shrubs for hedges or windbreaks, keep in mind both aesthetics and utility. If you wish to complement a formal garden design, choose stiff varieties or those that lend themselves to close clipping for a hedge; floppy or arched varieties are best for an informal garden. And be sure the mature size of the varieties you choose is appropriate for the location.

You can manipulate the sense of space on your property through the height of your hedges: Masses of tall, dense evergreens will make an area look smaller; a hedge of low shrubs or open and airy deciduous trees will create an expansive effect.

A hedge of fast-growing evergreens will screen an unsightly view or object. A more natural-looking alternative, however, would be to install a mixed selection of evergreens in clumps. To block unwelcome sightlines projecting from your neighbors' upper windows, consider a combination of tall columnar or pyramidal evergreens and twiggy deciduous trees such as hornbeam or *Pyrus calleryana* (Callery pear), whose high canopies will put the screening where you most need it.

If your property is large and deep, you can form a multilayered screen by planting tall trees behind lower-growing shrubs, or slow-growing evergreens on the boundary and fast-growing deciduous trees inside. When the purpose of a hedge is to delineate property lines without producing a closed-in look, deciduous shrubs can be very effective. Make sure, however, that such an installation fits in with the garden's overall design. To create a barrier that keeps your pets in and those of your neighbors out, plant fruiting shrubs that bear thorns or prickly leaves, such as barberry, hawthorn, rose, firethorn, or holly. These plants have the added benefit of providing food for wildlife.

Vines

The fastest way to block an ugly view or create a sense of privacy is to install a fence or trellis and grow a perennial vine on it. This almost instant barrier makes a good alternative to the dense shade and screening offered by a mid-size hedge. It can also enclose a space that is too small or narrow for trees or shrubs. Few vines, however, are evergreen, and many deciduous ones die back or need cutting back annually. And some varieties, such as trumpet vine, yellow jessamine, *Akebia quinata* (five-leaf akebia), *Actinidia chinensis* (kiwi fruit), and Japanese wisteria, are such sturdy, heavy growers they need pruning regularly to keep them from getting out of hand or even pulling down the structure they are growing on.

Most of these vines must be trained to climb a support, or be secured to it with wire or twine. Other fast growers, such as clematis, climbing hydrangea, cross-vine, *Polygonum aubertii* (China fleece vine), and star jasmine, twine and grip with tendrils. Vines that climb with extreme ease and cling to any vertical surface with suction roots include *Hedera colchica* 'Dentata' (Persian ivy), Boston ivy, Virginia creeper, *Euonymus fortunei* (winter creeper), and *Ficus pumila* (climbing fig).

Ornamental Grasses

With their graceful foliage and fluffy plumes, perennial ornamental grasses add form and texture to the landscape for most of the year. And their nodding seed heads and rustling leaves provide appealing sound and movement during the winter, when most of the garden is in the doldrums. Varieties range in height from 6 inches to 14 feet. The shorter varieties, such as *Carex morrowii* 'Aurea Variegata' (variegated Japanese sedge), *Arrhenatherum elatius* var. *bulbosum* (bulbous oat grass), *Festuca amethystina* (large blue fescue), and *Hakonechloa macra* 'Aureola'

EVERGREEN SHRUBS AND TREES

Abelia x *grandiflora* (glossy abelia)

Berberis julianae (wintergreen barberry)

Chamaecyparis lawsoniana 'Allumii' (Port Orford cedar)

x *Cupressocyparis leylandii* (Leyland cypress)

Euonymus alata (winged spindle tree)

Ilex x *altaclarensis* 'Wilsonii' (altaclara holly)

Ilex aquifolium (English holly)

Ilex x *attenuata* 'Fosteri' (Foster holly)

Juniperus chinensis (Chinese juniper)

Juniperus occidentalis (Sierra juniper)

Juniperus virginiana 'Skyrocket' (red cedar)

Ligustrum japonicum (waxleaf privet)

Pittosporum (pittosporum)

Prunus caroliniana 'Bright 'n' Tight' (Carolina cherry laurel)

Taxus (yew)

DECIDUOUS SHRUBS AND TREES

Carpinus betulus (European hornbeam)

Forsythia (golden-bells)

Viburnum (arrowwood)

VINES

Clematis armandii (Armand clematis)

Gelsemium sempervirens (yellow jasmine)

Hydrangea anomala ssp. *petiolaris* (climbing hydrangea)

Jasminum mesnyi (primrose jasmine)

Jasminum nudiflorum (winter jasmine)

Lonicera sempervirens (trumpet honeysuckle)

Rosa 'Cécile Brunner' (rose)

Wisteria (wisteria)

Capitalizing on Ornamental Grasses

Most ornamental grasses need not be divided for propagation; they are fast spreading or self-seeding. But like many other herbaceous perennials, they may start to look straggly and die off in the center after years of growth. When they do, it's time to divide them. Do this in early fall so the plants can reestablish themselves before the onslaught of winter; otherwise, wait until midspring.

There are many creative uses for divided clumps. Install low- to midheight grasses to control erosion on a slope, to replace a lawn, or to screen the base of a deck. They also add diversity in sunny herbaceous borders.

Use medium and tall varieties in place of shrubs to create a hedge. Where it may cost a small fortune to edge a sizable property with shrubs or trees, tall perennial grasses are an inexpensive and fast-growing alternative.

If space is limited, you can plant a compact, slow-growing variety, such as *Mis-canthus sinensis* 'Gracillimus' (maiden grass), *Carex morrowii* 'Aurea Variegata' (variegated Japanese sedge), or *Hakonechloa macra* 'Aureola' (golden variegated hakonechloa).

Consider planting some of the smaller grass varieties in containers so they can decorate your front entrance, deck, or patio. To keep the roots from freezing in extremely cold weather, you may have to overwinter the pots in a garage or cool basement.

(golden variegated hakonechloa), make striking combinations when planted as edging companions to low-growing creeping ground covers.

Among those grasses that grow to a middle height are *Pennisetum alopecuroides* (fountain grass), *Calamagrostis acutiflora* 'Stricta' (feather reed grass), *Cortaderia selloana* 'Pumila' (dwarf pampas grass), and *Miscanthus sinensis* 'Purpurascens'. The taller grasses, which can be planted as a privacy screen, include *Cortaderia selloana* (pampas grass), *Miscanthus sinensis* (eulalia), and *Erianthus ravennae* (Ravenna grass).

The leaf colors of most ornamental grasses range from creamy yellow to bright green. Some types have variegated hues, and others—including such low-growing species and cultivars as *Festuca glauca* (blue fescue), *Imperata cylindrica* 'Red Baron' (Japanese blood grass), *Ophiopogon planiscapus* 'Nigrescens' (black mondo grass), and *Carex elata* 'Bowles' Golden' (Bowles' golden sedge)—are distinctively colored.

Ornamental grasses are not only visually appealing but also desirable as fast-growing plants with minimal cultural requirements. In most regions they require no watering or fertilizing and will grow in poor soils. However, perennial varieties will need cutting back once a year in very early spring, before they start to send up new shoots.

Although ornamental grasses spread by root systems and seeds, they are easy to control. Simply remove the young volunteers as soon as they germinate in late summer or the following spring.

Lawns and Meadows

A lawn—even a small one—can be an asset to a garden. It will set off the house and separate the beds from the borders and the driveway. It will serve as a tranquil foil for the diversity of surrounding plants and garden elements. And it can provide a place for relaxation and play. Turf grass, however, needs constant attention. So you might want to consider replacing part of your lawn with an evergreen ground cover or giving over some of it to a sizable island bed planted with a combination of small trees, shrubbery, and ground covers.

The most carefree kind of open expanse is one that has been converted from a lawn into a wildflower meadow. Planted with native annuals and perennials, it requires no feeding or watering and need be mowed only once a year. It also provides food and shelter for butterflies, bees, and beneficial insects. In putting in a meadow, you will want to plant a variety of native flowers. Perennial wildflowers that are good in a wide variety of meadow environments include goldenrod, milkweed, aster, rudbeckia, *Echinacea purpurea* (purple coneflower), tansy, sunflower, yarrow, *Oenothera caespitosa* (twisted evening primrose), *Ranunculus* (buttercup), oxeye daisy, wild bergamot, *Phlox paniculata* (garden phlox), and *Liatris* (gay-feather). Although annual or biennial wildflowers such as *Centaurea cyanus* (cornflower) and Queen Anne's lace die at the end of their flow-

A CANVAS PAINTED IN HUES OF GRASS
The weeping green foliage of Pennisetum alopecuroides (fountain grass) softens the lines of the stonework and creates an intimate seating area in this garden near Baltimore. In the background, the golden foliage of Calamagrostis acutiflora 'Stricta' (feather reed grass) adds warmth and privacy to the scene.

ering season, they also work well. Because they self-seed prolifically, they will return year after year with almost the same certainty as perennials.

A Ground-Cover Carpet

Offering dense growth, year-round color, and interesting texture, ground covers make a fine alternative to turf grass. They can also define, separate, or unify portions of the landscape. When choosing a ground cover to replace an area of lawn, look for a type that meets your needs for speed of growth, ability to withstand light foot traffic, tolerance for sun or shade, and seasonal flower or foliage colors.

Ground covers that will accept moderate foot traffic include *Thymus praecox* (creeping thyme), wintergreen, ivy, winter creeper, bearberry, *Ajuga reptans,* and periwinkle. For shady areas, choose pachysandra, *Chrysogonum virginianum* (goldenstar), *Lamium maculatum* (spotted dead nettle), *Potentilla verna* (spring cinquefoil), or *Ophiopogon* (lilyturf). Ground covers that spread quickly in full sun and are effective in controlling erosion on a slope include *Verbena peruviana*, *Veronica repens, Cerastium tomentosum, Chamaemelum nobile, Hypericum calycinum, Lantana montevidensis,* and *Helianthemum nummularium.* One of the best ground covers to grow in moist or wet ground, whether sunny or shady, is *Lysimachia nummularia.* If the soil is moist and well drained, plant *Mentha requienii.*

Adding Color and Texture

You can ensure maximum year-round interest in your garden by weaving threads of seasonal color throughout its beds and borders. The first step is to sketch out color ideas on paper, so that when you are ready to plant you will be able to create a sense of unity throughout the garden. Your personal preferences will guide you in your initial choice of colors. You may lean toward hues from the warm end of the spectrum, such as red, orange, and yellow, rather than the cool end, which includes the greens, blues, and violets. Perhaps you prefer delicate tints over strong shades, and harmonious blendings over bright contrasts. Before you make any final decisions, however, there are a number of other things you must consider.

Color, Light, and Mood

How colors appear in your garden will depend on two factors—whether a planting is located in sun or shade and the way light changes from morning to night and through the seasons. Pastels stand out in the soft light of early morning or evening, for example, and fairly glimmer in the shade, but their pale presence is lost in bright midday sun, where strong, bright colors like reds and oranges do best. Colors that glow warmly in autumn light, such as bronze or purple, may look drab on hazy summer days or in the cold glare of winter.

One way to plan for successful seasonal colors is to observe the hues nature reveals over time. Spring is a symphony of pastel-blooming trees, shrubs, and bulbs, followed by deeper tints of blue, yellow, and pink as summer gets under way. Late summer is dominated by highly saturated colors—vibrant yellow, Day-Glo orange, hot red, deep pink, fuchsia, and violet. By contrast, fall is cloaked in muted shades of gold, bronze, rust, plum, and purple.

Certain color groupings will create different moods in the garden. Try planting pink, purple, or blue pastels interspersed with neutral whites and grays for a cooling and soothing effect. A garden theme mixing the neutral colors with various shades of green will create a cool retreat in the heat of summer. To add a little warmth, introduce soft creams and buttery yellows to the mix.

If you want a more vibrant atmosphere, choose strong yellows, golds, oranges, and reds. But use red with care; it is the most dominant color in the spectrum and can be overpowering. A backdrop of dark green foliage can tone down even the brightest reds, but a bright green background will make the reds pop out even more.

Color and Space

Through creative placement of colors, you can define spaces and change perspectives in a garden design. Cool colors lengthen distances, warm colors foreshorten them. Your choice of color groupings, therefore, should be based on the perspective you want to achieve.

A FOCAL POINT OF BRIGHT SEASONAL COLOR
Setting the landscape afire with its glowing orange-red fall foliage, a katsura tree (Cercidiphyllum japonicum) stands out from the subtler lime-yellow coloring of Hydrangea anomala ssp. petiolaris (climbing hydrangea) and Idesia polycarpa (iigiri tree).

A TAPESTRY OF ANNUALS AND PERENNIALS
Anchored by a Colorado blue spruce, drifts of Zinnia elegans 'Sun Red', orange Helichrysum bracteatum 'Bright Bikini' (strawflower), pink Phlox maculata 'Alpha' (wild sweet William), and yellow Lilium 'Citronella' put on a dazzling summer show. In the foreground, a broad green drift of Sedum spectabile 'Brilliant' (showy stonecrop) anchors the planting.

When planning beds and borders close to the house, consider how you can accentuate or complement the color of the roof, sides, or trim with foliage and flowers. Also, select herbaceous plants with colors that will tie in with those of adjacent small shrubs, ground covers, and larger plantings. This way, you will maintain a unified color theme.

You can also choose flower colors to attract butterflies and hummingbirds, which favor strong pinks, reds, yellows, and oranges. (Hummingbirds prefer tubular flowers; butterflies, flat and cup-shaped flowers.) To reduce the potentially overwhelming visual impact of these bright colors, use white flowers or dark green, gray, and variegated foliage to separate vivid pinks and reds from equally intense yellows and oranges.

Color from Bulbs and Annuals

To color your landscape from late winter into fall, be sure to include masses of small- and large-flowering bulbs in your design. Select different varieties that bloom simultaneously or those whose bloom times coincide with those of other flowering plants. For example, create a pleasing contrast by teaming up spring-blooming yellow tulips with blue forget-me-nots or with deep blue grape hyacinths. Or, for a harmonious combination, plant purple pansies next to pale lavender crocuses.

Many summer- and fall-flowering bulbs, such as lilies, dahlias, and begonias, bloom for several weeks and will brighten your beds and borders with a rich tapestry of hues ranging from deep pink to brick red, from apricot to bronze. For a blooming sequence that lasts from late winter through fall, plant a sunny border with a mixture of bulbs and perennials—daffodils, Siberian irises, flowering onion, peonies, daylilies, dahlias, rudbeckias, perennial phlox, asters, and chrysanthemums.

Because of their long bloom periods, which can span three seasons, annual bedding plants are good additions to planting schemes that focus on color. Choose their colors carefully, though, so that they will continue to complement the perennials and bulbs in the bed. You can also plant annuals to cover bare spots in the early years of a garden and to fill gaps between shrubs and trees.

Color in the Shade

Areas dominated by trees and shrubs are typically shady, and many varieties of annuals, perennials, and bulbs can brighten these shadowy spots. Begin with late-winter and early-spring bulbs that bloom before deciduous trees leaf out to block the sun. Snowdrops, crocuses, squill, Grecian windflowers, and daffodils are early bloomers that will naturalize into colorful masses.

For the rest of the growing season, fill spaces that receive partial or dappled shade with brightly colored, long-lasting, shade-tolerant perennials such as astilbe, foxglove, spurge, cardinal flower, alumroot, Virginia bluebells, monarda, St.-John's-wort, and red valerian *(Centranthus ruber)*. The most reliable annual for a shady nook is *Impatiens wallerana* (busy Lizzie). If you'd like to draw attention to a pocket of dark green shrubs, illuminate them with a grouping of white or pastel flowers, such as impatiens, columbine, lily of the valley, primrose, and bleeding heart.

Foliage Plants

Flowering plants bring a rainbow of colors to a border or bed, but herbaceous foliage plants also have their place. By no means confined to green, the foliage colors of these plants range all over the rest of the spectrum. Used in contrast with the blooms surrounding them, they can turn a merely pleasing border into a visual feast.

The texture of the foliage, which can vary from fine to coarse, also plays a major role. When foliage plants of different texture and shape are planted next to each other, for example, they add a dramatic dimension to the design. Ferns are a good example of plants with fine and feathery foliage. The leaves range in color from dark green to bright green, but one, *Athyrium nipponicum* 'Pictum', is dramatically edged in silver. Other fine, feathery-leaved plants include astilbe, *Artemisia* x 'Powis Castle', goatsbeard, *Perovskia* (Russian sage), yarrow, and *Dicentra eximia* 'Luxuriant'.

A good combination for a shade garden is to plant ferns beside smooth-leaved hostas. Depending on the variety, hosta leaves may be small and narrow or large and flat; tinted with blue, cream, yellow, chartreuse, or dark green; variegated with spots and stripes, or one intense solid color.

Other winning texture combinations include furry silver-gray lamb's ears planted with spiky gray-green lavender or green *Santolina;* the large, glossy, purple leaves of *Heuchera micrantha* 'Palace Purple' with the fragile, feathery leaves of achillea; the thick, vertical, sword-shaped leaves of *Yucca filamentosa* with the small, rounded leaves of *Sempervivum* (houseleek); and the narrow, stiff leaves of ornamental grasses with the low-growing lacy foliage of *Astilbe chinensis* 'Pumila'.

Flowers and Foliage for Desert Gardens

Rocky terrain, sandy soil, hot, dry summers, and winters where temperatures hover around freezing may sound like a hostile environment in which to grow flowers, but a number of attractive drought-tolerant plants are well suited to these desertlike conditions.

The most familiar desert plants are, of course, cacti. Some cacti are highly sculptural, and their flowers, although delicate and short-lived, may be quite spectacular. In the Scottsdale, Arizona, garden at left, *Opuntia phaeacantha* (Engelmann's prickly pear) lends an authentic desert look to a garden containing spiky *Hesperaloe parviflora* (red yucca) in the right foreground and polelike ocotillo at the back of the garden, along with other drought-tolerant plants.

Some of the more interestingly shaped desert plants are the cacti *Opuntia basilaris* (beavertail), *Ferocactus wislizenii* (fishhook cactus), and *Lemaireocereus thurberi* (organ-pipe cactus), and the succulents agave, yucca, jade plant, sempervivum, and hen-and-chickens.

Other drought-tolerant plants include ornamental grasses, artemisia, *Gaillardia pulchella* (blanket flower), *Callistemon citrinus* (crimson bottlebrush), *Baileya multiradiata* (desert marigold), *Delosperma cooperi* (iceplant), evening primrose, *Potentilla* (cinquefoil), *Euphorbia* (spurge), and *Eriogonum umbellatum* (sulfur flower).

Although they must be watered at planting time, drought-tolerant plants can go as long as 8 weeks before they will need more water. Irrigate them only when the soil is dry, since soil that remains moist will rot their roots. Resist watering during the shorter days of late fall and winter, when the plants are dormant, and cut back dead foliage and stalks in late winter or early spring, before new growth starts to show.

Planting Overview

When you are ready to commit your final planting plan to paper, you'll need to keep in mind how large each plant you choose will grow and how far and how fast it will spread. It takes about 3 years for most herbaceous perennials to spread into drifts, and 5 years for many shrubs to reach maturity. Depending on the growth rate of trees (slow, moderate, or fast) it can take anywhere from 8 to 20 years for them to reach significant size. You'll need to consider whether the trees you have in mind will eventually branch out so broadly that they'll turn your sunny garden into a shady one.

If you're planting slow-growing trees and shrubs, it's important to select a combination of evergreen and deciduous species that will continue to complement each other at maturity. Careful planning in the beginning will save you from the unpleasant and possibly expensive task of removing major plantings after several years of growth because they are crowding each other or simply no longer look good together.

Spacing shrubs to allow for future growth need not leave your garden looking bare and uninteresting during its first few years. To create fullness, you can interplant with perennials, annuals, and filler bulbs, such as tulips, hyacinths, or lilies. And once the shrubs start spreading, it's a simple matter to relocate the herbaceous plants as needed.

Planning for Seasonal Interest

To create a garden that provides four seasons of interest, you will need a mixture of plants that include some that are visually appealing throughout the year and others that bloom in different months. Before you break ground, your paper plan should indicate which plants produce long-lasting foliage or flowers and which overlap their blooming cycles.

Perhaps the surest way to formulate a successful year-round planting plan is to superimpose on your updated base map a different tissue overlay for each season. Indicate on each overlay which features—bloom color, leaf texture, distinctive bark, berries, and the like—will be prominent at which locations during that season.

Noting life cycles of flowers, trees, and shrubs will allow you to group plants to advantage. For ex-

A SUPERB BLENDING OF PLANTS
In this Connecticut garden, tulips and daffodils share a bed with perennials that will help disguise the bulbs' fading foliage. At the far end, a scarlet Japanese maple contrasts pleasantly with the pastel purple blossoms of a Higan cherry, while a backdrop of rhododendrons provides year-round greenery and the promise of summer flowers.

Tracking the Growth of a New Garden

A new bed, if properly planted, will show a lot of bare ground. In the bed at right, widely spaced astilbes thrust up white spires beneath a young Korean mountain ash tree. Three red Japanese barberry shrubs and a dwarf hinoki false cypress have space for modest growth, while the pink-flowered sedums, variegated hostas, and tiny ajuga plants require more room.

By the third year, the astilbes have filled in, the sedums have spread widely, the hostas have doubled in size, and the ajugas have put out runners in all directions, thickening into a ground cover. The canopy of the Korean mountain ash has expanded 3 to 5 feet, while the barberries and false cypress have yet to reach mature size.

The bed has attained a pleasing fullness by the fifth year. While the shrubs show steady but compact growth, the mountain ash continues to expand at 2 feet or so a year, toward its maximum size of 40 feet tall with a canopy 25 feet wide. The astilbes, sedums, and hostas require little maintenance or division, meaning that this bed need not be disturbed for many years to come.

ample, when daffodils have finished blooming, you will want their withering leaves to be out of view. The best way to accomplish this is to grow them in the midst of colorful foliage or tall swaths of annual or perennial flowers, which will come into full growth just as the bulb foliage begins to fade.

And although annuals have a life cycle of just a few months, they create a continuous flow of color from late spring to summer's end. Some, such as impatiens, scarlet sage, pot marigold, zinnia, cleome, cosmos, and zonal geranium, keep on producing blooms until they are killed by a hard frost. Overlapping with these warm-weather favorites are late-summer perennials, which also carry their colorful flowers until nipped by cold temperatures.

You can plan for even more fall color by choosing deciduous shrubs and trees with leaves that take on intensely brilliant hues and by planting perennials such as asters, *Sedum* x 'Autumn Joy' (stonecrop), goldenrod, *Chrysanthemum* x *morifolium* (florist's chrysanthemum), Japanese anemone, *Caryopteris* (bluebeard), *Colchicum autumnale* (autumn crocus), *Colchicum speciosum* 'Album' (showy autumn crocus), *Rosa* Meidiland varieties, and ornamental grasses.

93

Brightening Winter Months

In the winter, when fiery leaves no longer paint the landscape, you can still enjoy ample color in the various shades of evergreen foliage, tree and shrub bark, berries, dried grasses, and the seed heads of some perennials and shrubs. The bark of certain deciduous trees, such as birch, eastern sycamore, and *Stewartia pseudocamellia* (Japanese stewartia), and the shiny leaves of holly, bull bay, and ivy provide visual delights when most herbaceous plants have succumbed to frigid temperatures.

By late winter, small-bulb shoots are already pushing their way out of the soil. The delicate snowdrops are among the first to bloom, quickly followed by crocuses and other small bulbs and by the blossoming of shrubs such as witch hazel, forsythia, and *Prunus mume* (Japanese flowering apricot). From then on there is no stopping the show of spring-flowering squill, hyacinths, daffodils, and tulips. And if you have planned carefully, you can enjoy the sequential blooms of rhododendron species, flowering cherries, magnolias, dogwoods, lilacs, viburnums, and a host of other blooms that creep over the ground, wind their tendrils up fences, and dance over the landscape.

Putting in the Plants

Begin with the largest trees, which involve the greatest amount of digging and the most extensive trampling on surrounding soil. Because cultivated soil is easily compacted, don't till any soil for planting smaller shrubs and herbaceous plants until you are sure you no longer have any need to walk on it. After the large trees are in, add medium-sized shrubs and trees. Follow this stage by planting small decorative specimens, dwarf shrubs, perennials, vines, and ground covers and other filler plants, such as bulbs, annuals, and herbs.

When planting small shrubs, place them in groups of two, three, or even five if space allows. If they are slow growing, shrubs can be sited fairly close together to form a mass that makes a strong impression; you can also plant them farther apart at regular intervals to impart rhythm and continuity to a bed or border. Perennials look better when they are planted close to one another in groups of three or five; but if the plants are young, leave ample room between them. Annuals are more effective when planted in drifts or massed along the edges of a border. It doesn't matter if they crowd one another. Avoid planting flowers singly at random intervals, where their impact would be lost.

A DESIGN FOR SEASONAL COLOR AND TEXTURE
In this East Hampton, New York, garden, low-growing bird's-nest spruce, bloodleaf Japanese maple, and variegated hinoki false cypress (far right) furnish year-round interest. The ground-hugging lady's-mantle combined with the large ribbed leaves of hosta, the tall spires of foxtail lily, and the lacy heads of hydrangea contribute more seasonal texture. 'Just Joey' roses, 'Johnson's Blue' geraniums, and other perennials provide weeks of color.

Bringing It All Together

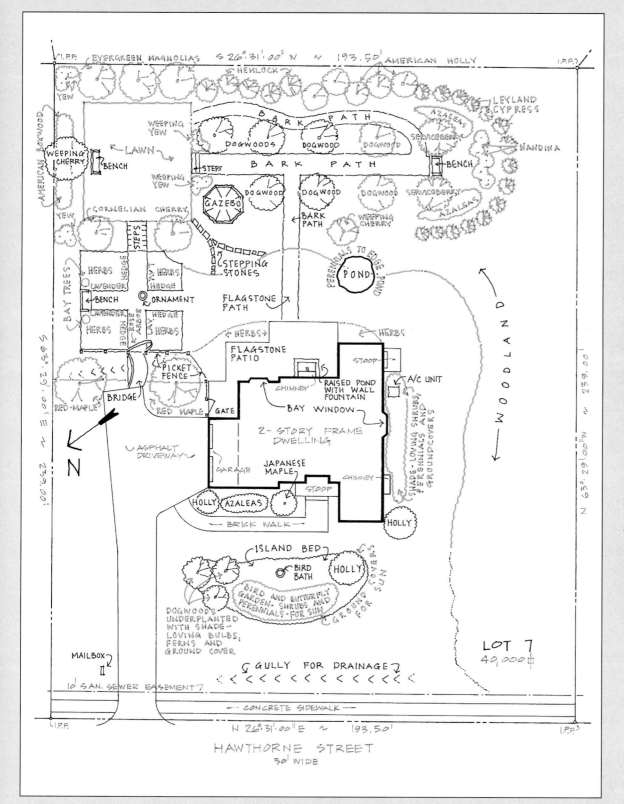

THE LAST STEP: SELECTING THE PLANTS

The final phase of this sample garden design is to impose a planting plan on the property map, which now incorporates in black ink the regrading, transplantings, and hardscape installations from the previous phase. The gardener, using green ink, has laid out an ambitious project that will probably take several years to complete. Included are a screen of ornamental trees along the rear property line, a foliage cul-de-sac in the south corner, a lawn framed by shrubs and ornamental trees on the new terrace in the east corner, a formal herb garden, a mixed shade border on the southwest side of the house, and a bird-and-butterfly garden in the existing bed at the front of the house.

95

Answers to Common Questions

I have many garden ideas for different parts of my property, but I have a hard time visualizing how they might all fit together. How can I work them out?

Go out into the landscape and try them. Place tall stakes where you think you would like trees; use hose, string, or powdered lime to define lawn shapes, paths, and beds; string up lines to represent fencing; spread out sheets or blankets where you might like a small paved area. Set outdoor furniture in places where you might want seating. Then look at these elements from different angles and keep making adjustments until you feel satisfied.

I don't intend to develop my whole property. Do I really need a plan for the entire area before I start a small front garden?

Making a cohesive plan for the whole property is essential, even if you don't expect to carry it all out or may change the plan later on. Individual projects like the front garden might end up well, but the cumulative effect of such efforts may not be fully satisfactory unless you have an overall plan.

Why do designers recommend looking at a garden in winter to determine what needs improvement?

Professionals see the garden first as a visual and spatial composition, and only secondarily as a collection of plants and garden elements. During warmer months the allure of foliage and flowers can distract a gardener from possible weaknesses in the composition. In winter it's easier to see plants as shapes or silhouettes and judge them in relation to other shapes (buildings, paving, walls) in the garden.

I've recently bought an older home with a rather boring landscape. I can't afford to redo the entire property at once. How can I phase the garden development over a period of, say, 5 years? In what order should I proceed?

Spend the first year getting to know your garden. Keep a notebook to record such data as when the plants bloom and how the sun strikes different areas throughout the day and in different seasons. Test the soil, and begin correcting any deficiencies. Bring in an arborist to evaluate the trees. The autumn and winter of the first year is a good time for removing diseased or poorly placed trees and planting new ones. The second year, put your money into "hardscape" items—an irrigation system, if needed, and patios, walkways, retaining walls, and fences. Protect trees during the construction process by surrounding the root zone with temporary fencing. Concentrate on shrubbery during the third year, thinning, transplanting, and adding color and texture. Use the fourth year to establish herbaceous beds. By the fifth year you should be ready to add the finishing touches—a sundial, perhaps, or garden art to serve as focal points.

I have planted different gardens in our large suburban lot over the years, but now I don't have the time to keep up all the areas as well as I would like to. How can I revamp the gardens so they will look good with less maintenance?

Categorize the different garden areas according to the levels of maintenance needed to keep each looking good: intensive, moderate, or casual. Are the intensive areas too many, too scattered, and too far away to be noticed or enjoyed? If so, concentrate your efforts where they matter. Let the farther reaches revert to woodland. Turn a mixed border into a low-maintenance shrub border. Replace a struggling woodland garden with a hardy ground cover. Put your main effort into pruning for shape a few key specimen trees and shrubs and intensively maintaining a close-in flower border.

I loved a planting scheme I saw in a garden book, but when I tried to copy it in my garden it didn't look right. How can I tell what will work in my garden?

Apart from incompatible cultural requirements among plants, the most common cause for an unsuccessful duplication of a garden scheme in another location is the difference in scale, proportion, and conformation of the surrounding space. When you see a design that you like, check to determine whether the setting of the locale where you want to duplicate it is similar to that of the original. You're almost certain to be disappointed, for example, if you pick out an arrangement set against a fenced-in corner for reproduction at the edge of a lawn opening onto woods.

DESIGN

I like formal garden styles, but I've heard that informal gardens require less maintenance. Is that true?

Formality or informality does not determine maintenance requirements. Whatever the style, complex garden patterns and intricate plant combinations take considerable effort to keep all the parts in balance. On the other hand, a simple ground shape like an oval lawn or a square terrace imparts a sense of formal order that can carry a casually maintained planting. A strong horizontal line like a wall, fence, or clipped hedge does the same thing on the vertical plane. And bold sweeps or groups will always look neater than a hodgepodge of unrelated materials scattered all over.

I was surprised to find on my trip to England that many houses there do not have foundation plantings. What is the purpose of foundation plantings, and are they really needed?

Foundation plantings gained widespread popularity in America during the Victorian era. Heavy evergreen shrubs helped stabilize the bulk of the then-new style of large Victorian houses. Foundation plantings have since acquired a life of their own and are used indiscriminately even when not needed. They are useful for hiding an ugly foundation, or when a house lacks a stable base of level ground, or when a softer transition is needed between house and ground. Otherwise, they are neither necessary nor desirable.

Many design books emphasize the importance of shape and mass in planting design, but I can't seem to get past the flower colors when I am making plant arrangements. How can I begin to see plants the way designers see them?

To see shape only, first try to look at your plant groupings as if they were all one color. Use a black-and-white photocopy of a garden view and trace an outline of trees, shrubs, and groups of smaller plants in the picture. Don't try to follow the outline shape in detail; generalize as much as possible, so that you end up with a diagram of circles, ovals, cones, horizontal lines, and so on. If the diagram turns out to be a series of boring circles, try adding vertical spikes or a taller cone shape to vary the composition. Once you have hit upon a pleasing combination of shapes, use this as the basis for working out a detailed planting plan, into which you can introduce texture and color.

I need immediate screening from my neighbors. Should I put in a fence along my property line?

This only makes sense when you want to mark your property or keep out intruders and animals. A more effective way of screening unwanted views is to place a fence or screen where it gives you the greatest protection. On a sloping lot, for example, a screen placed at the edge of an elevated terrace will be more effective than one at the property line, where you may be able to see over the fence from where you sit. Also, fences and screens are expensive garden elements, and you should take full advantage of their architectural features by locating them where you gain the most from the definition they provide, as near a terrace.

The only cool side of our house on summer evenings is the front yard. Is there any way we can make this into a quiet and private sitting area?

There's no rule that says a patio must open only off a back or side door. A front courtyard can be a wonderful place for dining outdoors or for reading the paper, and it can create a pleasant vista from a sitting room or dining room. If local building codes permit, you could build a walled front courtyard in a style that is compatible with the architecture of the house. In your planning, consider wind patterns, the effects of rain, cooling breezes, and drainage. If solid walls are not feasible, put in accent trees and shrubs of varying sizes and perhaps a section of decorative fencing. Complete the area with attractive furniture, add a small fountain to drown out traffic noises, and decorate with lots of colorful plants in containers.

Should a garden have a color scheme?

Yes. Nature can get away with combining every imaginable color in a wildflower meadow, but gardeners may ruin a landscape with clashing hues. One possible scheme is to repeat the colors of your living and dining rooms in the landscape. The colors of the exterior of your house are also important to consider in selecting a color theme for your garden. For example, if you have an orange brick house, avoid hot pinks or reds in favor of predominantly white-flowering trees, shrubs, and perennials, perhaps combined with blues, yellows, purples, and peachy tones. Against a neutral-colored house it's hard to go wrong with a pastel garden in tones of pink, with blue, yellow, and white accents. A bright red or an orange theme goes beautifully with a white house. If the house is dark or the site is heavily wooded, brighten it with lots of white and yellow.

CONSTRUCTION

The back of my lot slopes down so steeply from my house that the soil is washing away. I want to terrace the land for planters, but I'm concerned because the area is large and I might be creating a monster in terms of maintenance. What do you suggest?

Why not terrace the upper portion closest to your house and clothe the lower part in shrubs and ground covers? Plants with dense root systems, such as cotoneaster, *Hypericum calycinum* (St.-John's-wort), or juniper, will help prevent erosion. You would be well advised to call a landscape architect to prepare a plan for the terraced portion. A professional can help you select the most cost-effective material for a retaining wall and can engineer the wall to stand up to the force of soil and water pushing against it.

We plan to lay a new driveway and walkway, doing the work ourselves. We're trying to decide between natural brick and concrete pavers. What are the advantages and disadvantages of each? What should we know to do a professional job?

For residential use, the look of natural, or fired-clay, brick is generally preferable to that of concrete pavers. And both materials cost about the same, so for walkways and patios alone there's no real advantage in using pavers. A driveway is a different story. If you want to pave it in clay bricks you will need a reinforced concrete base, which may require hiring skilled labor, whereas interlocking concrete pavers need only a sand base that you can lay down yourselves. Thus, if you want the driveway and walkways to have the same surface, concrete pavers become the more cost-effective choice. Walkways should be laid with a slight crown along the center to shed water. Where they adjoin planting beds, lay them slightly higher than the soil level so that soil and mulches won't wash out onto the paving every time it rains. Slope all walks away from the house. Put down a layer of polyethylene or roofing felt before laying in the sand to reduce the chance of vegetation growing up between any cracks that may develop over the years.

We will be moving into a new house that is under construction. We want to plan for a garden, but cannot do it all right now. What should we do first?

Apart from having a plan, the most important first step is to grade the land to the contours you want while the equipment is still on site. This is the time to create flat spots for lawns or terraces, to shape the ground so that the house sits gracefully on it instead of perching awkwardly. Once the grading is done, you can add plantings and hardscape elements gradually over time.

PLANTS

We have a plan for our backyard that includes a flowering shrub border backed by an evergreen hedge. But we can't afford to execute the design with all large plants. How can we stay within our budget and still get some immediate effect?

It would be a mistake to try to spread out your budget evenly and compromise on the size of all the plants in your design. Instead, start off with a few large plants to carry the design until the rest grow in. Buy the hedge plants in larger sizes so that you get an effective backdrop right away. Buy moderate-sized plants of a few key shrubs that form a corner. The rest can be started out very small.

What are some good trees to plant in front of a new two-story townhouse on a very small lot?

Choose deep-rooted species; avoid such trees as sweet gum and Norway maple, which have greedy, shallow roots that compete with nearby shrubbery and make it impossible to grow grass. In the past few years nurseries have introduced several narrow-crowned, upright selections of familiar shade trees suitable for use in small gardens and as street plantings. Trees with less than a 15-foot spread include *Pyrus calleryana* 'Chanticleer' (Callery pear), pyramidal *Carpinus betulus* 'Fastigiata' (European hornbeam), *Quercus robur* 'Fastigiata' (English oak), or one of the several red maples selected for upright form, such as *Acer rubrum* 'Armstrong'.

How can I design for the most bloom in my perennial border?

First, make sure your border is large enough—at least 5 feet deep—to contain three tiers of plants for the front, middle, and back. Choose plants for a sequence of bloom over a long period, making sure that there will always be something in flower. Choose perennials with long bloom periods, and plant them in overlapping horizontal drifts rather than in blocks so the nonflowering gaps will look less obvious. Use annuals to fill in spaces left by plants whose foliage dies back after bloom. If you don't have room for a large bed, choose plants for a limited flowering season rather than diffusing the effect by trying to spread bloom over a longer period.

I have a tiny city garden that is walled in on all sides with almost no planting space around the patio. How can I make it a year-round garden that is full of plants that bloom in succession?

If you can't go outward go up: Plant the space thickly with climbers. Combine vines, so that when one is finished, another will bloom—for example, a planting of *Clematis montana,* 'New Dawn' climbing roses, and *Clematis paniculata (C. maximowicziana)* to cover spring, summer, and fall. Use bold foliage plants like *Yucca filamentosa* and *Mahonia bealei* for accents. Make a dense evergreen background by planting ivies or *Clematis armandii*. On the patio, set pots of annuals and bulbs in groups or arrange them on a baker's rack so you gain even more planting space.

Troubleshooting Guide

Even the best-tended gardens can fall prey to pests and diseases. To keep problems in check, regularly inspect your plants for warning signs, remembering that lack of nutrients, improper pH levels, and other environmental conditions can cause symptoms like those typical of some diseases. If wilting or yellowing appears on neighboring plants, the cause is probably environmental; pest and disease damage is usually more random.

This guide will help you identify and solve the most prevalent pest and disease problems. In general, good drainage and air circulation will help prevent infection, and the many birds and insects that prey on pests should be encouraged. Natural solutions to garden problems are best, but if you must use chemicals, treat only the affected plant. Try to use horticultural oils, insecticidal soaps, and the botanical insecticide neem; these products are the least disruptive to beneficial insects and will not destroy the soil balance that is the foundation of a healthy garden.

PESTS

PROBLEM: Leaves curl, become distorted and sticky, and may appear black and sooty. Buds and flowers are deformed, new growth is stunted, and leaves and flowers may drop.

CAUSE: Aphids are pear-shaped, semitransparent, wingless sucking insects about ⅛ inch long and ranging in color from green to red, pink, black, or gray. Aphids suck plant juices and through feeding may spread viral diseases. Infestations are worst in spring and early summer, when pests cluster on new shoots, the undersides of leaves, and around flower buds. Winged forms appear when colonies become overcrowded. Aphids secrete a sticky substance known as honeydew that fosters the growth on leaves of a black fungus called sooty mold.

SOLUTION: Spray plants frequently with a steady stream of water from a garden hose to knock aphids off and discourage them from returning. Ladybugs or lacewings, which eat aphids, may be introduced into the garden. In severe cases, prune away infested areas and use a diluted insecticidal soap solution or a recommended insecticide.
SUSCEPTIBLE PLANTS: VIRTUALLY ANY PLANT.

PROBLEM: Bark is loose and cracking and marked by many tiny holes. On some plants, holes may ooze a sticky sap or a sawdustlike substance. Twigs, buds, and branches above the site of infection usually die.

CAUSE: Borers are the larvae of many insects that bore into stems, twigs, and trunks of a variety of plants and feed on interior tissue. Adult females lay eggs on the surface of the plant, then bore holes into it and thrust the eggs inside, where the larvae later will feed undetected. Entry holes are usually too tiny to be noticed. In some species, the eggs are laid in the soil and the larvae invade plants through their roots.

SOLUTION: Keep trees and shrubs healthy. Avoid damaging them with the lawn mower or other garden tools, since borers are quite able to enter through wounds. Cut off and destroy all dead and dying branches. If a hole is large enough and borers are present, impale them on a thin piece of wire or fill a syringe with liquid *Bacillus thuringiensis* (Bt) and release into hole.
SUSCEPTIBLE PLANTS: MANY TREES, PARTICULARLY DOGWOOD; SHRUBS, ESPECIALLY LILAC AND RHODODENDRON.

PROBLEM: Leaves, buds, and flowers appear chewed. Entire plant may be defoliated.

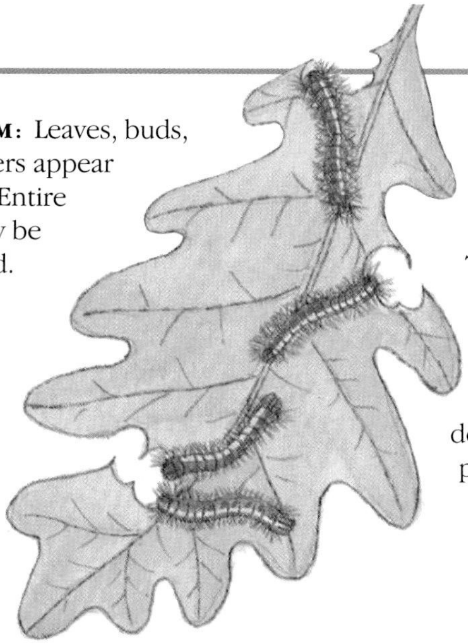

CAUSE: Caterpillars, the wormlike larvae of moths, butterflies, and sawflies, are voracious pests found in the garden, primarily in spring. They come in a variety of colors and can be smooth, hairy, or spiny. Gypsy moth caterpillars are particularly destructive. They can be recognized by five pairs of blue dots on their backs followed by six pairs of red dots.

SOLUTION: Handpick to control small populations. Destroy all visible cocoons and nests. Put up bands of sticky paper and traps to capture moving caterpillars. Bt kills many types without harming the plants. Some caterpillars are susceptible to insecticidal soap solutions sprayed directly on them. Neem, pyrethrins, and ryania can be used against gypsy moth caterpillars.
SUSCEPTIBLE PLANTS: MANY TREES AND SHRUBS.

PROBLEM: Leaves are stippled and blanched, with sticky brown droppings on the undersides. The plant loses color and vigor and appears stunted.

CAUSE: Lace bugs are sucking insects that feed primarily on the leaves of woody plants. They feed in clusters, draining leaves of their juices as droplets of brown waste accumulate around them. Each species will usually attack only one type of plant. Adults are about ⅛ inch long with lacy, nearly transparent wings. They lay black eggs on the undersides of leaves and along the midrib, usually near the tops of plants. Adults and eggs overwinter in garden debris.

SOLUTION: Spray plants regularly with a stream of water to knock off insects and droppings. For heavier infestations, apply an insecticidal soap solution or horticultural oil. Neem, pyrethrins, rotenone, and sabadilla are also effective against these pests.
SUSCEPTIBLE PLANTS: MANY TREES AND SHRUBS.

PROBLEM: Leaves are stippled or flecked, then discolor, curl, and wither. Webbing appears, particularly on undersides of leaves and on the branches of shrubs and trees.

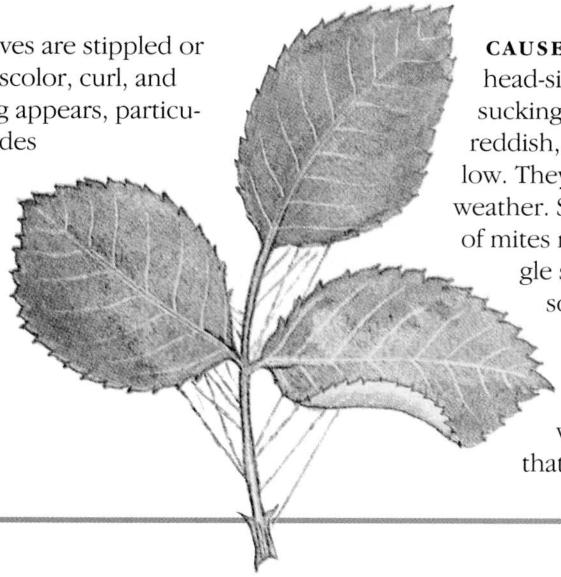

CAUSE: Mites are pin-head-sized, spiderlike sucking pests that can be reddish, pale green, or yellow. They flourish in hot, dry weather. Several generations of mites may occur in a single season. Adults of some species hibernate over the winter in sod and bark and on weeds and plants that retain foliage.

SOLUTION: Keep plants well watered and mulched, especially during hot, dry spells. Spray the undersides of leaves, where mites feed and lay eggs, with a stream of water or a diluted insecticidal soap solution, which controls the nymphs and adults but not the eggs. Apply horticultural oils and introduce ladybugs and lacewings, natural predators of mites, into the garden. For severe cases, use a miticide.
SUSCEPTIBLE PLANTS: MANY SHRUBS AND TREES.

PROBLEM: Branches, twigs, and leaves or needles of woody plants are covered with small, immobile, scaly patches that may be mistaken for a disease symptom. Plant growth is stunted, leaves discolor and drop. Leaves and fruit may be mottled.

CAUSE: Scale insects have shells that are either hard and armored or waxy and soft. They cling to plants, sucking the juices, and usually appear in clusters. They may be white, yellow, green, red, brown, or black. Adult females appear on stems or leaves as bumps. Males eventually develop wings and fly.

SOLUTION: Destroy severely infested stems or branches. Scrub scale off with a plastic scouring pad. Spray trees, shrubs, and roses with horticultural oil in early spring to smother eggs before plant growth begins. If insects appear in summer, control with insecticidal soap or spray with a chemical insecticide. *SUSCEPTIBLE PLANTS: SHRUBS, PARTICULARLY EUONYMUS AND EVERGREENS; ROSES; MANY TREES.*

DISEASES

PROBLEM: Red or brown sunken, watery lesions appear on stems and limbs. Tree branches may develop knotlike swellings known as girdles. Infected bark may exude a watery substance. Leaves or needles above the site of infection turn yellow or brown, then wilt and die. The entire limb will eventually die.

CAUSE: Cankers are caused by a fungus spread by spores transmitted in the air, in water, by some insects, and by contaminated gardening tools.

SOLUTION: There are no chemical preventives or cures; to help prevent the spread of the disease, cut away infected tree branches to the point where the wood no longer appears discolored. For shrubs, trim to below the canker. Destroy all diseased limbs. Disinfect pruning tools with alcohol or a 10 percent bleach solution after each cut. *SUSCEPTIBLE PLANTS: MANY TREES, INCLUDING BIRCH, DOGWOOD, ELM, MAPLE, MAGNOLIA, OAK, PINE, POPLAR, SPRUCE, SWEET GUM; SHRUBS, INCLUDING AZALEA, FORSYTHIA, QUINCE; ROSES.*

PROBLEM: Leaves develop small yellow, brown, or black spots surrounded by a rim of discolored tissue. Spots often join to form large, irregular blotches. An entire leaf may turn yellow, wilt, and drop. Spotting usually starts on lower leaves and moves upward.

CAUSE: Leaf-spot diseases are caused by a number of fungi and bacteria. All can become particularly severe in wet weather because they are spread by splashing water.

SOLUTION: Remove and destroy infected leaves as they appear. Clean up all fallen leaves before winter. Water only in the morning. Provide good air circulation. There is no cure for infected leaves, but a fungicide applied when buds open can protect healthy foliage. *SUSCEPTIBLE PLANTS: MANY, INCLUDING AZALEA, BARBERRY, CRAPE MYRTLE, EUONYMUS, FORSYTHIA, LILAC, PRIVET, QUINCE; ASH, BIRCH, DOGWOOD, GOLDEN RAIN TREE, SWEET GUM, TULIP TREE; CLEMATIS, WISTERIA.*

PROBLEM: Leaves are covered with spots or a film of grayish white powdery matter. Leaves may distort, curl, discolor, and finally drop off.

CAUSE: Powdery mildews are fungal diseases that thrive when nights are cool and days are hot and humid. The problem is often noticeable in late summer and fall.

SOLUTION: Provide good air circulation and full sun. Water from overhead and only in the early morning. Fungicides may help prevent spreading; also effective are summer-oil sprays and antitranspirants, which decrease the amount of water lost through the leaves. *SUSCEPTIBLE PLANTS: ANY TYPE OF PLANT.*

PROBLEM: Leaves may be sparse, yellowed, or misshapen, and may wilt and drop prematurely. Overall growth of plant is stunted, and limbs and twigs may die. In trees, bark becomes spongy and develops fan-shaped growths that resemble mushrooms.

CAUSE: Root rot is caused by a variety of fungi, many of which thrive in heavy, wet soil where they can persist for several years.

SOLUTION: Remove and discard infected plants, roots, and surrounding soil. For trees, also remove stumps. If you cannot remove all surrounding soil, wait for several years before replanting. Incorporate composted tree bark into remaining soil to suppress fungus growth. Improve drainage. Water early in the day and allow soil to dry between waterings.
SUSCEPTIBLE PLANTS: ANY TYPE OF PLANT.

PROBLEM: Plants suddenly lose their color, turn yellow, and wilt. Entire branches may die back. Roots are damaged or deformed and have small knotty growths and swellings.

CAUSE: Soil nematodes—colorless microscopic worms that live in the soil and feed on roots—inhibit a plant's intake of nitrogen. Damage is at its worst in warm, sunlit, sandy soils that are moist.

SOLUTION: Only a laboratory test can confirm the presence of nematodes. Be suspicious if roots are swollen or stunted. There are no chemical controls; dispose of infected plants and the soil that surrounds them, or solarize the soil. Grow resistant species or cultivars. Add nitrogen fertilizer.
SUSCEPTIBLE PLANTS: VIRTUALLY ANY PLANT.

PROBLEM: One side or one branch of a plant may wilt. Leaves turn yellow, then brown, and finally wilt and die. Trees die branch by branch. Wilt progresses up from the bottom of the plant and out toward branch tips. A cross section of a tree branch will reveal a dark ring or rings.

CAUSE: Verticillium wilt is a fungal disease that can be confirmed only by a laboratory test. The fungus thrives in cool, moist soil, entering the plant through the roots and spreading via plant veins and tissue, where it discolors the plant and cuts off the flow of water and nutrients.

SOLUTION: There are no organic or chemical controls. Once the soil is infected, the only countermeasure is to plant resistant varieties. If infection in a tree is detected early, fertilize and water to encourage natural recovery, and prune away damaged parts. If infection is severe, the tree cannot be saved. Do not replant the same species, as the soil will remain contaminated.
SUSCEPTIBLE PLANTS: MANY SHRUBS, INCLUDING AZALEA, BARBERRY, HYDRANGEA, NANDINA, AND SMOKEBUSH; MANY TREES, INCLUDING ELM, MAGNOLIA, AND JAPANESE AND OTHER MAPLES.

Plant Selection Guide

Organized by plant type, this chart provides information needed to select species and varieties that will thrive in the particular conditions of your garden. For additional information on each plant, refer to the encyclopedia that begins on page 110.

PERENNIALS AND GRASSES

Plant	Z3	Z4	Z5	Z6	Z7	Z8	Z9	Z10	Dry	Moist	Full Sun	Part. Shade	Shade	Spring	Summer	Fall	Winter	Under 3ft	3-6ft	6-10ft	10-20ft	Over 20ft	Form	Foliage	Flowers	Fruit/Seeds	Bark/Twigs
ARTEMISIA X 'POWIS CASTLE'			✓	✓	✓	✓			✓		✓							✓						✓			
BERGENIA CORDIFOLIA	✓	✓	✓	✓	✓	✓				✓	✓	✓		✓				✓						✓	✓		
CALAMAGROSTIS ACUTIFLORA 'STRICTA'			✓	✓	✓	✓			✓	✓	✓				✓				✓				✓	✓	✓		
CYRTOMIUM FALCATUM					✓	✓	✓		✓			✓	✓					✓						✓			
FARGESIA MURIELAE			✓	✓	✓	✓			✓			✓									✓		✓	✓			
HELLEBORUS NIGER		✓	✓	✓	✓					✓			✓			✓	✓	✓						✓	✓		
HEMEROCALLIS 'STELLA D'ORO'		✓	✓	✓	✓	✓	✓		✓	✓	✓	✓			✓	✓		✓							✓		
HEUCHERA MICRANTHA 'PALACE PURPLE'		✓	✓							✓	✓	✓			✓			✓						✓			
HOSTA 'KROSSA REGAL'	✓	✓	✓	✓	✓	✓				✓		✓	✓		✓				✓				✓	✓			
IRIS SIBIRICA 'CAESAR'S BROTHER'	✓	✓	✓	✓	✓	✓	✓			✓	✓			✓					✓				✓	✓	✓		
LAVANDULA ANGUSTIFOLIA			✓	✓	✓	✓	✓		✓		✓				✓			✓						✓	✓		
LAVANDULA STOECHAS					✓	✓	✓	✓	✓		✓				✓			✓						✓	✓		
MISCANTHUS SINENSIS 'ZEBRINUS'			✓	✓	✓	✓			✓	✓	✓					✓				✓			✓	✓	✓		
PENNISETUM SETACEUM 'RUBRUM'					✓	✓	✓	✓	✓	✓	✓				✓			✓					✓	✓	✓		
POTENTILLA NEPALENSIS 'MISS WILMOTT'			✓	✓	✓					✓	✓	✓			✓			✓							✓		
RUDBECKIA FULGIDA 'GOLDSTURM'	✓	✓	✓	✓	✓	✓	✓			✓	✓	✓			✓	✓		✓							✓		
SEDUM X 'AUTUMN JOY'	✓	✓	✓	✓	✓	✓	✓	✓	✓	✓	✓				✓	✓		✓					✓	✓	✓		

GROUND COVERS

Plant	Z3	Z4	Z5	Z6	Z7	Z8	Z9	Z10	Dry	Moist	Full Sun	Part. Shade	Shade	Spring	Summer	Fall	Winter	Under 3ft	3-6ft	6-10ft	10-20ft	Over 20ft	Form	Foliage	Flowers	Fruit/Seeds	Bark/Twigs
CALLUNA VULGARIS 'MRS. RONALD GRAY'		✓	✓	✓	✓				✓		✓	✓			✓			✓					✓	✓	✓		
CEANOTHUS GRISEUS VAR. HORIZONTALIS					✓	✓	✓	✓	✓		✓			✓				✓							✓		
COTONEASTER DAMMERI 'SKOGHOLM'			✓	✓	✓				✓	✓	✓	✓		✓				✓					✓	✓			
COTONEASTER SALICIFOLIUS 'AUTUMN FIRE'			✓	✓	✓				✓	✓	✓	✓		✓				✓					✓	✓	✓	✓	
ERICA CARNEA 'SPRINGWOOD PINK'			✓	✓	✓				✓	✓	✓					✓	✓	✓							✓		
EUONYMUS FORTUNEI 'COLORATA'		✓	✓	✓	✓				✓	✓	✓	✓	✓					✓						✓			
HYPERICUM CALYCINUM			✓	✓	✓	✓			✓		✓	✓			✓	✓		✓							✓		
JUNIPERUS HORIZONTALIS 'WILTONII'	✓	✓	✓	✓	✓	✓	✓		✓		✓	✓						✓					✓	✓			
JUNIPERUS PROCUMBENS	✓	✓	✓	✓	✓	✓	✓		✓		✓	✓						✓						✓			
LIRIOPE MUSCARI 'VARIEGATA'				✓	✓	✓	✓	✓	✓	✓	✓	✓	✓			✓		✓						✓	✓	✓	
MAHONIA REPENS			✓	✓	✓	✓			✓			✓	✓	✓				✓						✓	✓	✓	

Plant selection guide table.

VINES

Plant	Zone 3	Zone 4	Zone 5	Zone 6	Zone 7	Zone 8	Zone 9	Zone 10	Dry	Moist	Full Sun	Partial Shade	Shade	Spring	Summer	Fall	Winter	Under 3 Ft.	3-6 Ft.	6-10 Ft.	10-20 Ft.	Over 20 Ft.	Form	Foliage	Flowers	Fruit/Seeds	Bark/Twigs
CLEMATIS ARMANDII					✓	✓	✓			✓	✓	✓		✓							✓			✓	✓		
CLEMATIS PANICULATA		✓	✓	✓	✓					✓	✓	✓				✓					✓				✓		
GELSEMIUM SEMPERVIRENS			✓	✓	✓	✓				✓	✓	✓		✓						✓					✓		
HYDRANGEA ANOMALA SSP. PETIOLARIS		✓	✓	✓	✓					✓	✓	✓	✓		✓						✓				✓		✓
IPOMOEA ALBA								✓		✓	✓				✓	✓				✓					✓		
LONICERA HECKROTTII		✓	✓	✓	✓	✓	✓		✓	✓	✓	✓			✓					✓					✓		
ROSA 'NEW DAWN'	✓	✓	✓	✓	✓	✓	✓	✓		✓	✓				✓					✓					✓		
WISTERIA FLORIBUNDA		✓	✓	✓	✓	✓	✓			✓	✓	✓		✓								✓			✓		

DECIDUOUS SHRUBS

Plant	Zone 3	Zone 4	Zone 5	Zone 6	Zone 7	Zone 8	Zone 9	Zone 10	Dry	Moist	Full Sun	Partial Shade	Shade	Spring	Summer	Fall	Winter	Under 3 Ft.	3-6 Ft.	6-10 Ft.	10-20 Ft.	Over 20 Ft.	Form	Foliage	Flowers	Fruit/Seeds	Bark/Twigs
ABELIA X 'EDWARD GOUCHER'			✓	✓	✓	✓	✓	✓		✓	✓	✓			✓	✓			✓					✓	✓		
ACER PALMATUM 'DISSECTUM'		✓	✓	✓	✓					✓	✓	✓		✓					✓				✓	✓			✓
BERBERIS THUNBERGII 'CRIMSON PYGMY'		✓	✓	✓	✓	✓			✓	✓	✓			✓			✓	✓						✓		✓	
CHAENOMELES SPECIOSA 'CAMEO'		✓	✓	✓	✓	✓			✓	✓	✓			✓					✓						✓	✓	
COTINUS COGGYGRIA 'VELVET CLOAK'		✓	✓	✓	✓				✓	✓	✓				✓						✓			✓	✓		
ENKIANTHUS CAMPANULATUS		✓	✓	✓						✓	✓	✓		✓						✓				✓	✓		
EUONYMUS ALATA 'COMPACTA'		✓	✓	✓	✓				✓	✓	✓	✓	✓	✓						✓			✓			✓	✓
FORSYTHIA X INTERMEDIA 'SPECTABILIS'			✓	✓	✓	✓			✓	✓	✓			✓						✓			✓		✓		
HAMAMELIS X INTERMEDIA 'ARNOLD PROMISE'		✓	✓	✓	✓					✓	✓	✓					✓			✓				✓	✓		
HYDRANGEA ARBORESCENS 'ANNABELLE'	✓	✓	✓	✓	✓	✓				✓	✓	✓	✓		✓				✓						✓		
JASMINUM NUDIFLORUM			✓	✓	✓	✓	✓	✓	✓	✓	✓	✓					✓		✓				✓		✓		✓
LAGERSTROEMIA INDICA 'SEMINOLE'			✓	✓	✓	✓			✓	✓	✓				✓					✓			✓		✓		✓
LIGUSTRUM OVALIFOLIUM 'AUREUM'		✓	✓	✓	✓	✓	✓		✓	✓	✓	✓			✓						✓		✓	✓	✓		
MYRICA PENSYLVANICA	✓	✓	✓	✓					✓	✓	✓			✓						✓			✓			✓	
POTENTILLA FRUTICOSA 'KLONDIKE'	✓	✓	✓	✓					✓	✓	✓				✓	✓	✓	✓						✓	✓		
PUNICA GRANATUM 'LEGRELLEI'					✓	✓	✓		✓	✓	✓				✓					✓					✓	✓	
RHODODENDRON MUCRONULATUM		✓	✓	✓	✓					✓		✓				✓	✓	✓	✓					✓	✓		
RHODODENDRON SCHLIPPENBACHII		✓	✓	✓	✓					✓		✓		✓					✓					✓	✓		
ROSA RUGOSA 'HANSA'	✓	✓	✓	✓						✓	✓				✓			✓						✓	✓	✓	
SPIRAEA X BUMALDA 'GOLD FLAME'	✓	✓	✓	✓	✓					✓	✓				✓		✓	✓						✓	✓		
STEWARTIA OVATA			✓	✓	✓	✓	✓			✓	✓	✓			✓						✓				✓		✓
SYRINGA PATULA 'MISS KIM'	✓	✓	✓	✓	✓	✓				✓	✓			✓					✓					✓	✓		
VIBURNUM PLICATUM VAR. TOMENTOSUM			✓	✓	✓	✓			✓	✓	✓	✓		✓						✓			✓	✓	✓	✓	
VITEX AGNUS-CASTUS 'ROSEA'					✓	✓	✓		✓	✓	✓				✓	✓				✓	✓				✓		

EVERGREEN SHRUBS

	Zone 3	Zone 4	Zone 5	Zone 6	Zone 7	Zone 8	Zone 9	Zone 10	Dry	Moist	Full Sun	Partial Shade	Shade	Spring	Summer	Fall	Winter	Under 3 FT	3-6 FT	6-10 FT	10-20 FT	Over 20 FT	Form	Foliage	Flowers	Fruit/Seeds	Bark/Twigs
	ZONES								**SOIL**		**LIGHT**			**BLOOM SEASON**				**PLANT HEIGHT**					**NOTED FOR**				
AUCUBA JAPONICA 'VARIEGATA'				✓	✓	✓	✓			✓		✓	✓						✓					✓		✓	
BERBERIS BUXIFOLIA VAR. NANA		✓	✓	✓	✓					✓	✓	✓	✓	✓				✓						✓	✓	✓	
BERBERIS JULIANAE		✓	✓	✓	✓					✓	✓	✓	✓	✓					✓					✓	✓	✓	
CHAMAECYPARIS OBTUSA 'NANA GRACILIS'		✓	✓	✓	✓					✓	✓	✓							✓				✓	✓			
CISTUS X HYBRIDUS					✓	✓	✓	✓	✓		✓			✓					✓						✓		
CISTUS X PURPUREUS					✓	✓	✓	✓	✓		✓				✓				✓						✓		
COTONEASTER SALICIFOLIUS				✓	✓	✓				✓	✓	✓		✓						✓			✓	✓		✓	
ERIOBOTRYA JAPONICA					✓	✓	✓			✓	✓	✓				✓				✓	✓			✓		✓	
ESCALLONIA X LANGLEYENSIS 'APPLE BLOSSOM'					✓	✓	✓			✓	✓	✓		✓	✓	✓			✓					✓	✓		
EUONYMUS FORTUNEI 'EMERALD GAIETY'		✓	✓	✓	✓	✓			✓	✓	✓	✓	✓					✓					✓	✓			
FATSIA JAPONICA					✓	✓	✓			✓			✓			✓				✓			✓	✓	✓		
HEBE 'AUTUMN GLORY'					✓	✓	✓	✓	✓		✓				✓	✓		✓							✓		
ILEX CORNUTA 'BERRIES JUBILEE'				✓	✓	✓				✓	✓	✓		✓					✓					✓		✓	
JUNIPERUS CHINENSIS 'MINT JULEP'	✓	✓	✓	✓	✓	✓	✓		✓	✓	✓								✓				✓	✓			
LIGUSTRUM JAPONICUM					✓	✓	✓	✓	✓	✓	✓	✓	✓	✓						✓	✓			✓	✓	✓	
MAHONIA BEALEI				✓	✓	✓				✓			✓				✓		✓					✓	✓	✓	
NANDINA DOMESTICA 'HARBOUR DWARF'				✓	✓	✓				✓	✓	✓	✓				✓	✓					✓	✓	✓	✓	
PICEA ABIES 'NIDIFORMIS'	✓	✓	✓	✓	✓					✓	✓	✓						✓					✓	✓			
PIERIS JAPONICA 'VARIEGATA'			✓	✓	✓					✓		✓	✓	✓					✓	✓			✓	✓	✓		
PITTOSPORUM TOBIRA					✓	✓	✓	✓	✓	✓	✓	✓		✓						✓				✓			
PRUNUS LAUROCERASUS 'OTTO LUYKEN'				✓	✓	✓	✓			✓	✓	✓	✓	✓					✓					✓	✓		
RAPHIOLEPIS INDICA					✓	✓	✓			✓	✓	✓		✓					✓					✓	✓		
RHODODENDRON 'SCARLET WONDER'			✓	✓	✓					✓		✓	✓	✓			✓	✓						✓	✓		
ROSMARINUS OFFICINALIS 'LOCKWOOD DE FOREST'				✓	✓	✓	✓	✓	✓	✓	✓	✓		✓		✓	✓	✓					✓	✓	✓		
VIBURNUM DAVIDII					✓	✓	✓			✓	✓	✓		✓				✓						✓	✓	✓	

DECIDUOUS TREES

	Zone 3	Zone 4	Zone 5	Zone 6	Zone 7	Zone 8	Zone 9	Zone 10	Dry	Moist	Full Sun	Partial Shade	Shade	Spring	Summer	Fall	Winter	Under 3 FT	3-6 FT	6-10 FT	10-20 FT	Over 20 FT	Form	Foliage	Flowers	Fruit/Seeds	Bark/Twigs
ACER GRISEUM		✓	✓	✓	✓					✓	✓	✓		✓							✓			✓			✓
ACER RUBRUM 'OCTOBER GLORY'	✓	✓	✓	✓	✓	✓	✓			✓	✓	✓		✓								✓		✓			✓
BETULA NIGRA		✓	✓	✓	✓	✓	✓			✓	✓	✓		✓								✓	✓	✓			✓
CARPINUS BETULUS 'COLUMNARIS'		✓	✓	✓	✓					✓	✓	✓		✓								✓	✓				✓
CHILOPSIS LINEARIS					✓	✓	✓	✓	✓		✓				✓					✓	✓				✓	✓	
CLADRASTIS KENTUKEA		✓	✓	✓	✓	✓				✓	✓	✓		✓								✓	✓	✓	✓		✓
CORNUS ALTERNIFOLIA	✓	✓	✓	✓	✓					✓	✓	✓		✓							✓		✓	✓	✓	✓	

	Zone 3	Zone 4	Zone 5	Zone 6	Zone 7	Zone 8	Zone 9	Zone 10	Dry	Moist	Full Sun	Partial Shade	Shade	Spring	Summer	Fall	Winter	Under 3 ft	3-6 ft	6-10 ft	10-20 ft	Over 20 ft	Form	Foliage	Flowers	Fruit/Seeds	Bark/Twigs
DECIDUOUS TREES																											
CORNUS KOUSA VAR. CHINENSIS		✓	✓	✓	✓					✓	✓	✓		✓	✓						✓		✓	✓	✓	✓	✓
FAGUS SYLVATICA 'AUREA PENDULA'		✓	✓	✓	✓					✓	✓	✓		✓							✓		✓	✓			✓
FRAXINUS AMERICANA 'CHAMPAIGN COUNTY'	✓	✓	✓	✓	✓	✓	✓		✓	✓	✓			✓								✓	✓		✓		
GLEDITSIA TRIACANTHOS VAR. INERMIS 'IMPERIAL'		✓	✓	✓	✓				✓	✓	✓			✓								✓	✓	✓			
KOELREUTERIA PANICULATA			✓	✓	✓	✓			✓	✓	✓				✓							✓	✓		✓	✓	
LAGERSTROEMIA INDICA 'NATCHEZ'					✓	✓	✓	✓		✓	✓				✓	✓					✓		✓		✓	✓		✓
MAGNOLIA STELLATA 'ROYAL STAR'		✓	✓	✓	✓	✓				✓	✓	✓					✓			✓			✓		✓	✓	
MAGNOLIA VIRGINIANA			✓	✓	✓	✓	✓			✓	✓	✓		✓						✓	✓		✓	✓	✓	✓	
MALUS 'RED JADE'		✓	✓	✓	✓					✓	✓			✓						✓			✓		✓	✓	✓
PHELLODENDRON AMURENSE	✓	✓	✓	✓	✓	✓			✓	✓	✓			✓								✓	✓				✓
PISTACIA CHINENSIS			✓	✓	✓	✓	✓		✓	✓	✓			✓								✓	✓		✓		✓
POPULUS TREMULOIDES	✓	✓	✓	✓	✓				✓	✓	✓			✓								✓	✓	✓			✓
PRUNUS MUME			✓	✓	✓	✓				✓	✓	✓					✓			✓					✓	✓	
PYRUS CALLERYANA 'CHANTICLEER'			✓	✓	✓	✓			✓	✓	✓			✓							✓		✓	✓	✓	✓	
QUERCUS SHUMARDII			✓	✓	✓	✓	✓		✓	✓	✓			✓								✓	✓	✓			
SAPINDUS DRUMMONDII			✓	✓	✓	✓			✓		✓	✓		✓								✓	✓		✓	✓	✓
STEWARTIA PSEUDOCAMELLIA			✓	✓	✓					✓	✓	✓			✓							✓	✓		✓	✓	✓
STYRAX JAPONICUS			✓	✓	✓					✓	✓	✓		✓								✓	✓	✓		✓	✓
SYRINGA RETICULATA	✓	✓	✓	✓						✓	✓				✓							✓	✓		✓		
TAXODIUM DISTICHUM		✓	✓	✓	✓	✓				✓	✓			✓								✓	✓	✓	✓		✓
ULMUS PARVIFOLIA		✓	✓	✓	✓	✓	✓			✓	✓					✓						✓	✓		✓		✓
ZELKOVA SERRATA 'GREEN VASE'			✓	✓	✓				✓	✓	✓											✓	✓	✓			✓
EVERGREEN TREES																											
ABIES CONCOLOR	✓	✓	✓	✓	✓				✓	✓												✓	✓	✓			
CEDRUS DEODARA				✓	✓				✓	✓	✓											✓	✓	✓			
X CUPRESSOCYPARIS LEYLANDII 'SILVER DUST'				✓	✓	✓	✓	✓	✓	✓	✓											✓	✓	✓	✓		
CUPRESSUS SEMPERVIRENS					✓	✓	✓		✓		✓											✓	✓	✓			✓
ILEX OPACA			✓	✓	✓	✓	✓			✓	✓	✓		✓								✓	✓		✓		
ILEX VOMITORIA					✓	✓	✓	✓	✓	✓	✓	✓		✓							✓		✓			✓	✓
PICEA GLAUCA	✓	✓	✓	✓						✓	✓	✓										✓	✓	✓			
PINUS CONTORTA VAR. CONTORTA					✓	✓	✓	✓		✓	✓											✓	✓	✓			
PINUS NIGRA		✓	✓	✓	✓				✓	✓	✓											✓	✓	✓			
TAXUS X MEDIA 'HICKSII'		✓	✓	✓	✓				✓	✓	✓	✓									✓		✓	✓	✓		

A Zone Map of the U.S. and Canada

A plant's winter hardiness is critical in deciding whether it is suitable for your garden. The map below divides the United States and Canada into 11 climatic zones based on average minimum temperatures, as compiled by the U.S. Department of Agriculture. Find your zone and check the zone information in the plant selection guide *(pages 104-107)* or the encyclopedia *(pages 110-149)* to help you choose the plants most likely to flourish in your climate.

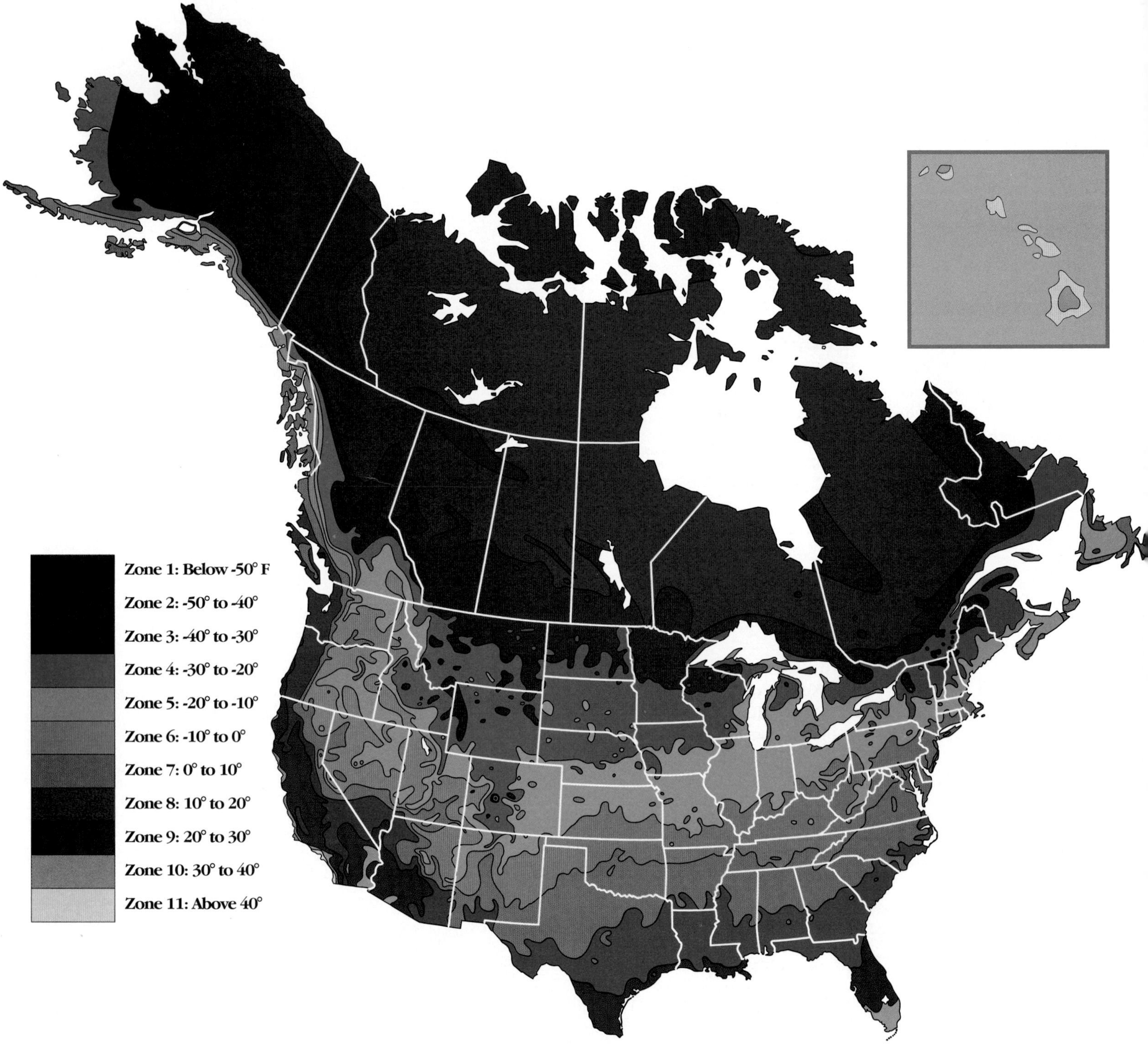

Zone 1: Below -50° F
Zone 2: -50° to -40°
Zone 3: -40° to -30°
Zone 4: -30° to -20°
Zone 5: -20° to -10°
Zone 6: -10° to 0°
Zone 7: 0° to 10°
Zone 8: 10° to 20°
Zone 9: 20° to 30°
Zone 10: 30° to 40°
Zone 11: Above 40°

Cross-Reference Guide to Plant Names

Adam's-needle—*Yucca*
Alumroot—*Heuchera*
Appalachian tea—
  Ilex glabra
Apple—*Malus*
Apricot—*Prunus*
Arrowwood—*Viburnum*
Ash—*Fraxinus*
Aspen—*Populus*
Azalea—*Rhododendron*
Bamboo—*Fargesia*
Bamboo—*Nandina*
Barberry—*Berberis*
Barberry—*Mahonia*
  aquifolium
Bayberry—*Myrica*
Bear's-breech—*Acanthus*
Beech—*Fagus*
Belle de nuit—
  Ipomoea alba
Birch—*Betula*
Blueblossom—*Ceanothus*
Blue brush—*Ceanothus*
Boxleaf veronica—*Hebe*
Bridal wreath—*Spiraea*
Buckeye—*Aesculus*
Burning bush—
  Euonymus alata
Candleberry—*Myrica*
Carmel creeper—
  Ceanothus
Cassina (cassine)—
  Ilex vomitoria
Cedar (Atlas, deodar)—
  Cedrus
Cedar (Oregon, Port
  Orford)—*Chamaecyparis*
Cedar (red)—*Juniperus*
Chaste tree—*Vitex*
Cherry—*Prunus*
Chokeberry—
  Malus floribunda
Christmas rose—*Helleborus*
Cinquefoil—*Potentilla*
Coneflower—*Rudbeckia*
Coral bells—*Heuchera*
Cork tree—*Phellodendron*
Cornelian cherry—
  Cornus mas
Crab apple—
  Malus floribunda

Crape myrtle—
  Lagerstroemia
Cypress (bald, red,
  swamp)—*Taxodium*
Cypress (false, Lawson)—
  Chamaecyparis
Cypress (Italian, Mediter-
  ranean)—*Cupressus*
Cypress (Leyland)—
  x *Cupressocyparis*
Daylily—*Hemerocallis*
Desert catalpa—*Chilopsis*
Desert willow—*Chilopsis*
Dogwood—*Cornus*
Elm—*Ulmus*
Eulalia—*Miscanthus*
Evening trumpet flower—
  Gelsemium
False cypress—
  Chamaecyparis
Fir—*Abies*
Flag—*Iris*
Fleur-de-lis—*Iris*
Flowering quince—
  Chaenomeles
Flowering willow—
  Chilopsis
Formosa rice tree—*Fatsia*
Fountain grass—
  Pennisetum
Foxtail grass—*Pennisetum*
Gallberry—*Ilex glabra*
Gladwin—*Iris foetidissima*
Golden-bells—*Forsythia*
Golden rain tree—
  Koelreuteria
Green osier—*Cornus*
Hawthorn—*Raphiolepis*
Heath—*Erica*
Heather—*Calluna*
Heather—*Erica carnea*
Hedge plant—*Ligustrum*
Hellebore—*Helleborus*
Holly—*Ilex*
Holly fern—*Cyrtomium*
Honeysuckle—*Lonicera*
Hornbeam—*Carpinus*
Horse chestnut—*Aesculus*
Inkberry—*Ilex glabra*
Ironwood—*Carpinus*
Japanese aralia—*Fatsia*

Japanese medlar—
  Eriobotrya
Japanese plum—*Eriobotrya*
Japanese quince—
  Chaenomeles
Jasmine (jessamine)—
  Gelsemium
Jasmine (jessamine)—
  Jasminum
Juniper—*Juniperus*
Laurel (cherry, English,
  Portugal)—*Prunus*
Laurel (Japanese,
  spotted)—*Aucuba*
Laurel (purple)—
  Rhododendron
Laurel (swamp)—*Magnolia*
Lavender—*Lavandula*
Lenten rose—*Helleborus*
Lilac—*Syringa*
Lily-of-the-valley bush—
  Pieris
Lilyturf—*Liriope*
Ling—*Calluna*
Live-forever—*Sedum*
Locust—*Gleditsia*
Loquat—*Eriobotrya*
Maiden grass—*Miscanthus*
Maple—*Acer*
Mock orange—*Pittosporum*
Mock orange—*Prunus*
Moonflower (moon vine)—
  Ipomoea alba
Morning glory—*Ipomoea*
Mountain camellia—
  Stewartia
Mountain grape—*Mahonia*
Mountain rosebay—
  *Rhododendron cataw-
  biense*
Mugwort—*Artemisia*
Needle palm—*Yucca*
Oak—*Quercus*
Oregon grape—*Mahonia*
Paper plant—*Fatsia*
Pear—*Pyrus*
Pig squeak—*Bergenia*
Pine—*Pinus*
Pinyon—*Pinus edulis*
Plantain lily—*Hosta*
Pomegranate—*Punica*

Poplar—*Liriodendron*
Poplar—*Populus*
Possom haw—*Ilex decidua*
Pride of India—
  Koelreuteria
Privet—*Ligustrum*
Quiverleaf—*Populus*
Redroot—*Ceanothus*
Reed grass—*Calamagrostis*
Rockrose—*Cistus*
Rockrose—*Helianthemum*
Rosemary—*Rosmarinus*
Sage tree—*Vitex*
Savin—*Juniperus*
Sevenbark—*Hydrangea*
Siberian tea—*Bergenia*
Silver grass—*Miscanthus*
Smoke tree (smokebush)—
  Cotinus
Snowbell—*Styrax*
Soapberry—*Sapindus*
Sorbet—*Cornus mas*
Spindle tree—*Euonymus*
Spruce—*Picea*
St.-John's-wort—*Hypericum*
Stonecrop—*Sedum*
Storax—*Styrax*
Sun rose—*Helianthemum*
Swamp (sweet) bay—
  Magnolia virginiana
Sweet gum—*Liquidambar*
Tulip magnolia—
  Liriodendron
Tulip tree—*Liriodendron*
Venetian sumac—*Cotinus*
Virgin's-bower—*Clematis*
Wax myrtle—*Myrica*
Whitewood—*Liriodendron*
Wig tree—*Cotinus*
Wild China tree—*Sapindus*
Wild lilac—*Ceanothus*
Wild orange—*Prunus*
Wild pepper—*Vitex*
Winter begonia—*Bergenia*
Winterberry—*Ilex decidua*
Witch hazel—*Hamamelis*
Wormwood—*Artemisia*
Yaupon—*Ilex vomitoria*
Yellowwood—*Cladrastis*
Yew—*Taxus*
Zebra grass—*Miscanthus*

Encyclopedia of Plants

Presented here in compact form is pertinent information on most of the plants mentioned in this volume. Each genus is listed alphabetically by its Latin botanical name, followed by pronunciation of the Latin and, in bold type, its common name or names. If you know a plant only by a common name, see the cross-reference chart on page 109 or the index.

A botanical name generally consists of the genus and a species, both usually printed in italics. Species may also have common names, which appear in parentheses, and many species contain one or more cultivars, whose names appear between single quotation marks. An "x" preceding the name indicates a hybrid.

"Hardiness" refers to the zones described on the USDA Plant Hardiness Zone Map for the United States and Canada (page 109). Plants grown outside recommended zones may do poorly or fail to survive.

Abelia
(a-BEE-li-a)
ABELIA

Abelia x 'Edward Goucher'

Hardiness:	*Zones 6-10*
Plant type:	*shrub*
Height:	*3 to 6 feet*
Interest:	*form, flowers, foliage*
Soil:	*moist, well-drained, acid*
Light:	*partial shade to full sun*

Abelia's fountainlike sprays of glimmering foliage lend airy grace and fine texture to borders and hedges. Tiny bell-shaped or tubular flowers bloom from early summer to frost. The small, pointed, richly green leaves are bronze when young and often turn bronze or bronzy purple again in fall. In the northern parts of its range, abelia is semi-evergreen.

Selected species and varieties: *A.* x *grandiflora* (glossy abelia)—rounded shrub 3 to 6 feet high (to 8 feet in the South) and equally wide, with small pinkish white flowers. *A.* x 'Edward Goucher', the result of a cross between *A.* x *grandiflora* and *A. schumannii,* forms a 4- to 5-foot-tall shrub with equal spread bearing pinkish lavender flowers. *A. schumannii*—mauve-pink flowers amid downy, blunt-pointed leaves; hardy to Zone 7.

Growing conditions and maintenance: Abelia flowers best when provided with at least a half-day of sunlight each day. It tolerates less-than-ideal soil. Prune in late winter or early spring; flowers are borne on new growth.

Abies
(AY-beez)
FIR

Abies concolor

Hardiness:	*Zones 3-7*
Plant type:	*tree*
Height:	*30 to 50 feet or more*
Interest:	*form, foliage*
Soil:	*moist to dry, well-drained*
Light:	*full sun*

White fir develops into a grand evergreen pyramid ideal as a specimen, screen, or vertical accent. The upper branches are upright in habit; the middle and lower, horizontal to descending. The trees bear flat, aromatic needles that have blunt tips and a glaucous coating. Greenish or purplish cones, up to 6 inches long, mature to a brown hue and fall apart when ripe.

Selected species and varieties: *A. concolor* (white fir, Colorado fir)—30 to 50 feet high (but reaching 100 feet under ideal conditions) by 15 to 30 feet wide, having a central trunk with whorled branches and producing bluish green, grayish green, or silvery blue needles up to 2½ inches long; 'Compacta' is a densely branched dwarf usually 3 feet high, with 1½-inch blue needles, acquiring an attractively irregular form as it matures.

Growing conditions and maintenance: Although white firs accept dry, rocky soils, they grow better in deep, sandy or gravelly loams. They withstand drought, heat, cold, and air pollution better than other firs. They tolerate light shade but fare best in full sun. Mulch well with shredded bark, woodchips, or leaves.

Acanthus
(a-KAN-thus)
BEAR'S-BREECH

Acanthus spinosus

Hardiness: *Zones 7-10*

Plant type: *perennial*

Height: *3 to 4 feet*

Interest: *form, foliage, flowers*

Soil: *well-drained, acid*

Light: *full sun to partial shade*

Valued for its bold sculptural effects, bear's-breech forms spreading clumps of broad, shiny, deeply lobed leaves up to 2 feet long that arise from the base of the plant and tall, stiff spikes of tubular flowers borne well above the foliage in summer. The flowers and seed heads are effective in arrangements.

Selected species and varieties: *A. spinosus* (spiny bear's-breech)—dense flower spikes, usually mauve but sometimes white, bloom on 3- to 4-foot stalks over arching, deeply cut, thistlelike leaves.

Growing conditions and maintenance: Give bear's-breech the full sun it loves except where summers are hot, when some shade is advisable. Plant 3 feet apart, and propagate by seed or by division in early spring or fall after the plant has bloomed at least 3 years. Tolerant of moderate drought, bear's-breech abhors wet winter soil. Once established, this plant is difficult to remove from a site, as bits of fleshy roots inadvertently left behind easily grow into new plants.

Acer
(AY-ser)
MAPLE

Acer griseum

Hardiness: *Zones 2-9*

Plant type: *shrub or tree*

Height: *6 to 75 feet*

Interest: *foliage, form, fruit*

Soil: *moist, well-drained*

Light: *full sun to partial shade*

The genus *Acer* includes a diverse group of deciduous plants ranging from towering trees with brilliant fall foliage to small, picturesque specimens ideal as centerpieces for ornamental beds. The mid-size maples included here are good specimen or patio trees. Flowers are usually inconspicuous, followed by winged seeds.

Selected species and varieties: *A. ginnala* (Amur maple, fire maple)—15 to 25 feet tall, usually branched close to the ground, with a canopy wider than its height, bearing serrated medium to dark green three-lobed leaves 1½ to 3 inches long that unfurl early in spring along with small, fragrant, yellowish white flower panicles, followed by winged fruits, often red, that persist to late fall; Zones 2-8. *A. griseum* (paperbark maple)—oval- to round-crowned tree 20 to 30 feet tall with up to an equal spread, clad in exfoliating reddish brown bark and producing dark green to blue-green leaves with three leaflets that may turn red in fall; Zones 4-8. *A. macrophyllum* (bigleaf maple, Oregon maple)—three- to five-lobed leaves 8 to 12 inches wide that turn bright yellow to orange in fall on a wide-crowned, 45-

to 75-foot-tall tree with fragrant greenish yellow flowers in nodding clusters that appear with the leaves in spring; hardy to Zone 5. *A. nigrum* [also classified as *A. saccharum* ssp. *nigrum*] (black maple)—a 60- to 75-foot-tall tree closely related to the sugar maple with drooping lobed leaves 3 to 6 inches wide that turn a brilliant yellow in fall; Zones 4-8. *A. palmatum* (Japanese maple)—slow-growing tree or multistemmed shrub 15 to 25 feet tall and at least as wide, with deeply cut leaves having five, seven, or nine lobes, and young stems that are reddish purple to green and become gray with age, Zones 5-8; 'Bloodgood' grows

Acer palmatum 'Dissectum'

upright to 15 or 20 feet with maroon or reddish purple leaves that turn scarlet in fall, blackish red bark, and attractive red fruit; 'Dissectum' (threadleaf Japanese maple) is a small, pendulous, lacy shrub usually 6 to 8 feet tall, with drooping green-barked branches that bear very finely divided pale green leaves with up to 11 lobes that turn yellow in fall; 'Dissectum Atropurpureum' has a moundlike appearance similar to 'Dissectum', with lacy purple-red new leaves that fade to green or purple-green and turn crimson or burnt orange in fall, as well as tortuous branching that is most apparent in winter. *A. rubrum* (red maple, scarlet maple, Canadian maple)—a medium-fast-growing tree to 60 feet tall, and sometimes much taller, with ascending branches forming an irregular, oval to rounded crown 20 feet wide and with reddish twigs bearing red 1-inch flowers in early spring followed by red winged seeds, then small, shiny, three- to five-lobed green leaves yielding a dazzling fall color that is unreliable in the species but consistent among cultivars; 'Autumn Blaze' [*A. x freemanii*] is a fast-growing cultivar reaching 50 feet tall by 40 feet wide exhibiting superb orange-red fall color on its dense, oval to rounded crown, hardy to Zone 4; 'October Glory' has a round crown and vivid bright orange to red foliage in midfall, holding late into the season and coloring well in the South. *A. saccharum* (sugar maple, rock maple)—60 to 75 feet tall with a spread about two-thirds the height in a symmetrical crown bearing greenish yellow flowers in spring and three- or five-lobed medium to dark

Acer rubrum 'October Glory'

green leaves that turn yellow, burnt orange, or reddish in fall; Zones 3-8.

Growing conditions and maintenance: Most maples can withstand occasional drought; red maples grow naturally in wet soil. Bigleaf maples prefer a cool, moist climate like that of their native Pacific Northwest. Sugar and red maples prefer slight acidity but tolerate other soil types. *A. rubrum* 'Autumn Blaze' is said to be slightly more drought tolerant than true red maple cultivars. Amur and paperbark maples tolerate a wide range of acid and alkaline soils. Japanese maples need highly organic loam; amend the soil with peat moss or leaf mold before planting. The finely divided foliage of threadleaf maples often shows leaf burn in hot, dry climates; find a spot sheltered from strong winds, late spring frosts, and searing sun. Amur and sugar maples tolerate some shade. Large maples have extensive, fibrous root systems that crowd the soil's surface in search of water and nutrients, making it difficult to sustain significant plantings beneath them.

Aesculus
(ES-kew-lus)
BUCKEYE

Aesculus glabra

Hardiness: *Zones 3-7*

Plant type: *tree*

Height: *20 to 40 feet*

Interest: *foliage, form, buds*

Soil: *moist, well-drained, slightly acid*

Light: *full sun to partial shade*

One of the first trees to leaf out in spring, the buckeye (also called horse chestnut) is a low-branched, round-topped tree with deep green five-fingered compound leaves that turn a vibrant orange in fall. Its large greenish yellow spring flowers are usually lost amid the foliage. The fruit is a brown seed capsule with a prickly cover, considered by some to be a good-luck charm. Buckeyes cast deep shade, discouraging grass below. Plant them in a naturalized area or a mulched bed where leaf, flower, and fruit litter will not be a nuisance. The seeds are poisonous.

Selected species and varieties: *A. glabra* (Ohio buckeye, fetid buckeye)—20 to 40 feet tall with an equal spread, bearing medium to dark green leaflets 3 to 6 inches long that open bright green, followed by flower panicles up to 7 inches long, and later 1- to 2-inch oval fruit.

Growing conditions and maintenance: A native of rich bottom lands and riverbanks, the Ohio buckeye prefers deep loam. Mulch well to conserve moisture; dry soil causes leaf scorch. Prune in the early spring.

Artemisia
(ar-tem-IS-ee-a)
WORMWOOD

Artemisia x 'Powis Castle'

Hardiness: *Zones 5-8*

Plant type: *perennial*

Height: *3 feet*

Interest: *foliage*

Soil: *poor, well-drained to dry*

Light: *full sun*

Wormwood (also called mugwort) exhibits aromatic, feathery silver-gray foliage that is useful as an accent or filler in perennial beds, blending especially well with blue, lavender, and pink flowers and softening harsh tones. It also lends variety to an all-green landscape. Forms range from woody evergreen shrubs, 4 to 5 feet high and good for background effects, to feathery mounds scarcely 6 inches high, suitable for edging and ground cover. Most species have inconspicuous flowers.

Selected species and varieties: *A.* x 'Powis Castle'—lacy mound 4 feet wide with a woody base, composed of finely divided steel gray to silvery leaves up to 4 inches long on woolly stems, and no flowers.

Growing conditions and maintenance: Plant *A.* x 'Powis Castle' 2 to 3 feet apart. Most wormwood becomes unkempt in moist, fertile soil and does poorly in heat and humidity. It tolerates very light shade, although it much prefers full sun. Cut back in late fall or early spring to keep plants shapely. Propagate by tip cuttings in spring or stem cuttings in late summer and fall.

Aucuba
(aw-KEW-ba)
AUCUBA

Aucuba japonica 'Variegata'

Hardiness: *Zones 7-10*

Plant type: *evergreen shrub*

Height: *6 to 10 feet*

Interest: *foliage, fruit*

Soil: *moist, well-drained, fertile*

Light: *partial to deep shade*

A rounded, upright shrub with large, leathery leaves that are often marked with gold or yellow, aucuba brightens shady areas. An excellent transition plant between woodland and garden, it is also useful for hedges and borders. If a male plant is nearby, female aucubas produce scarlet berries that last all winter but are often hidden by the foliage. Leaf color remains unchanged throughout the seasons.

Selected species and varieties: *A. japonica* (Japanese aucuba, Japanese laurel, spotted laurel)—lustrous medium to dark green leaves 3 to 8 inches long and up to 3 inches wide that dominate tiny purple flowers borne in erect panicles in early spring and ½-inch-wide bright red berries; 'Variegata' (gold-dust plant) is female and has deep green leaves heavily sprinkled with yellow.

Growing conditions and maintenance: Aucuba prefers slightly acid loam but will tolerate other soils. Once established, it withstands moderate drought. Full shade is best to maintain leaf color; direct sun—particularly in warmer climates—tends to blacken the foliage. Prune to control height and maintain shape.

Berberis
(BER-ber-is)
BARBERRY

Berberis x gladwynensis 'William Penn'

Hardiness: *Zones 4-8*

Plant type: *shrub*

Height: *18 inches to 8 feet*

Interest: *foliage, fruit*

Soil: *well-drained*

Light: *full sun to light shade*

Barberries are dense, somewhat stiff-limbed shrubs that produce bright yellow flowers in spring and red, blue, or black fruit. All are more or less thorny, with spines occurring along their stems, and some leaves also have spiny margins. Deciduous forms exhibit bright fall foliage and colorful berries that persist through winter. Barberries are useful as hedges, barriers, foundation plants, or specimens. Varieties with red or yellow leaves provide dramatic contrast in green landscapes and work especially well in combination with low-growing junipers.

Selected species and varieties: *B. buxifolia* var. *nana* (dwarf Magellan barberry)—spiny leaves up to 1 inch long on an evergreen shrub 18 inches tall and 24 inches wide, usually bearing orange-yellow flowers and purple berries; hardy to Zone 5. *B.* x *gladwynensis* 'William Penn'—mounded evergreen 4 feet high and wide, with showy flowers and lustrous dark green foliage that turns bronze in winter; hardy to Zone 6, but deciduous north of Zone 8. *B. julianae* (wintergreen barberry)—evergreen mound with upright habit, 6 to 8 feet high and wide,

with often light-colored stems bearing spines up to 1 inch long and narrow, spiny leaves 2 to 3 inches long that may turn bronze or dark reddish in color in winter, profuse bloom in spring, and ⅓-inch bluish black berries that may linger into fall; hardy to Zone 5. *B. thunbergii* (Japanese barberry)—multibranched deciduous shrub, 3 to 6 feet tall and 4 to 7 feet wide, producing bright green leaves that appear early to hide small flower clusters and turn orange, red, and reddish purple in fall as ⅓-inch bright red berries form; 'Aurea' grows 3 to 4 feet tall, with vivid yellow leaves in the growing season but relatively few flowers and fruit; var. *atropurpurea* 'Crimson Pygmy' [sometimes referred to as 'Little Gem', 'Little Beauty', 'Little Favorite', or 'Atro-

Berberis thunbergii

purpurea Nana'] has maroon to purplish red summer foliage and grows to 2 feet tall and 3 feet wide; var. *atropurpurea* 'Rose Glow' reaches 5 to 6 feet tall and produces foliage opening rosy pink with splotches of darker red-purple changing later to solid red-purple.

Growing conditions and maintenance: Evergreen barberries grow best in moist, slightly acid soil in sites that are protected from drying winds and strong sun. Deciduous barberries adapt to almost any soil and are tolerant of drought and urban pollution. They show their best fall color in full sun. The red and yellow forms revert to green in shade. Pruning is usually not necessary. Although *B. vulgaris* (common barberry) serves as an alternate host for black stem rust, a destructive disease of wheat, the varieties listed here are safe to grow.

Bergenia
(ber-JEN-ee-a)
BERGENIA

Bergenia cordifolia

Hardiness: *Zones 3-8*

Plant type: *perennial or ground cover*

Height: *12 to 18 inches*

Interest: *foliage, flowers*

Soil: *moist, well-drained*

Light: *full sun to partial shade*

Striking foliage and flowers make bergenia a standout in perennial beds and edgings. Slowly creeping by rhizomes, it is effective when used to cover small areas or planted in masses along the edge of a stream. The cabbagelike leaves are evergreen in warmer climates and may turn burgundy in winter.

Selected species and varieties: *B. cordifolia* (heartleaf bergenia, pig squeak)—deep pink, pale pink, or white flower racemes borne just above the 12- to 18-inch clump of puckered, leathery heart-shaped leaves, up to 12 inches long, with saw-toothed edges. *B. crassifolia* (leather bergenia, Siberian tea, winter begonia)—fleshy oval or spoon-shaped leaves, smaller than those of heartleaf bergenia, and spikes of lavender-pink flowers held well above the foliage, hardy to Zone 4; 'Redstar' has rose-purple flowers and reddish winter foliage.

Growing conditions and maintenance: Bergenia tolerates any well-drained soil but maintains the best foliage color in poor soil. Provide afternoon shade in hot climates. After several years, divide plants in early spring to rejuvenate.

Betula
(BET-u-la)
BIRCH

Betula nigra

Hardiness: *Zones 2-9*

Plant type: *tree*

Height: *40 to 70 feet*

Interest: *bark, form, foliage*

Soil: *moist, acid*

Light: *full sun*

Birches grace the landscape with trunks of decorative bark and airy canopies of medium to dark green finely toothed leaves that flutter in the slightest breeze and turn yellow in fall before dropping. Male and female flowers, called catkins, are borne on the same tree. Birches create a light dappled shade and are lovely in groups or singly as specimens.

Selected species and varieties: *B. nigra* (river birch, red birch, black birch)—40 to 70 feet tall with a spread almost equal to its height, usually multitrunked, with cinnamon brown bark, peeling when young and becoming deeply furrowed into irregular plates with age, and nearly triangular leaves to 3½ inches long that often show brief fall color; Zones 4-9. *B. papyrifera* (paper birch, canoe birch, white birch, cluster birch)—a low-branched tree with reddish brown bark when young aging to creamy white and peeling thinly to reveal reddish orange tissue beneath, growing 50 to 70 feet tall by 25 to 45 feet in spread, and bearing 2- to 4-inch roundish, wedge-shaped leaves turning a lovely yellow in fall; Zones 2-7. *B. pendula* (European white birch, silver birch, warty birch, common birch)—graceful, drooping branches on a 40- to 50-foot-tall by 20- to 35-foot-wide tree with the bark on trunk and main limbs changing slowly from whitish to mostly black-on-white with age, golden brown twigs and slender branches bearing serrated, almost diamond-shaped leaves 1 to 3 inches long that hold later in the fall than do the other species but often show little fall color, Zones 2-7; 'Dalecarlica' (cutleaf weeping birch, Swedish birch) has pendulous branches that arc to touch the ground and dangling, deeply lobed and sharply toothed leaves.

Growing conditions and maintenance: Give birches optimum growing conditions and keep a sharp eye out for insects

Betula papyrifera

or disease. Although river birches can thrive in periodic flooding, most species need good drainage and grow best in loose, rich, acid loams. Paper birch and European white birch tolerate neutral soils, but river birch must have acid soil. Amend soil with peat moss, leaf mold, or finished compost. Add sand if the soil is heavy. Mulch to retain moisture and to protect from lawn-mower damage. All birches bleed heavily in late winter or early spring; prune in summer or fall. Bottom branches on paper birch can easily be removed to create a high-branched specimen tree. Although river birch and paper birch are resistant to the bronze birch borer, European white birch is quite susceptible and may succumb if a routine spraying program is not followed. Most birches live about 50 years.

Calamagrostis
(kal-a-ma-GROS-tis)
REED GRASS

Calamagrostis acutiflora 'Stricta'

Hardiness: *Zones 6-9*

Plant type: *ornamental grass*

Height: *5 to 7 feet*

Interest: *form, foliage, flowers*

Soil: *adaptable*

Light: *full sun*

This dense, picturesque clump of narrow, arching leaves and feathery flower plumes on tall, upright stems supplies a striking vertical accent to the garden. One of the first ornamental grasses to bloom, feather reed grass is a fine multiseason specimen, singly or in groups, for perennial beds, borders, or streamside plantings. It also blends well with rocks and provides interesting wintertime contrast with dark green, broadleaved evergreens.

Selected species and varieties: *C. acutiflora* 'Stricta' (feather reed grass)—2-foot-wide clumps of matte green leaves ½ inch wide arch below 4-foot shafts bearing 15-inch-long flower panicles in early summer, the foliage at first pinkish green, turning tan in summer, and maturing to golden brown and lasting all winter.

Growing conditions and maintenance: An undemanding perennial, feather reed grass grows as well in heavy, wet soils as in poor, dry soils. Little attention is required. Cut the clump to within 6 inches of the ground before new growth begins in spring. Propagate by division in spring.

Calluna
(ka-LOO-na)
HEATHER, LING

Calluna vulgaris 'Corbett's Red'

Hardiness: *Zones 4-7*

Plant type: *shrub or ground cover*

Height: *24 inches*

Interest: *flowers, form*

Soil: *moist, well-drained, acid, sandy*

Light: *full sun to partial shade*

Scotch heather produces a sea of wavy bloom when its tiny spikes of urn-shaped flowers begin blooming in midsummer. Minute, scalelike, evergreen leaves are closely pressed to dense colonies of floating stems and may turn bronze in winter. Let this fine-textured plant form a thick mat in sunny locations where ground cover is needed, or tuck it into rock gardens and edgings.

Selected species and varieties: *C. vulgaris* (Scotch heather)—variable height up to 2 feet, spreading 2 feet or more, and bearing purplish pink flower clusters up to 1 foot long until fall; 'Else Frye' has double white flowers and reaches 18 inches; 'H. E. Beale' grows 2 feet high with silvery pink flowers; 'Mrs. Ronald Gray', 4 inches high with reddish flowers.

Growing conditions and maintenance: Heathers grow best in loam of low fertility. Good drainage is critical. Plant in full sun for best flowering and protect from drying winds. Mulch to conserve moisture, and water during dry spells. Prune faded flowers and stem tips to reduce legginess.

Carpinus
(car-PY-nis)
HORNBEAM

Carpinus betulus 'Fastigiata'

Hardiness: *Zones 4-7*

Plant type: *tree*

Height: *30 to 60 feet*

Interest: *foliage, form, bark*

Soil: *well-drained*

Light: *full sun to partial shade*

A deciduous tree with crisp summer foliage, smooth gray bark, and a well-contoured winter silhouette, hornbeam (also called ironwood) makes a handsome specimen tree. Because it has dense foliage that takes well to pruning, however, it is often used as a hedge or screen. The dark green leaves may turn yellow or brown in fall. Hornbeam has extremely hard wood that was once used to make ox yokes.

Selected species and varieties: *C. betulus* (European hornbeam, common hornbeam)—pyramidal when young, maturing to a rounded crown, 40 to 60 feet tall under average conditions with a spread of 30 to 40 feet, bearing sharply toothed leaves 2½ to 5 inches long and 1 to 2 inches wide that remain unusually pest free; 'Columnaris' has a densely branched, steeple-shaped outline; 'Fastigiata' grows 30 to 40 feet tall with a spread of 20 to 30 feet, an oval to vaselike shape, and a forked trunk.

Growing conditions and maintenance: A highly adaptable and trouble-free plant, European hornbeam tolerates a wide range of soil conditions.

Ceanothus
(see-a-NO-thus)
WILD LILAC, REDROOT

Ceanothus arboreus

Hardiness: *Zones 7-11*

Plant type: *tree, shrub, or ground cover*

Height: *18 inches to 25 feet*

Interest: *flowers*

Soil: *well-drained to dry*

Light: *full sun*

Wild lilacs are widely used on slopes and in masses in West Coast gardens. They improve the soil by fixing nitrogen. Evergreen forms bloom in spring.

Selected species and varieties: *C. arboreus* (Catalina mountain lilac, feltleaf ceanothus)—blue plumes on a 25-foot-tall shrub or tree with 4-inch evergreen leaves; Zones 9-10. *C. x delilianus*—3-foot deciduous shrub with 4- to 6-inch blue flowers in summer and fall and dark green leaves 3 inches long; 'Gloire de Versailles' grows 6 feet tall with fragrant lavender-blue flowers; hardy to Zone 7. *C. griseus* var. *horizontalis* (Carmel creeper)—18 to 30 inches tall and 5 to 15 feet wide with light blue flower clusters 1 inch wide and glossy 2-inch-long evergreen leaves; hardy to Zone 8. *C. thyrsiflorus* 'Skylark' (blueblossom)—dark blue spikes bloom over a long season on a broad 3- to 6-foot-tall shrub with 2-inch-long evergreen leaves; hardy to Zone 8.

Growing conditions and maintenance: Wild lilacs thrive on rocky slopes that usually stay dry all summer. Plant them in light, sandy soil, and water only during their first season. Fast drainage is a must.

Cedrus
(SEE-drus)
CEDAR

Cedrus deodora

Hardiness: *Zones 6-9*

Plant type: *evergreen tree*

Height: *100 to 150 feet*

Interest: *form, foliage*

Soil: *well-drained*

Light: *full sun*

Cedars grow into magnificent specimen trees, their sweeping branches and great height best displayed on broad lawns.

Selected species and varieties: *C. atlantica* (Atlas cedar)—slowly reaches more than 100 feet tall and two-thirds as wide, appearing open and spindly when young but maturing into a flat-topped shape with bluish green or sometimes green to silvery blue inch-long needles and 3-inch-long cones that take 2 years to mature; 'Glauca' (blue Atlas cedar) has rich blue needles. *C. deodara* (deodar cedar)—pyramidal and more attractive when young than Atlas cedar, becoming flat topped and broad with age, growing 40 to 70 feet tall with a nearly equal spread but sometimes reaching 150 feet, with light blue to grayish green needles up to 1½ inches long, a gracefully drooping habit, and 3- to 4-inch cones; Zones 7-8.

Growing conditions and maintenance: Give both species ample room to develop in a site protected from strong winds. Atlas cedar grows best in moist, deep loam but will tolerate other soils as long as they are well drained. A moderately dry site is best for deodar cedar.

Chaenomeles
(kee-NOM-e-lees)
FLOWERING QUINCE

Chaenomeles speciosa 'Texas Scarlet'

Hardiness: *Zones 4-8*

Plant type: *deciduous shrub*

Height: *3 to 10 feet*

Interest: *flowers*

Soil: *moist to dry, acid*

Light: *full sun*

A thorny, rounded spreading shrub, flowering quince's best attribute is its showy profusion of early-spring flowers before the foliage appears. The small, yellowish green quincelike fruits that ripen in fall can be used for jams and jellies but cannot be eaten raw. The shrub's dense, twiggy branching makes a coarse winter silhouette. Budded stems can be used for late-winter arrangements.

Selected species and varieties: *C. speciosa* (common flowering quince, Japanese quince)—6 to 10 feet tall with equal or greater width, usually with red or scarlet, but sometimes pink or white, flowers and lustrous dark green leaves that open bronzy red; 'Cameo' produces peachy pink double flowers; 'Nivalis', white flowers; 'Texas Scarlet', profuse tomato red flowers on a 3- to 5-foot plant.

Growing conditions and maintenance: Flowering quince adapts to most soils except the very alkaline. Full sun produces the best bloom. Restore vigor and improve flowering by cutting out older branches. Leaf spot and too much spring rain can cause a loss of foliage, but some leaf drop by midsummer is normal.

Chamaecyparis
(kam-ee-SIP-a-ris)
FALSE CYPRESS

Chamaecyparis obtusa

Hardiness: *Zones 4-8*

Plant type: *shrub or tree*

Height: *4 to 75 feet*

Interest: *form, foliage*

Soil: *well-drained, fertile, acid to neutral*

Light: *full sun to partial shade*

False cypresses are coniferous evergreen specimen trees with fan-shaped, flattened branch tips and scalelike foliage.

Selected species and varieties: *C. lawsoniana* (Lawson false cypress, Lawson cypress, Port Orford cedar)—40 to 60-foot columnar tree with massive central trunk, short ascending branches with drooping tips, and glaucous green to dark green foliage, Zones 5-7; 'Allumii' grows a narrow silvery blue spire to 30 feet. *C. obtusa* (hinoki false cypress, hinoki cypress)—dark green slender pyramid growing 50 to 75 feet tall; 'Crippsii' forms a broad pyramid with drooping golden yellow branch tips; 'Gracilis' takes a narrow conical form, 6 to 10 feet tall; 'Nana Gracilis' has very dark green foliage arranged in slightly curved sprays, making for an attractive accent plant 4 to 6 feet tall and 3 to 4 feet wide.

Growing conditions and maintenance: Although hinoki false cypress is moderately tolerant of light shade and drier climates, most other species prefer full sun in cool, moist climates. Provide partial shade in hot regions and protect from drying wind. Amend soil with peat moss or leaf mold to hold moisture.

Chilopsis
(kill-OP-sis)
DESERT WILLOW

Chilopsis linearis

Hardiness: *Zones 8-10*

Plant type: *shrub or tree*

Height: *10 to 25 feet*

Interest: *flowers, foliage*

Soil: *dry, sandy*

Light: *full sun*

Showy, trumpet-shaped spring flowers resembling snapdragons bloom in clusters at the tips of desert willow's branches in spring and often sporadically until fall. Its open, branching and willowlike leaves, evergreen in milder climates, lend an airy appearance. A heavy crop of thin, foot-long pods persists through winter. Desert willow can be trained into a graceful specimen for dry gardens.

Selected species and varieties: *C. linearis* (desert catalpa, flowering willow)—shrubby habit, 10 to 25 feet tall and 10 to 15 feet wide, with twisted branches bearing narrow 6- to 12-inch-long leaves and fragrant lilac, rosy pink, purple, or white flowers with curled lobes and white or yellow markings.

Growing conditions and maintenance: Native to arid lands of the Southwest, desert willow enjoys light soil that is very well drained. Prune to develop a tree form or to eliminate shagginess.

Cistus
(SIS-tus)
ROCKROSE

Cistus x purpureus

Hardiness: *Zones 8-10*

Plant type: *shrub*

Height: *3 to 5 feet*

Interest: *flowers, foliage*

Soil: *dry to well-drained*

Light: *full sun*

Rockroses provide long-lasting color for desert areas or seaside gardens. Useful in rock gardens or mixed borders, massed, or as a ground cover on banks, these mounding shrubs with aromatic leaves bear flowers resembling single roses that last only a day but bloom sporadically for several weeks. Because the downy, mostly evergreen foliage is resistant to burning, rockroses are often planted in fire-hazard areas.

Selected species and varieties: *C. x hybridus* (white rockrose)—1½-inch-wide white flowers with yellow centers in late spring contrast with crinkly gray-green leaves to 2 inches long on a shrub 3 to 5 feet high and wide, sometimes spreading 6 to 8 feet. *C. x purpureus* (orchid rockrose)—compact shrub 4 feet tall and wide, with wrinkled dark green leaves 1 to 2 inches long and reddish purple flowers, each petal with a red blotch at its base, 3 inches wide, in early to midsummer.

Growing conditions and maintenance: Rockroses grow well in poor, dry soil and accept heat, ocean spray, and alkaline or even slightly acid soils.

Cladrastis
(cla-DRAS-tis)
YELLOWWOOD

Cladrastis kentukea

Hardiness: *Zones 4-8*

Plant type: *tree*

Height: *30 to 50 feet*

Interest: *flowers, foliage, form, bark*

Soil: *well-drained*

Light: *full sun*

An excellent deciduous shade tree for small landscapes, yellowwood produces long, hanging panicles of fragrant flowers in mid- to late spring and a broad canopy of bright green foliage that turns yellow in fall. The bark is smooth and gray. Open, delicate zigzag branching creates an airy form. The color of the interior wood gives the tree its name. Flowering is best every second or third year.

Selected species and varieties: *C. kentukea* [formerly called *C. lutea*] (American yellowwood, Kentucky yellowwood, virgilia)—low-branching habit with a rounded crown 40 to 55 feet wide, producing 3- to 4-inch long compound leaves opening bright yellowish green before darkening slightly later, with flower clusters up to 14 inches long, and thin brown seedpods 4 to 5 inches long in fall.

Growing conditions and maintenance: Although it occurs naturally on rich, limestone soils, American yellowwood adapts to a wide range of soil types from acid to alkaline and is remarkably pest free. Once established, it is drought tolerant. Prune only in summer to prevent heavy sap bleeding.

Clematis
(KLEM-a-tis)
VIRGIN'S-BOWER

Clematis montana var. rubens

Hardiness: *Zones 5-9*

Plant type: *woody vine*

Height: *4 to 30 feet*

Interest: *flowers, fragrance*

Soil: *moist, well-drained, fertile*

Light: *partial shade to full sun*

Gracefully twining stems and showy flowers in white, pink, or purple make clematis an excellent choice for covering trellises, fences, arbors, and even unsightly rock piles. Clematis has no true petals; the showy parts of the flower are the sepals. Dark green leaves with three heart-shaped leaflets 1 to 4 inches long appear at the end of leafstalks that curl around a support; the foliage develops no fall color. There are more than 230 species of clematis; the small-flowered types are hardy, prolific bloomers. A vine from one of the perfumed varieties can scent a room.

Selected species and varieties: *C. armandii*—fast-growing evergreen vine with large, leathery green leaves and fragrant white flowers up to 2½ inches wide with four to seven sepals, borne in panicles in spring; Zones 7-9. *C. montana* (anemone clematis)—a vigorous climber 20 to 25 feet tall, with four-sepaled white flowers up to 2½ inches wide in late spring to early summer, appearing singly or in groups of up to five and sometimes vanilla scented, Zones 5-8; var. *rubens* produces 2¼-inch fragrant rosy red flow-

ers later than the species and purplish bronze foliage that opens with a purplish red tinge, hardy to Zone 5; 'Tetrarose' grows purplish pink 3-inch-wide flowers with ruby stamens and bronzy foliage that is less colorful than that of var. *rubens*. *C. paniculata* [now classified by some authorities as *C. maximowicziana;* often confused by nurseries with *C. dioscoreifolia* or *C.d.* var. *robusta*] (sweet autumn clematis)—rampant grower up to 30 feet, producing fragrant 1-inch-wide white flowers with six to eight narrow sepals, borne at every joint

Clematis paniculata

in drooping panicles in late summer to fall and blooming so profusely—particularly in male plants—that the entire plant appears to be covered with white; followed by gray, pinwheel-like seed heads that persist well into winter; Zones 5-8.

Growing conditions and maintenance: Clematis performs best when its roots remain cool and moist but its top is in the sun. Plant against a north-facing wall or in the shade of low shrubs, allowing it to clamber up to the sun. Sweet autumn clematis tolerates bright shade. Amend soil liberally with leaf mold, peat moss, or compost. Although fairly adaptable, clematis prefers neutral or slightly alkaline conditions. Mulch well or underplant with a surface-rooting ground cover. Provide a structure, wire netting, or support. Fertilize monthly during the growing season. Prune severely for the first several years. Spring-blooming clematis, which flowers on old wood, can be pruned after blooming; species that bloom in summer or autumn flower on new wood and should be pruned in late fall or early spring.

Cornus
(KOR-nus)
DOGWOOD

Cornus florida

Hardiness: *Zones 3-9*

Plant type: *large shrub or small tree*

Height: *15 to 30 feet*

Interest: *flowers, foliage, fruit, form, bark*

Soil: *well-drained*

Light: *bright shade to full sun*

Dogwoods can turn the spring landscape into a fairyland and in fall provide bright red fruit for birds. They may also offer red to reddish purple fall foliage, colorful bark, and low, layered branching for an attractive winter silhouette.

Selected species and varieties: *C. alternifolia* (pagoda dogwood, green osier)—strongly fragrant yellowish white flowers borne in flat clusters 1½ to 2½ inches wide on a horizontally branched tree growing 15 to 25 feet tall with a greater spread and tierlike habit, also bearing fruit that matures from green to red to blue-black; Zones 3-7. *C. florida* (flowering dogwood)—small tree with broad crown, usually 20 to 30 feet tall with an equal or greater spread, producing white flowerlike bracts lasting 10 to 14 days in spring before the leaves emerge, followed in fall by small glossy red fruits borne in clusters of at least three to four; Zones 5-9. *C. kousa* (kousa dogwood)—large shrub or small tree 20 to 30 feet tall and wide with exfoliating gray, tan, and brown bark and tiered branching, flowering in late spring after the leaves appear and lasting for up to 6 weeks, followed by pink to red fruit

up to 1 inch wide in late summer to fall, when the leaves turn reddish purple or scarlet, Zones 5-8; var. *chinensis* (Chinese dogwood)—grows to 30 feet and has larger bracts than the species. *C. mas* (cornelian cherry, sorbet)—multistemmed shrub or small, oval to round tree 20 to 25 feet tall and 15 to 20 feet wide, branching nearly to the ground with attractive exfoliating gray to brown bark, bearing small clusters of yellow flowers for 3 weeks in early spring and bright red fruit in midsummer that is partly hidden by the lustrous dark green leaves, 2 to 4 inches long, that usually show little fall color; Zones 4-8.

Growing conditions and maintenance: Give flowering and pagoda dogwoods a moist, acid soil enriched with leaf mold,

Cornus mas

peat moss, or compost. Partial shade is best in hotter areas. Mulch to keep soil cool and prevent lawn-mower damage, which invites invasion by dogwood borers. Kousa dogwood prefers loose, sandy, acid soil, rich with organic matter, in sunny locations. It is more drought tolerant than flowering dogwood. Although adaptable to a wide range of soil types, cornelian cherry prefers moist, rich sites in sun or partial shade and is probably the best performer of the dogwoods for the Midwest. Susceptible to the usually fatal anthracnose, which has killed many dogwoods on the East Coast, flowering dogwood has a better chance of staying healthy if stress is reduced. The other dogwoods listed here appear not to be affected. For colder climates, the best bud hardiness in flowering dogwoods occurs in trees native to those regions.

Cotinus
(ko-TYE-nus)
SMOKE TREE

Cotinus coggygria 'Velvet Cloak'

Hardiness: *Zones 5-9*

Plant type: *shrub*

Height: *10 to 15 feet*

Interest: *fruiting panicles*

Soil: *well-drained*

Light: *full sun*

For most of the summer and early fall, smokebush almost explodes with puffy, smoky pink plumes, actually hairs arising from the 6- to 8-inch fruiting stalks as the tiny yellowish flowers fade. An eye-catching accent plant that often has colorful fall foliage, smokebush also works well in borders and groupings.

Selected species and varieties: *C. coggygria* (common smokebush, smoke plant, Venetian sumac, wig tree)—a loose and open multistemmed deciduous shrub, 10 to 15 feet wide, bearing 1½- to 3-inch-long leaves that unfurl pink-bronze in midspring, mature to medium blue-green, and sometimes show yellow-red-purple fall color and branched puffs changing to gray; 'Royal Purple' has purplish maroon leaves with scarlet margins, eventually turning scarlet all over; 'Velvet Cloak', purple plumes and velvety dark purple leaves throughout the summer before changing to reddish purple in fall.

Growing conditions and maintenance: Tolerant of a wide range of soils, smokebush demands only that a site be well drained. Too-rich or too-moist soil reduces bloom and subdues leaf color.

Cotoneaster
(ko-toe-nee-AS-ter)
COTONEASTER

Cotoneaster microphyllus

Hardiness: *Zones 5-8*

Plant type: *evergreen shrub or ground cover*

Height: *1 to 15 feet*

Interest: *foliage, fruit, form*

Soil: *well-drained*

Light: *full sun to partial shade*

Red berries decorate the stiff, spreading branches of cotoneasters in fall and winter, and the tiny, deep green leaves lend a fine texture to the garden in all seasons. White or pink flowers, often quite small, appear in spring. Usually spreading at least as wide as their height, cotoneasters are used as fast-growing ground covers that are ideal for slopes, rock gardens, and walls; in masses; or as shrubs good for borders and screens. Cotoneasters can also be trained into espaliers.

Selected species and varieties: *C. dammeri* (bearberry cotoneaster)—prostrate form, 12 to 18 inches high, an excellent ground cover because it roots wherever its branches touch soil and spreads quickly to 6 feet wide, with white flowers up to ½ inch wide, a light crop of red berries, and narrow, 1-inch-long, lustrous dark green leaves that may become tinged with red-purple in winter, Zones 5-8; 'Skogholm' grows vigorously to 1½ to 3 feet high, spreading several feet each year. *C. lacteus* (red cluster-berry, parney cotoneaster)—a 6- to 10-foot shrub with a handsome fruit display persisting through winter and 2- to 3-

inch-wide white flower clusters in spring, sometimes partly hidden by the foliage; Zones 6-8. *C. microphyllus* (littleleaf cotoneaster, rockspray cotoneaster)—a nearly prostrate shrub, usually 24 inches high or less, spreading up to 10 feet wide with ¼- to ½-inch-long glossy leaves, tiny white flowers, and red fruit; Zones 5-8. *C. salicifolius* (willowleaf cotoneaster)—a shrub with an arching habit, growing 10 to 15 feet tall with a smaller spread and producing narrow, willowlike leaves 1½ to 3½ inches long that are lustrous dark green in summer becoming plum-purple in winter, flat 2-inch-wide white flower

Cotoneaster salicifolius

heads often masked by the foliage, and tiny, long-lasting bright red fruit, Zones 6-8; 'Autumn Fire' forms a 2- to 3-foot-high ground cover with 1½- to 2-inch very glossy leaves turning reddish purple in winter and scarlet fruit; 'Repens' has lustrous 1-inch leaves on a prostrate ground cover to 12 inches tall.

Growing conditions and maintenance: Bearberry cotoneaster is tolerant of most well-drained soils and is easily grown. Willowleaf and parney cotoneasters need moist, well-drained, acid to nearly neutral soil. Mature plants will tolerate drought, seashore conditions, and wind; dry or poor soil often produces the best fruiting. Cotoneaster is susceptible to fire blight, a blackened die-off of branch tips which, if not treated, is fatal to the plant; littleleaf cotoneaster may be more susceptible in the South. Other pests are borers, red spiders, and lace bugs. Prune only to control the plant's shape.

x Cupressocyparis
(kew-press-oh-SIP-ar-iss)
LEYLAND CYPRESS

x Cupressocyparis leylandii 'Silver Dust'

Hardiness: *Zones 6-10*

Plant type: *evergreen tree*

Height: *60 to 70 feet*

Interest: *foliage, form*

Soil: *adaptable*

Light: *full sun*

A dense, towering, columnar or pyramidal tree when left unchecked, x *Cupressocyparis*—a hybrid of *Cupressus* and *Chamaecyparis*—produces some of the fastest-growing and finest-textured screen or hedge plants available. The fanlike arrangement of bluish green scalelike needles appears soft and feathery.

Selected species and varieties: x *C. leylandii* (Leyland cypress)—a cross between *Cupressus macrocarpa* (Monterey cypress) and *Chamaecyparis nootkatensis* (Alaska cedar) that grows 3 feet a year or more to 70 feet tall and usually 10 to 18 feet wide, with reddish brown scaly bark; cultivars include silvery green, variegated, and golden yellow forms; 'Silver Dust' has creamy white markings on green foliage.

Growing conditions and maintenance: Leyland cypress grows best in moist, well-drained, moderately fertile loams but is very tolerant of almost any soil. Provide protection from drying winter winds. It is best transplanted from a container; field-grown plants are hard to ball and burlap. Unaffected by serious pests, it also resists sea winds and cold damage.

Cupressus
(kew-PRESS-us)
CYPRESS

Cupressus sempervirens

Hardiness: *Zones 7-9*

Plant type: *evergreen tree*

Height: *30 to 40 feet*

Interest: *form, foliage, bark*

Soil: *dry to well-drained*

Light: *full sun*

These graceful, fine-textured trees make handsome specimens, screens, or windbreaks. Their aromatic foliage consists of scalelike leaves closely pressed on braided-cord stems. Reddish brown exfoliating bark becomes dark brown and furrowed with age. Cones with shieldlike scales are 1 inch across.

Selected species and varieties: *C. glabra* [sometimes labeled by nurseries as *C. arizonica,* which is actually a separate species] (smooth-barked Arizona cypress)—a dense, bushy pyramid 30 to 40 feet tall and 15 to 20 feet wide with soft green, gray-green, or blue-green foliage. *C. sempervirens* (Italian cypress, Mediterranean cypress)—a slender column 30 or more feet tall, with horizontal branches and dark green foliage; cultivars include bright green, gold, and blue forms.

Growing conditions and maintenance: Best suited to the West and the Southwest, cypress enjoys mild to hot, dry climates and needs no supplemental water once established. Soil must be perfectly drained. When grown in its natural habitat, cypress is generally insect and disease free. It is short-lived in the Southeast.

Cyrtomium
(sir-TOH-mee-um)
HOLLY FERN

Cyrtomium falcatum

Hardiness: *Zones 8-10*

Plant type: *perennial*

Height: *1 to 2 feet*

Interest: *foliage*

Soil: *moist, well-drained, acid, organic*

Light: *partial to full, deep shade*

The shiny deep green leathery fronds of holly fern rise in a spiral from an erect crown and arch gracefully. This vase-shaped, woody evergreen is ideal for the north side of walls, the foreground of partly shaded foundation plantings, and woodland gardens in dappled light.

Selected species and varieties: *C. falcatum* (Japanese holly fern)—1 to 2 feet high and 2 feet wide, displaying 3-inch-long glossy leaflets with prominent margin points on fronds up to 2½ feet long that are greenish yellow when new and mature to dark green.

Growing conditions and maintenance: Holly fern is easier to grow than many ferns and is more tolerant of low humidity, partial sun, and exposed sites. Plant in moist, loose soil well amended with peat moss, leaf mold, or compost. Use sand to improve drainage of heavy clay soil. Holly fern is usually free of insects and disease. Propagate by dividing in spring or summer.

Enkianthus
(en-kee-AN-thus)
ENKIANTHUS

Enkianthus campanulatus

Hardiness: *Zones 4-7*

Plant type: *shrub or small tree*

Height: *6 to 30 feet*

Interest: *foliage, flowers*

Soil: *moist, well-drained, acid, organic*

Light: *full sun to partial shade*

Pendulous clusters of dainty flowers in spring and brilliant fall foliage make this deciduous shrub a stand-alone specimen or a welcome addition to groups of acid-loving rhododendrons and azaleas.

Selected species and varieties: *E. campanulatus* (redvein enkianthus)—narrow, upright habit, 6 to 8 feet tall in cold areas, to 30 feet in warmer climates, with layered branches bearing at their tips tufts of 1- to 3-inch-long medium green leaves that turn bright red to orange and yellow in fall, and producing long-stalked clusters of pale yellow or light orange bell-shaped flowers with red veins in late spring as the leaves develop, the blooms sometimes persisting for several weeks; hardy to parts of Zone 4. *E. perulatus* (white enkianthus)—6 feet high and wide, with white urn-shaped flower clusters in midspring before the foliage appears, the bright green 1- to 2-inch-long leaves turning scarlet in fall; hardy to Zone 5.

Growing conditions and maintenance: Mix peat moss or leaf mold into the soil before planting. Mulch to retain moisture. Pruning is rarely necessary.

Erica
(ER-i-ka)
HEATH

Erica carnea 'Winter Beauty'

Hardiness: *Zones 6-9*

Plant type: *evergreen shrub or ground cover*

Height: *to 16 inches*

Interest: *flowers, buds*

Soil: *moist, well-drained*

Light: *full sun to partial shade*

Spring heath produces a mass of colorful flower spikes from winter to spring above a spreading evergreen carpet of bright green needlelike foliage. Use singly in rock gardens and flower beds, or plant in masses to cover a sunny slope or to edge a path.

Selected species and varieties: *E. carnea* (spring heath, snow heather)—prostrate branches with upright branchlets up to 16 inches high and spreading 2 to 6 feet wide bearing bell-shaped flowers of white, pink, rose, red, or purple in nodding clusters; 'Springwood Pink' grows 6 to 8 inches high with clear pink flowers; 'Springwood White', 6 to 8 inches high with pure white flowers and bronze new growth; 'Winter Beauty', to 5 inches high with a profusion of dark pink flowers.

Growing conditions and maintenance: Plant in sandy loam amended with peat moss or leaf mold. Heath usually fares poorly in heavy clay. Mulch to conserve moisture for the shallow roots, and water during dry periods. Spring heath prefers acid soil, but unlike many other heaths, tolerates slight alkalinity. Prune after flowering to encourage compactness.

Eriobotrya
(air-ee-o-BOT-ree-a)
LOQUAT

Eriobotrya japonica

Hardiness: *Zones 8-10*

Plant type: *shrub or tree*

Height: *15 to 25 feet*

Interest: *foliage, fruit, fragrance*

Soil: *moist, well-drained*

Light: *full sun to partial shade*

Lustrous wrinkled evergreen leaves that are sometimes a foot long create interesting textural effects in the landscape. Stiff panicles of fragrant, but not showy, woolly flowers form in fall or winter, and by late spring edible yellow-orange fruits are ready to be picked in the Deep South. Loquat can be used as an accent, or it can be trained into a patio tree or espalier.

Selected species and varieties: *E. japonica* (Chinese loquat, Japanese plum, Japanese medlar)—a tree or rounded multistemmed shrub 15 to 25 feet tall and wide, with supple branches bearing heavily veined 6- to 12-inch-long toothy leaves that are deep green above and a rust color on the undersides, with five-petaled dull white ½-inch-wide flowers borne in 6-inch clusters and covered with brown fuzz, and pear-shaped fruit almost 2 inches long in the southern half of its range.

Growing conditions and maintenance: Loquat prefers moist loam but tolerates moderately alkaline soils and occasional drought. Provide protection from wind. Feed only lightly; rampant new growth is subject to fire blight.

Escallonia
(es-ka-LOAN-ee-a)
ESCALLONIA

Escallonia x langleyensis 'Apple Blossom'

Hardiness: *Zones 8-10*

Plant type: *evergreen shrub*

Height: *3 to 5 feet*

Interest: *flowers, foliage, fragrance*

Soil: *well-drained*

Light: *full sun*

Escallonia produces short clusters of pink, white, or red funnel-shaped flowers amid glossy, often sweetly fragrant foliage over a long blooming season. A good choice for coastal gardens, escallonia is often used for hedges or screens and in masses.

Selected species and varieties: *E.* x *langleyensis* 'Apple Blossom'—a dense, sprawling shrub 3 to 5 feet high, with arching branches bearing large leaves and pink buds opening to pinkish white flowers throughout the warm months. *E.* 'Pride of Donard'—dense, broad-spreading habit with rosy pink flowers throughout the year in mild climates. *E. rubra* 'C. F. Ball' (red escallonia)—a compact, upright shrub to 5 feet tall, good for hedging, with very glossy leaves and bright red flowers in 1- to 3-inch clusters blooming freely during warm seasons.

Growing conditions and maintenance: A native of Chile, escallonia thrives in salt spray and coastal winds. *E.* x *langleyensis* 'Apple Blossom', however, does not do well in fully exposed locations. Escallonia likes average soils and withstands some drought but is intolerant of high alkalini-

Euonymus
(yew-ON-i-mus)
SPINDLE TREE

Euonymus alata 'Compacta'

Hardiness: *Zones 4-9*

Plant type: *shrub, ground cover, or vine*

Height: *4 inches to 70 feet*

Interest: *foliage, form*

Soil: *well-drained*

Light: *full sun to deep shade*

This broad genus includes deciduous shrubs that produce dazzling fall foliage and a cleanly defined winter silhouette as well as evergreen ground covers, shrubs, and clinging vines. Inconspicuous flowers form in spring, and hidden pink to red fruit capsules, which are usually hidden, split to expose orange seeds in fall, attracting birds. In its varied forms, euonymus provides structure to the garden. Use burning bush *(E. alata)* for hedges that need no trimming or for massing. Japanese euonymus is suitable for hedges and tall foundation plants. Winter creeper euonymus can climb a brick wall or cover a bank.

Selected species and varieties: *E. alata* [also listed as *E. alatus*] (winged spindle tree, winged euonymus, burning bush) —a slow-growing, wide-spreading, flat-topped shrub of variable height, usually 15 to 20 feet tall and wide, with soft green leaves 1 to 3 inches long that turn brilliant red in fall, yellow-green flowers in spring, and small red fruits borne under the leaves, Zones 4-8; 'Compacta' [also listed as 'Compactus'] (dwarf burning bush) grows 10 feet tall, its slender branches exhibiting less prominent corky ridges and forming a denser, more rounded outline; hardy to Zone 5. *E. fortunei* (winter creeper euonymus)— an evergreen ground cover 4 to 6 inches high or a climbing vine 40 to 70 feet high, with lustrous dark green, silvery veined, vaguely serrated inch-long oval leaves; 'Colorata' [also listed as 'Coloratus'] is a ground cover with glossy leaves lacking silver veins and turning plum-purple in winter; 'Emerald Gaiety' leaves have irregular white margins that turn pink in

Euonymus fortunei 'Emerald Gaiety'

winter on a mounding, loosely erect shrub to 5 feet tall, or vine if near a structure. *E. japonica* [also listed as *E. japonicus*] (Japanese spindle tree, Japanese euonymus)—dark green, leathery, waxy leaves 1 to 3 inches long and slightly toothed on a dense, oval evergreen shrub usually 5 to 10 feet tall and half as wide, with greenish white flowers in early summer and ineffective pinkish fruits, Zones 7-9; 'Albo-marginata' [also listed as 'Albo-marginatus'] bears leaves with narrow white margins.

Growing conditions and maintenance: Euonymus does well in all except very wet soils and accepts severe pruning. Although burning bush shows fall color in full shade, brighter hues seem to develop in full sun. Winter creeper euonymus needs snow cover or shade to withstand Zone 4 winters; it is used as a substitute for ivy in semiarid climates. Japanese euonymus shows great tolerance for salt spray and seaside conditions. All except burning bush are susceptible to scale, a destructive insect.

Fagus
(FAY-gus)
BEECH

Fagus sylvatica 'Atropunicea'

Hardiness: *Zones 3-9*

Plant type: *tree*

Height: *50 to 70 feet or more*

Interest: *form, foliage*

Soil: *moist, well-drained, acid*

Light: *full sun to dappled shade*

Long-lived beeches have massive trunks clad in smooth gray bark. In spring, as inconspicuous flowers form, silky leaves unfurl, turning bronze or ochre in the fall. Nuts are small but edible. Shallow rooted, often with branches sweeping the ground, beeches usually inhibit grass.

Selected species and varieties: *F. grandifolia* (American beech)—50 to 70 feet tall and almost as wide, with light gray bark and toothy leaves 2 to 5 inches long, dark green above and light green below. *F. sylvatica* (common beech, European beech, red beech)—usually 50 to 60 feet tall and 35 to 45 feet wide, with elephant-hide bark, branching close to the ground, Zones 4-7; 'Atropunicea' ['Atropurpurea'] (purple beech, copper beech) has black-red new leaves that turn purple-green; 'Aurea Pendula' is a weeping form with yellow new leaves aging to yellow-green; 'Dawyck Purple' grows in a narrow column with deep purple leaves.

Growing conditions and maintenance: Although both species listed here enjoy acid soil, European beech adapts to most soils. Best growth occurs in full sun.

Fargesia
(far-JEEZ-ee-a)
BAMBOO

Fargesia murielae

Hardiness: *Zones 5-9*

Plant type: *woody grass*

Height: *10 to 15 feet or more*

Interest: *form, foliage*

Soil: *adaptable*

Light: *partial shade*

Narrow, tapered dark green leaves flutter from purplish sheaths on slender purplish gray culms, or canes, that arch as they mature and spread to form mounded clumps. Use as a dramatic color and vertical accent in ornamental beds. Cut canes make good garden stakes.

Selected species and varieties: *F. murielae* [also classified as *Thamnocalamus spathaceus*] (umbrella bamboo)—slender bright green canes to 12 feet tall, aging to yellow, bend at the top under the weight of rich green leaves 3 to 5 inches long that turn yellow in fall before dropping; hardy to Zone 6. *F. nitida* [also classified as *Sinarundinaria nitida*] (clump bamboo, hardy blue bamboo, fountain bamboo)—hollow dark purple canes ½ inch in diameter and 10 to 15 feet tall (reaching 20 feet under optimum conditions) are coated with a bluish white powder when young and, after the first year, produce leaves to 7 inches long with bristly margins on one side.

Growing conditions and maintenance: As clumps begin to develop above soil level, divide and replant. Clump bamboo is less invasive than umbrella bamboo.

Fatsia
(FAT-see-a)
JAPANESE ARALIA

Fatsia japonica

Hardiness: *Zones 8-10*

Plant type: *shrub*

Height: *6 to 10 feet*

Interest: *foliage, flowers*

Soil: *moist, well-drained*

Light: *shade*

A bold, dramatic plant with a tropical effect, Japanese aralia creates a rounded mound of deeply lobed dark green leaves up to 14 inches wide. In midautumn, round clusters of tiny white flowers form on long stalks, followed by round black fruit that persists through winter.

Selected species and varieties: *F. japonica* (Japanese fatsia, Formosa rice tree, paper plant, glossy-leaved paper plant)—moderate to fast grower 6 to 10 feet high and wide, usually with open, sparsely branched habit displaying lustrous evergreen leaves with seven to nine prominent lobes on 4- to 12-inch-long stalks, and flowers clustered in 1½-inch-wide spheres on white stalks, several spheres forming a showy, branched cluster.

Growing conditions and maintenance: Although fatsia tolerates clay and sandy soils, it grows best in light soils high in organic matter. Protect from drying winds and exposure to sun, even in winter. Leaves are easily burned or desiccated. Prune to control legginess.

Forsythia
(for-SITH-ee-a)
GOLDEN-BELLS

Forsythia x intermedia

Hardiness: *Zones 6-9*

Plant type: *shrub*

Height: *10 feet*

Interest: *flowers*

Soil: *average*

Light: *full sun*

Useful in shrub borders, masses, and banks, forsythia produces a burst of yellow bloom in fountainlike sprays in early spring before the slender, toothy leaves appear. A showy shrub for only one season and bland for the rest of the year, forsythia is best blended into shrub borders or planted alone or in drifts in the lawn.

Selected species and varieties: *F. x intermedia* (border forsythia)—12 feet wide with upright, arching canes that bear 1- to 1½-inch pale to deep yellow flowers singly or in groups of up to six, followed by tapered, medium to dark green leaves 3 to 5 inches long that sometimes turn dull olive or purple in fall; 'Spectabilis' bears a profusion of richly hued, bright yellow flowers at the stem axils and is easily the showiest-blooming cultivar. *F. suspensa* var. *sieboldii* (weeping forsythia)—arching habit with long, trailing branches and less flowering than border forsythia.

Growing conditions and maintenance: Forsythia tolerates almost any soil but does best in loose loam. Best flowering occurs in full sun. Prune after bloom by removing old canes. For best effect, avoid formal shearing.

Fraxinus
(FRAK-si-nus)
ASH

Fraxinus pennsylvanica

Hardiness: *Zones 2-9*

Plant type: *tree*

Height: *45 to 80 feet*

Interest: *foliage*

Soil: *wet to dry*

Light: *full sun*

Ashes are moderate- to fast-growing trees that give light shade. In fall, the leaves may crumble after they drop, requiring little if any raking. Small greenish yellow flowers are borne on separate male and female trees in spring. Paddle-shaped winged seeds on female trees germinate easily and may become a nuisance. Select a male clone or a seedless variety.

Selected species and varieties: *F. americana* (white ash)—to 80 feet tall with an open, rounded crown, with compound leaves, dark green above and pale below, that turn a rich yellow, then maroon to purple in fall, hardy to Zone 3; 'Champaign County', to 45 feet, with a dense canopy of leaves. *F. pennsylvanica* (red ash, green ash)—50 to 60 feet tall with an irregular crown half as wide, bearing shiny green leaves that may turn yellow in fall, to Zone 3; 'Patmore', a seedless form, grows 45 feet tall, with a symmetrical, upright-branching crown; to Zone 2.

Growing conditions and maintenance: Though ashes prefer moist, well-drained soil, white ash tolerates dry and moderately alkaline soils, and green ash adapts to wet and dry soils and high salt.

Gelsemium
(jel-SEE-mee-um)
CAROLINA JASMINE

Gelsemium sempervirens

Hardiness: *Zones 6-9*

Plant type: *woody vine*

Height: *10 to 20 feet*

Interest: *flowers, fragrance*

Soil: *moist, well-drained*

Light: *full sun to light shade*

Carolina jasmine is a twining evergreen vine that produces fragrant yellow funnel-shaped flowers in late winter to early spring. Allow it to cover fences, trellises, or unsightly features, or use it as a rambling ground cover. Planted at the base of a tree, it scrambles up the trunk. Tucked into the top of a retaining wall, it spills flowers and foliage over the side. Caution: All parts of the plant are poisonous to humans and livestock.

Selected species and varieties: *G. sempervirens* (Carolina yellow jessamine, false jasmine, evening trumpet flower)—a vigorous grower with slender, wiry stems bearing 1½-inch-long flowers singly or in clusters in the axils of narrow, lance-shaped dark green leaves 1 to 3½ inches long that turn yellowish green or dull purplish in winter.

Growing conditions and maintenance: Carolina yellow jessamine grows best in highly organic soils similar to its native woodland loams but tolerates average soils, from acid to slightly alkaline. Best flowering occurs in full sun. If vine becomes top-heavy, cut back severely.

Gleditsia
(gle-DIT-see-a)
HONEY LOCUST

Gleditsia triacanthos

Hardiness: *Zones 3-9*

Plant type: *tree*

Height: *to 70 feet*

Interest: *foliage, form*

Soil: *well-drained*

Light: *full sun*

Leafing late in spring on a wide-spreading canopy of arching branches, honey locust produces bright green ferny foliage, creating light to dappled shade during a short season. Inconspicuous fragrant flowers in late spring are followed by 12- to 18-inch reddish brown to brown strap-shaped pods, usually viewed as a nuisance. When the leaves turn yellow and fall in early autumn, they crumble into the grass and mostly disappear.

Selected species and varieties: *G. triacanthos* var. *inermis* (thornless honey locust, sweet locust)—highly variable size, from 30 to 70 feet tall and equally wide ranging in spread, with a short trunk and an open crown bearing doubly compound leaves with oblong leaflets ⅓ to 1½ inches long and greenish yellow flowers; 'Imperial' [also called 'Impcole'] is a seedless version that grows to 35 feet high and wide; Zones 4-7.

Growing conditions and maintenance: Honey locusts grow best in moist, rich loam but tolerate acid and alkaline soils, drought, and salt. Under average conditions, they grow 2 feet per year or more but may be insect and disease prone.

125

Hamamelis
(ha-ma-MEL-lis)
WITCH HAZEL

Hamamelis x intermedia 'Arnold Promise'

Hardiness: *Zones 5-8*

Plant type: *shrub or small tree*

Height: *15 to 20 feet*

Interest: *flowers, foliage, fragrance*

Soil: *moist, well-drained*

Light: *partial shade to full sun*

Witch hazel brightens and perfumes the winter landscape with yellow to red ribbonlike flowers, then dazzles the fall garden with colorful foliage. Seed capsules explode on maturity in late fall, shooting seeds many feet away. Best located where their scent and bright flowers can be appreciated at close range, witch hazels are underused in American gardens.

Selected species and varieties: *H.* x *intermedia*—an upright-spreading shrub flowering yellow, red, or burnt orange on bare branches and bearing medium green leaves 3 to 4 inches long that turn yellow to red in fall; 'Arnold Promise', one of the best blooming cultivars, produces fragrant clear yellow flowers, each straplike petal up to 1 inch long, in late winter as well as reddish orange fall foliage; 'Jelena' [also called 'Copper Beauty'] produces copper-colored flowers and orange-red fall color.

Growing conditions and maintenance: Witch hazel grows best in slightly acid soil enriched with organic matter. If the plant becomes open, prune to encourage dense growth. Propagate by layering if a shrub, with cuttings if a tree.

Hebe
(HEE-bee)
HEBE

Hebe buxifolia 'Patty's Purple'

Hardiness: *Zones 8-10*

Plant type: *shrub*

Height: *2 to 5 feet*

Interest: *flowers, foliage, form*

Soil: *well-drained*

Light: *full sun to partial shade*

Native to New Zealand, hebes are rounded, leathery-leaved evergreen shrubs that produce spikes of white, pink, red, lavender, or purple flowers 2 to 4 inches long at the ends of the branches. Their small, glossy leaves, densely arranged on stems, make these fine-textured spreading shrubs good candidates for shrub borders, hedges, edgings, rock gardens, and perennial beds.

Selected species and varieties: *H.* 'Autumn Glory'—a mounding form 2 to 3 feet high and 2 feet wide, with glossy dark green leaves 1½ inches long tinged with red when young, and dark lavender-blue flower spikes, 2 inches long and sometimes branched, blooming profusely from midsummer through fall. *H. buxifolia* 'Patty's Purple' (boxleaf veronica)—1-inch-long purple clusters and leaves scarcely ½ inch long, growing to 5 feet.

Growing conditions and maintenance: Hebes need good drainage and prefer either acid or alkaline soil of average fertility. They thrive in cool coastal gardens, and need partial shade where summers are hot. Prune after flowering to avoid legginess. They are tolerant of salt spray.

Helianthemum
(hee-lee-AN-the-mum)
SUN ROSE, ROCKROSE

Helianthemum nummularium

Hardiness: *Zones 5-7*

Plant type: *evergreen shrub or ground cover*

Height: *6 to 12 inches*

Interest: *flowers*

Soil: *dry, poor, well-drained, alkaline*

Light: *full sun*

Sun roses provide a colorful cover for dry, sunny slopes, look good tumbling out of a crevice in a rock wall, and brighten rock gardens. From late spring to early summer, flowers resembling wild roses with five crepe-paper-like petals cover a low-growing mound with trailing stems. Varieties come in yellow, orange, red, rose, pink, apricot, salmon, peach, white, bicolors, and in double flowers.

Selected species and varieties: *H. nummularium* (yellow sun rose)—a sprawling mound, 12 to 24 inches wide, with trailing stems that bear grayish green leaves 1 to 2 inches long with silvery undersides and 1-inch-wide flowers with broad petals and prominent stamens.

Growing conditions and maintenance: Sun roses like dry, poor, gravelly or sandy soils and do not grow well in fertile soils. Good drainage is essential. Prune in early spring to encourage dense growth, and prune again after flowering to get a second flush of bloom in late summer. Protect with mulch over the winter. Propagate by division in spring or by soft stem cuttings.

Helleborus
(hell-e-BOR-us)
HELLEBORE

Helleborus orientalis

Hardiness: *Zones 4-9*

Plant type: *perennial*

Height: *15 to 24 inches*

Interest: *flowers, foliage*

Soil: *moist, well-drained, organic*

Light: *bright full shade*

Cup-shaped flowers in subtle hues and many-fingered evergreen foliage are hellebore's trademarks. Plant in borders and along paths where its quiet, sometimes off-season beauty can be enjoyed.

Selected species and varieties: *H. argutifolius* [also classified as *H. corsicus* and *H. lividus* ssp. *corsicus*] (Corsican hellebore)—clusters of 18- to 24-inch-tall yellowish green flowers tinged with white bloom in early spring above gray-green leaves; Zones 7-8. *H. niger* (Christmas rose)—15 inches tall, with pink-tinged white flowers to 2½ inches across with yellow stamens, blooming generally in winter to early spring but sometimes in late fall; Zones 4-8. *H. orientalis* (Lenten rose)—bears cream, pink, plum, brownish purple, chocolate brown, or nearly black flowers 2 inches wide in clusters of two to six in early to midspring on 18-inch plants, although size and bloom time may be as variable as color.

Growing conditions and maintenance: Cover loosely with mulch in severe winters. Propagation by division is difficult; roots are brittle, and older plants may fail to bloom for a year after being disturbed.

Hemerocallis
(hem-er-o-KAL-is)
DAYLILY

Hemerocallis 'Stella d'Oro'

Hardiness: *Zones 3-9*

Plant type: *perennial*

Height: *12 to 18 inches*

Interest: *flowers*

Soil: *average, well-drained*

Light: *full sun to partial shade*

Trumpet-shaped, lilylike flowers, available in nearly every color but blue, rise above dense mounds of arching, grasslike leaves on naked branched stems called scapes. Each bloom lasts only a day, but a scape may hold many buds, and flowering can last for weeks or even months. One of the longest bloomers of any daylily, 'Stella d'Oro' flowers from late spring until frost on 12- to 18-inch stalks, which makes it a miniature, as some daylilies top 4 feet. The large hybrids are useful for naturalized areas, ground covers, banks, and borders. Smaller varieties are ideal for border fronts and rock gardens.

Selected species and varieties: *H.* 'Stella d'Oro'—slightly fragrant, bell-like blossoms 2½ inches wide, with lightly ruffled lemon yellow petals curled slightly back to reveal a golden yellow throat.

Growing conditions and maintenance: Daylilies tolerate a range of soil types, but a too-rich soil will produce much foliage and few flowers. Set crowns ½ to 1 inch below soil surface. Propagate or rejuvenate by dividing the tuberous roots every 3 to 5 years in fall or early spring.

Heuchera
(HEW-ker-a)
ALUMROOT

Heuchera micrantha 'Palace Purple'

Hardiness: *Zones 3-8*

Plant type: *perennial*

Height: *12 to 30 inches*

Interest: *flowers, foliage*

Soil: *moist, well-drained, fertile*

Light: *partial shade to full sun*

Mounds of handsome lobed leaves make alumroot useful for rock gardens, edgings, and perennial beds. Delicate bell-shaped flowers on wiry stems bloom in late spring and summer.

Selected species and varieties: *H.* x *brizoides*—bears red, pink, or white blooms on 12- to 30-inch stems and dark green leaves; 'Pluie de Feu' ('Rain of Fire') grows to 18 inches tall, with red flowers. *H. micrantha* 'Palace Purple' (small-flowered alumroot)—15- to 18-inch-high mound of wrinkled leaves that are deep purple-red in spring and fall, fading to purplish bronze-green in hot weather, with pinkish white flowers but grown primarily for its foliage. *H. sanguinea* (coral bells)—12 to 18 inches tall, with dark green leaves and pink, white, or red flowers among the hybrids; Bressingham Hybrids have rose-colored flowers.

Growing conditions and maintenance: Alumroot grows best in shade in warmer climates. Supplement soil with peat moss, leaf mold, or finished compost. As stems become woody, the plant falls open in the center. Divide every 3 to 4 years after flowering or in the fall.

Hosta
(HOS-ta)
PLANTAIN LILY

Hosta 'Gold Standard'

Hardiness: *Zones 3-9*

Plant type: *perennial*

Height: *15 inches to 4 feet*

Interest: *foliage, flowers*

Soil: *moist, well-drained, slightly acid*

Light: *partial to bright full shade*

Hostas are prized mainly for their spreading clumps of attractive foliage, making them ideal for textural and color accents in perennial beds and borders. Trumpet-shaped flowers appear in summer.

Selected species and varieties: *H.* 'Francee'—dark green heart-shaped leaves with white margins, to 18 inches tall, with lavender flowers on 2-foot stems. *H.* 'Gold Standard'—veined yellow leaves with green margins to 2½ feet tall, with violet flowers. *H.* 'Krossa Regal'—4 feet tall, with veined blue leaves up to 8 inches long and 5 inches wide and lilac flowers atop 5-foot stalks. *H. sieboldiana* 'Frances Williams' [also called 'Yellow Edge']—to 3 feet tall, bearing foot-long crinkled leaves with yellow margins and lilac flowers amid the leaves.

Growing conditions and maintenance: Good drainage is essential, especially in winter. Although most hostas thrive in deep shade, variegated and blue forms need bright shade to hold their color. *H.* 'Francee' tolerates some sun. Remove flowers to improve foliage and prevent crossbreeding. Propagate by division in fall or early spring.

Hydrangea
(hy-DRANE-jee-a)
HYDRANGEA

Hydrangea arborescens 'Annabelle'

Hardiness: *Zones 3-9*

Plant type: *deciduous shrub or vine*

Height: *3 to 80 feet*

Interest: *flowers, foliage, bark*

Soil: *moist, well-drained*

Light: *bright full shade to full sun*

Hydrangeas produce flowers that change color through their bloom period, usually from white to purplish pink, then to brown. Most are shrubs, but the climbing hydrangea is a vine with twining stems and aerial roots that cling to rough surfaces. The flower clusters of hydrangeas consist of small, starlike, fertile flowers surrounded by larger, showier, sterile flowers, 1 to 1½ inches wide. The long-lasting blossoms are valued for fresh and dried arrangements and wreaths. All hydrangeas are coarse in texture, and some offer colorful fall foliage and attractive exfoliating bark.

Selected species and varieties: *H. anomala* ssp. *petiolaris* (climbing hydrangea)—climbs to a height of 60 to 80 feet, with flat-headed white flowers 6 to 10 inches wide, toothy leaves up to 4 inches wide, and attractive reddish brown peeling bark; Zones 4-7. *H. arborescens* (hills-of-snow, wild hydrangea, sevenbark, smooth hydrangea)—a rounded, fast-growing shrub, 3 to 5 feet high and wide, bearing serrated oval leaves up to 8 inches long, and 4- to 6-inch-wide, almost flat flower clusters with few sterile (e.g.,

showy) blooms, borne on new growth; 'Annabelle' produces symmetrical, extremely showy flower clusters up to 1 foot across. *H. paniculata* (panicle hydrangea)—a fast-growing, upright, often unkempt large shrub or small tree, 10 to 25 feet high and 10 to 20 feet wide, bearing minimally decorative flower panicles, 6 to 8 inches long that change from white to purplish pink in mid- to late summer, Zones 3-8; 'Grandiflora' (peegee hydrangea) is a far showier cultivar with mostly sterile flowers in panicles 12 to 18 inches long. *H. quercifolia* (oakleaf hydrangea)—a moderate-growing, 4- to 6-foot-high mound with shoots arising from the base but with few branches,

Hydrangea quercifolia

bearing erect flower panicles 4 to 12 inches long from mid- to late summer, rich brown, flaky bark on older stems, and large three- to seven-lobed deep green leaves that turn red, brownish orange, and purple in fall; hardy to Zone 5.

Growing conditions and maintenance: Hydrangeas are intolerant of drought at any time of year and wilt under hot afternoon sun in warmer climates. The heavy flower heads of *H. arborescens* 'Annabelle' can force stems to the ground. For better form, cut to the ground in late winter and feed lightly; flowers will form on new growth by early summer. It can be grown as a herbaceous perennial in colder climates. Peegee hydrangea produces its largest blooms and a cleaner form when all but five to 10 shoots are removed. Prune oakleaf hydrangeas after flowering, removing weak branches.

Hypericum
(hy-PER-i-kum)
ST.-JOHN'S-WORT

Hypericum calycinum

Hardiness: *Zones 5-9*

Plant type: *shrub or ground cover*

Height: *1 to 3 feet*

Interest: *flowers*

Soil: *average to poor*

Light: *full sun to partial shade*

St.-John's-wort bears brilliant yellow five-petaled flowers. Creeping St.-John's-wort spreads by stolons and rooting stems to create a thick carpet of dark green semievergreen leaves and is useful for covering difficult hillsides. Shrubbier forms are suited for borders and edgings.

Selected species and varieties: *H. calycinum* (creeping St.-John's-wort, Aaron's-beard)—18 inches tall and spreading to 2 feet wide, with rising and trailing stems bearing 3-inch flowers from midsummer to early autumn, when foliage turns purplish; Zones 5-8. *H.* 'Hidcote' —3 feet tall and wide, blooming profusely with fragrant 2- to 3-inch-wide flowers from early summer to fall; hardy to Zone 6. *H.* x *moseranum* (gold flower, Moser's St.-John's-wort)—12- to 24-inch-high mound with arching reddish branches bearing 2½-inch golden yellow flowers from midsummer to fall; hardy to Zone 7 and often grown as a perennial.

Growing conditions and maintenance: St.-John's-wort grows well in poor, sandy, or gravelly soils and requires little care. Cold winters often kill plant tops, but subsequent flowering is not affected.

Ilex
(EYE-lex)
HOLLY

Ilex aquifolium 'Argenteo-marginata'

Hardiness: *Zones 4-10*

Plant type: *shrub or tree*

Height: *2 to 50 feet*

Interest: *foliage, fruit, form*

Soil: *moist, well-drained*

Light: *full sun to partial shade*

The genus produces a broad range of mostly evergreen plants in all sizes and shapes. Dense, lustrous foliage and a neat habit make shrub hollies ideal foundation plants, hedges, and background plants. The taller hollies make lovely specimen plants and effective screens. Tiny, sometimes fragrant, spring flowers are inconspicuous. In most species, a female plant must be within 100 feet of a male to set fruit.

Selected species and varieties: *I.* x *altaclarensis* 'Wilsonii' (Altaclara holly)—a 30-foot-tall tree with spiny leaves up to 5 inches long and 3 inches wide and red fruit; Zones 7-9. *I. aquifolium* (common holly, English holly)—30 to 50 feet tall, with fragrant whitish flowers in spring, wavy leaves with spines, and red berries, Zones 6-9; 'Argenteo-marginata', a female, has dark green leaves edged with white; 'Boulder Creek', also a female, glossy black-green leaves. *I.* x *attenuata* 'Fosteri' (Foster Hybrids)—small pyramidal trees 10 to 25 feet high with small red berries; Zones 6-9. *I. cornuta* (Chinese holly, horned holly)—a dense, rounded shrub 8 to 10 feet tall, with spiny rectan-

gular leaves up to 4 inches long, small, fragrant spring flowers, and bright red berries lasting until late winter, Zones 7-9; 'Berries Jubilee' has large berry clusters and grows 6 to 10 feet tall; 'Carissa' is 3 to 4 feet tall and up to 6 feet wide, bearing oval leaves with only one spine; 'Needlepoint' has narrow, twisted leaves and a single spine. *I. crenata* (Japanese holly, box-leaved holly)—a dense, multi-

Ilex cornuta

branched rounded shrub that grows slowly to 5 to 10 feet high and wide, with lustrous oval leaves ½ to 1 inch long and small black berries hidden under the foliage, Zones 5-8; 'Convexa' is a very dense cultivar that eventually grows to 9 feet tall and more than twice as wide, with ½-inch-long curved leaves and heavy fruit; 'Green Island' has an open habit, growing to 4 feet tall and 6 feet wide; 'Helleri' is 2 to 3 feet tall by 5 feet wide with ½-inch dull, very dark green leaves; 'Microphylla' has an upright habit and leaves smaller than the species. *I. decidua* (possom haw, winterberry)—a deciduous shrub or small tree to 15 feet, with glossy green leaves turning yellow in fall and orange to red berries that linger until the next spring; Zones 5-9. *I. glabra* (inkberry, Appalachian tea)—an upright, multibranched rounded shrub 6 to 8 feet tall by 8 to 10 feet wide, becoming open with age, with narrow-oval leaves 1 to 2 inches long and bearing small black berries, partly hidden by the leaves, from fall to the following spring, Zones 4-9; 'Compacta', a female, is a more tightly branched form 4 to 6 feet tall. *I.* x *meserveae* (Meserve Hybrids)—a group of dense, bushy shrubs 8 to 12 feet tall, with lustrous dark green or bluish green leaves on deep purple stems, hardy to Zone 4; 'Blue Prince', a male, forms a broad pyramid; 'Blue Princess', known to grow as much as 15 feet high and 10 feet wide, has dark blue-green leaves and red berries. *I. opaca* (American holly)—a 40- to 50-foot tree, pyramidal when young, becoming open and irregular over time, with dull to dark yellow-green leaves and bright red berries persisting into winter; Zones 5-9. *I. pedunculosa* (long-stalked holly)—a moderately dense, large shrub or small tree, 15 to 20 feet tall, with dark green leaves, 1 to 3 inches long, and red berries borne on long stems in fall, usually not lasting into winter; Zones 5-8. *I.* x 'Sparkleberry'—forms a narrow column,

Ilex pedunculosa

with small red berries that persist well into winter and nearly black bark. *I. vomitoria* (yaupon, cassina—15 to to 20 feet tall and less in width, with attractively irregular branches, gray to white bark, and a heavy fruit crop lasting till spring, Zones 7-10; 'Nana' grows 5 feet high and wide, with fruit often hidden by the foliage.

Growing conditions and maintenance: Although hollies tolerate partial shade, they prefer full sun. Most evergreen hollies do not endure hot, windy, or dry climates. For best results, provide a loose, well-drained loam. Chinese holly tolerates most soils and withstands drought. Japanese holly prefers moist, slightly acid soils. Inkberry, found naturally in swamps, thrives in wet, acid soils. American holly needs very well drained, acid loam in wind-protected areas. Long-stalked holly tolerates heavy soils and drying wind. Yaupon withstands dry to wet sites and tolerates alkalinity. All species readily accept pruning.

Ipomoea
(eye-po-MEE-a)
MOONFLOWER

Ipomoea alba

Hardiness:	*Zones 10-11*
Plant type:	*vine*
Height:	*15 to 20 feet*
Interest:	*flowers, fragrance*
Soil:	*moist, well-drained, sandy*
Light:	*full sun*

Fragrant nocturnal flowers bloom amid large heart-shaped leaves on this tropical vine that is usually grown as an annual in cooler climates. Moonflowers are excellent for covering trellises, arbors, and fences, and also in hanging baskets.

Selected species and varieties: *I. alba* [also listed as *Calonyction aculeatum*] (moonflower)—a perennial, part-woody/part-herbaceous quick-climbing vine that can reach 20 feet, with shiny, bright green leaves up to 8 inches long and white trumpet-shaped flowers up to 6 inches long and wide, opening after sundown and closing before noon the next day, blooming from midsummer to frost.

Growing conditions and maintenance: Amend heavy soils with sand, and add only a modest amount of organic matter; too-rich soil will produce lush foliage but few flowers. Plant seeds 12 to 18 inches apart in a sunny location after all danger of frost has passed, or start seeds indoors in individual pots 4 to 6 weeks before the last frost date and then transplant gently. Germination takes 5 to 7 days; to speed sprouting, nick the seed coats or soak the seeds in water for 2 days.

Iris
(EYE-ris)
FLAG, FLEUR-DE-LIS

Iris sibirica 'Caesar's Brother'

Hardiness:	*Zones 3-9*
Plant type:	*perennial*
Height:	*18 inches to 5 feet*
Interest:	*flowers, fruit*
Soil:	*moist, well-drained, fertile*
Light:	*partial shade to full sun*

Most irises are valued for their blooms, but the species described here offer the unusual: Gladwin is prized not for flowers but for its showy fruit pods used in dried arrangements; yellow flag is a perfect choice for stream or pond borders; Siberian iris has grasslike foliage.

Selected species and varieties: *I. foetidissima* (Gladwin, stinking iris, roast beef plant)—18 inches tall, with evergreen leaves that are malodorous when crushed and small, purplish gray flowers followed by large, red-seeded fruit pods; Zones 6-9. *I. pseudacorus* (yellow iris, yellow flag)—2-inch-wide bright yellow flowers flecked with brown on 5-foot stalks in late spring or early summer and green fruit capsules, Zones 3-9; 'Variegata' has yellow-striped leaves. *I. sibirica* (Siberian iris)—4 feet tall, violet to blue flowers 3 to 4 inches wide above slender bright green arching leaves in early summer, Zones 3-9; 'Caesar's Brother' has deep purple flowers on 3-foot stems.

Growing conditions and maintenance: Iris enjoys moisture-retentive soil rich in organic matter; yellow flag prefers wet soil. Divide in late summer or fall.

Jasminum
(JAZ-min-um)
JASMINE, JESSAMINE

Jasminum mesnyi

Hardiness: *Zones 6-10*

Plant type: *shrub, ground cover, or vine*

Height: *3 to 15 feet*

Interest: *flowers, stems, form, foliage*

Soil: *well-drained, average to poor*

Light: *full sun to partial shade*

A perfect solution for slopes with poor soil, jasmine forms a wide-spreading mound of arching stems that bear bright yellow trumpetlike flowers and triplets of dark green leaflets. Branches root wherever they contact the soil and can soon cover a large area. Jasmine can also be trained to climb a support, where it may reach 15 feet. In winter, the naked green stems are effective, especially when allowed to trail over a wall.

Selected species and varieties: *J. mesnyi* (primrose jasmine, Japanese jasmine, yellow jasmine)—5 to 6 feet high, with flowers up to 1¾ inches wide, often semi-double to double, from early spring sporadically to midsummer, and leaflets 1 to 3 inches long; Zones 8-9. *J. nudiflorum* (winter jasmine)—1-inch-wide single flowers bloom erratically on warm days in winter before 1-inch leaflets appear, the thicket of arching vines reaching 3 to 4 feet high and 4 to 7 feet wide.

Growing conditions and maintenance: Winter jasmine tolerates neglect and even moderate drought. Cut back almost to the ground every 3 to 5 years to restore vigor. Best bloom occurs in full sun.

Juniperus
(joo-NIP-er-us)
JUNIPER

Juniperus conferta

Hardiness: *Zones 2-9*

Plant type: *tree, shrub, or ground cover*

Height: *6 inches to 60 feet*

Interest: *foliage, form*

Soil: *light, well-drained*

Light: *full sun*

Junipers vary from wide, flat mats that hug the ground to tall, thin spires good for accents or corner plantings. Their scalelike evergreen foliage ranges in color from green to silvery blue to yellow and sometimes assumes a different shade in winter. Female plants produce small blue berries. Tall forms make good screens and windbreaks.

Selected species and varieties: *J. chinensis* (Chinese juniper)—usually a narrow, conical tree 50 to 60 feet high with green to bluish to gray-green foliage, Zones 3-9; 'Mint Julep' is a fountain-shaped shrub 4 to 6 feet tall with greater spread, bearing arching branches and bright green foliage; 'Old Gold' has ascending branches with bronze-gold foliage and grows to 3 feet tall by 4 feet wide; 'Pfitzeriana Glauca' has bluish foliage becoming purplish blue in winter, normally 5 feet high by 10 feet wide but often larger. *J. conferta* (shore juniper)—a shrub spreading 6 to 9 feet and 1 to 1½ feet high with soft, needlelike bluish green foliage in summer turning bronzy or yellow-green in winter; Zones 6-9. *J. horizontalis* (creeping juniper, creeping savin)—1 to 2 feet high by 4 to 8 feet wide, with trailing branches bearing glaucous green, blue-green, or blue plumelike foliage turning plum-purple in winter, Zones 3-9; 'Wiltonii' (blue rug juniper) forms a flat mat less than 6 inches high, spreading up to 8 feet, with grayish blue foliage. *J. occidentalis* (Sierra juniper, California juniper)—shrub or tree to 40 feet, with glaucous green foliage; hardy to Zone 5. *J. procumbens* [sometimes classified as *J. chinensis* var. *procumbens*] (Japanese garden juniper)—1 to 2 feet high and 10 to 15 feet wide, with bluish green to gray-green foliage; 'Nana', a dwarf of the species, forms a low, rounded, compact mat 6 to 12 inches high and spreading up

Juniperus horizontalis 'Wiltonii'

to 12 feet, with overlapping branches of bluish green foliage turning purplish in winter. *J. sabina* (savin)—a vase-shaped shrub 4 to 6 feet high by 5 to 10 feet wide, with dark green foliage turning a drab green tinged with yellow in winter; 'Broadmoor' grows 2 to 3 feet high with a 10-foot spread, bearing soft gray-green foliage in short upright sprays; hardy to Zone 4. *J. scopulorum* (Rocky Mountain juniper, Colorado red cedar)—a narrow pyramidal tree growing 30 to 40 feet high and 3 to 15 feet wide, with foliage ranging from light green to dark blue-green; 'Skyrocket' forms a narrow spire, 10 to 15 feet tall, with bluish foliage.

Growing conditions and maintenance: Tolerant of almost any soil as long as it is well drained, junipers do best in moist, light soils. Loosen heavy soils with sand. Most junipers tolerate drought and pollution. Shore junipers grow well in seaside gardens. Savin and Chinese junipers accept limestone soils.

Koelreuteria
(kol-roo-TEER-ee-a)
GOLDEN RAIN TREE

Koelreuteria paniculata 'September'

Hardiness: *Zones 5-9*

Plant type: *tree*

Height: *30 to 40 feet*

Interest: *flowers, foliage, form*

Soil: *well-drained*

Light: *partial shade to full sun*

A delightful small tree to shade a garden bench or patio, the golden rain tree produces airy sprays of yellow flowers in early summer on wide-spreading branches. Greenish balloon-shaped seed capsules turn yellow, then brown and papery in fall; the color change takes about 2 months. The dense canopy consists of large compound leaves that are medium bright green, changing to yellow before dropping in fall. Sparse branching gives the tree a coarse look in winter.

Selected species and varieties: *K. paniculata* (golden rain tree, varnish tree)—rounded crown with spread equal to or greater than its height, bearing 6- to 18-inch-long leaves composed of seven to 15 toothed and lobed leaflets 1 to 3 inches long, purplish red when opening, and flower clusters 12 to 15 inches long and wide; 'September' flowers in late summer and is less hardy than the species.

Growing conditions and maintenance: Golden rain tree tolerates a wide variety of conditions including drought. It grows best—about 1½ feet per year—in soil well amended with peat moss or leaf mold. Provide shelter from wind.

Lagerstroemia
(la-gur-STREE-mee-a)
CRAPE MYRTLE

Lagerstroemia indica 'Seminole'

Hardiness: *Zones 7-9*

Plant type: *shrub or tree*

Height: *7 to 25 feet*

Interest: *flowers, bark*

Soil: *moist, well-drained*

Light: *full sun*

Crape myrtle's large clusters of crinkly flowers in pink, white, rose, or purple come in late summer at a time when little else may be in bloom. In fall, the dark green leaves turn red, orange, and yellow, all on the same plant. As the light gray bark ages, it exfoliates, revealing dark gray and brown underbark. Crape myrtle is often grown as a specimen.

Selected species and varieties: *L. indica* (common crape myrtle)—a fast-growing multistemmed shrub or tree 15 to 25 feet tall, with flower clusters 6 to 8 inches long; 'Natchez' reaches 20 feet tall and wide, with cinnamon brown exfoliating bark and white flower clusters 6 to 12 inches long from early summer to fall, when glossy dark green leaves turn orange and red; 'Seminole' bears medium pink flowers for 6 to 8 weeks beginning in midsummer on a 7- to 8-foot shrub.

Growing conditions and maintenance: Amend soil with peat moss or leaf mold. At its northern limits, crape myrtle is grown as a herbaceous perennial; when severe cold kills the plant to the ground, it returns the next spring with abundant, lush new growth.

Lavandula
(lav-AN-dew-la)
LAVENDER

Lavandula angustifolia 'Hidcote'

Hardiness: *Zones 5-10*

Plant type: *shrub*

Height: *1 to 4 feet*

Interest: *form, fragrance, flowers*

Soil: *well-drained to dry, neutral to alkaline*

Light: *full sun*

The gray-green woolly foliage of lavender, prized for its fragrance, contrasts well with both dark green and blue plants in the landscape. Dainty flower spikes top tightly packed upright stems in late spring to summer. Lavender is used in edgings, rock gardens, and perennial beds, and its fine-textured evergreen foliage softens the landscape. The species can also be trimmed into a low hedge.

Selected species and varieties: *L. angustifolia* (English lavender, common lavender)—blue-violet flowers in whorls 2 to 3 inches tall bloom at the top of 1- to 2-foot (occasionally 4-foot) stems that are lined with narrow 1- to 2-inch leaves, Zones 5-9; 'Hidcote', 12 to 15 inches tall, has dense deep purple spikes and silvery leaves. *L. stoechas* (Spanish lavender)—1½ to 3 feet tall with 1-inch leaves and short dark purple spikes topped with tufts of petal-like bracts; Zones 8-10.

Growing conditions and maintenance: Fast drainage is essential; loosen heavy soils with sand, and do not fertilize. Set plants 12 to 18 inches apart. Cut back in early spring to encourage dense growth. Propagate by division in spring.

Ligustrum
(li-GUS-trum)
PRIVET, HEDGE PLANT

Ligustrum japonicum

Hardiness: *Zones 6-10*

Plant type: *shrub*

Height: *6 to 15 feet*

Interest: *foliage, flowers, fruit*

Soil: *adaptable*

Light: *full sun or shade*

Privet is grown primarily for its dense habit and lustrous foliage, which is highly amenable to heavy shearing. Usually used for hedges, screens, and foundation plants, privet can also be tailored into topiary specimens. White flowers, often considered malodorous, bloom in late spring or early summer, followed by black or blue-black berries.

Selected species and varieties: *L. japonicum* (Japanese privet, waxleaf privet, waxleaf ligustrum)—an upright, dense evergreen shrub 6 to 12 feet tall and up to 8 feet wide with 2- to 6-inch-high pyramidal flower clusters offsetting very dark green leaves 1½ to 4 inches long; Zones 7-10. *L. ovalifolium* 'Aureum' (California privet)—yellow leaves with a green spot in the center when planted in sun, heavily scented flower clusters 2 to 4 inches wide in summer, and shiny black berries on 10- to 15-foot densely arranged upright stems, semi-evergreen to evergreen in warmer climates.

Growing conditions and maintenance: Easily grown and undisturbed by insects or disease, privet adapts to almost any soil except those that are constantly wet.

Liquidambar
(li-kwid-AM-bar)
SWEET GUM

Liquidambar styraciflua

Hardiness: *Zones 5-9*

Plant type: *tree*

Height: *60 to 120 feet*

Interest: *foliage*

Soil: *moist, slightly acid*

Light: *full sun*

The sweet gum is a neatly conical tree whose star-shaped leaves linger till late fall and turn lovely shades of yellow, purple, and scarlet. Its name is derived from the fragrant, gummy sap, used in making perfume. The bark is deeply furrowed and resembles cork. Spiny globe-shaped fruits drop from late fall to early spring, a liability for patios, walkways, and barefoot walks in the grass.

Selected species and varieties: *L. styraciflua* (American sweet gum, red gum, bilsted)—narrow-pyramidal in youth, maturing into a semirounded crown with a spread two-thirds the height, the branches edged with corky wings and bearing glossy rich medium green leaves 4 to 7½ inches long and wide, with five to seven finely serrated, pointed lobes.

Growing conditions and maintenance: Although native to rich, moist bottom lands, sweet gum is tolerant of poor soils if they are neutral to slightly acid and reasonably moist. The roots need plenty of room to develop. Plant in spring in soil amended with peat moss or leaf mold. Sweet gum usually takes 2 to 5 years to become established. Prune in winter.

Liriodendron
(lir-ee-o-DEN-dron)
TULIP TREE

Liriodendron tulipifera

Hardiness: *Zones 4-9*

Plant type: *tree*

Height: *70 to 100 feet or more*

Interest: *foliage, form*

Soil: *moist, well-drained, slightly acid*

Light: *full sun*

A giant suitable only for large areas, the tulip tree is a columnar to oval deciduous tree with distinctive bright green foliage that turns golden yellow in fall. In mid- to late spring, tuliplike greenish white flowers with a deep orange blotch at the base of the petals appear high on the tree after the foliage unfurls. Conelike clusters of winged fruit persist into winter.

Selected species and varieties: *L. tulipifera* (yellow poplar, tulip magnolia, tulip poplar, whitewood)—fast growing with a spread of 35 to 50 feet and the potential of topping 100 feet tall, pyramidal when young, bearing lobed leaves up to 8 inches wide and long opening early in spring, and cup-shaped flowers 2½ inches wide with six petals, borne singly at or near branch tips.

Growing conditions and maintenance: Give tulip trees a moist, deep loam with plenty of room to grow. They prefer slightly acid soils but will tolerate neutral to slightly alkaline soils. Leaves occasionally turn black with a mold that grows on the sweet, sticky substance secreted by scale and aphids. In ideal soil, tulip trees may grow 2½ to 3 feet per year.

Liriope
(li-RYE-o-pee)
LILYTURF

Liriope muscari 'Variegata'

Hardiness: *Zones 6-10*

Plant type: *perennial*

Height: *12 to 18 inches*

Interest: *foliage, flowers, fruit*

Soil: *moist to dry, fertile*

Light: *full shade to full sun*

Lilyturf's foliage forms fountainlike tufts that spread into clumps. Flowers resembling grape hyacinths, 6 to 8 inches long, bloom on 5- to 12-inch stems for several weeks in summer and are replaced by black berries in fall. Lilyturf is useful in edgings and rock gardens or as a ground cover beneath large trees or shrubs.

Selected species and varieties: *L. muscari* (big blue lilyturf)—12 to 18 inches tall to 12 inches across, with ½- to ¾-inch-wide blades and violet-purple spikes; 'Majestic' has very dark green leaves, 12 to 15 inches tall, and large flowers; 'Monroe's White', white flowers; 'Variegata', leaves with creamy margins and lilac flowers; hardy to Zone 7.

Growing conditions and maintenance: Although lilyturf tolerates deep shade, full sun, and periodic drought, it grows best in dappled shade rooted in moist loam. *L. muscari* 'Monroe's White' requires shade. Set clumps 8 to 12 inches apart. In early spring, before new growth begins, clip old leaves, taking care not to cut into crowns. Evergreen in the South, the foliage usually turns brown and disheveled in winter in colder regions.

Lonicera
(lon-ISS-er-a)
HONEYSUCKLE

Lonicera heckrottii

Hardiness: *Zones 4-9*

Plant type: *shrub or vine*

Height: *4 to 20 feet*

Interest: *flowers, fruit, foliage*

Soil: *moist to dry, average*

Light: *partial shade to full sun*

Honeysuckles produce abundant medium green foliage studded with fragrant flowers and berries often liked by birds.

Selected species and varieties: *L. heckrottii* (goldflame honeysuckle)—a climbing vine to 20 feet high, with buds opening to yellow inside, the outside slowly changing to pink, borne in terminal clusters, followed by sparse red fruit amid oval leaves that are evergreen in Zone 9. *L. nitida* 'Baggesen's Gold' (yellow box honeysuckle)—gold evergreen leaves on a 4- to 6-foot dense mound with white flowers and bluish fruits; hardy to Zone 7. *L. pileata* (privet honeysuckle)—an evergreen or semi-evergreen spreading shrub to 4 feet tall with horizontal branches bearing small yellowish white flowers and purple fruit amid narrow ½- to 1-inch-long leaves; Zones 6-8. *L. sempervirens* (trumpet honeysuckle)—unscented scarlet flowers with yellow-orange throats and red berries on a twining vine to 20 feet.

Growing conditions and maintenance: Honeysuckles are easy to grow in almost any soil. Provide vines with a support. Privet and box honeysuckles do well in seashore conditions.

Magnolia
(mag-NO-lee-a)
MAGNOLIA

Magnolia stellata 'Royal Star'

Hardiness: *Zones 4-9*

Plant type: *shrub or tree*

Height: *10 to 80 feet*

Interest: *flowers, fragrance, fruit, foliage, form*

Soil: *moist to wet, acid, fertile*

Light: *partial shade to full sun*

Large or small, magnolias of any size make outstanding accent or specimen plants, their showy flowers sweet with fragrance in spring or summer, and their fat, conelike fruit capsules splitting open to expose red seeds in fall. The smaller forms make excellent patio or shade trees; the stately bull bay needs a broad lawn for best development and display of its huge leathery leaves and 8- to 12-inch cup-shaped flowers.

Selected species and varieties: *M. grandiflora* (bull bay, southern magnolia, evergreen magnolia)—dense evergreen pyramid 60 to 80 feet high and 30 to 50 feet wide, branching close to the ground, bearing fragrant creamy white six-petaled waxy flowers in late spring to summer against lustrous dark green leaves 5 to 10 inches long, and fruit capsules 3 to 5 inches long, Zones 7-9; 'Bracken's Brown Beauty', a densely branched, compact form to 30 feet tall, produces leathery leaves 6 inches long that are lustrous dark green above and rusty brown below, with 5- to 6-inch-wide flowers and 2- to 3-inch fruits; 'Little Gem' has a shrubby habit with smaller leaves and 3-

to 4-inch flowers that bloom from summer to fall on a 20-foot specimen. *M. stellata* (star magnolia)—dense, roundish to oval form, 15 to 20 feet high and 10 to 15 feet wide, with fuzzy gray winter buds opening to fragrant white 3- to 4-inch flowers, each with 12 to 18 strap-shaped petals, in late winter or early spring before the satiny dark green 2- to 4-inch leaves appear, Zones 4-8; 'Royal Star' has 25 to 30 pure white petals in each flower. *M. virginiana* (sweet bay, laurel magnolia, swamp laurel, swamp bay, swamp

Magnolia virginiana

magnolia)—creamy white, lemon-scented nine- to 12-petaled flowers 2 to 3 inches wide in late spring or early summer, followed by showy dark red seed clusters to 2 inches long, borne on a multistemmed deciduous or semi-evergreen shrub of open, spreading habit, 10 to 20 feet high and wide in the North, to 60 feet in the South, where it is evergreen; Zones 5-9.

Growing conditions and maintenance: *M. virginiana* grows well in wet soils; the other magnolias need moist, well-drained loam. Amend the soil with peat moss or leaf mold before planting. Mulch to conserve moisture and keep the roots cool. Feed with an acid fertilizer no later than midsummer to allow new growth time to harden off. Star magnolia's buds are easily killed by late winter freezes; provide a sheltered spot, and avoid southern exposure that would encourage buds to swell early. Bull bay can be a messy tree, dropping large leaves in spring and fall that are slow to decay; *M. grandiflora* 'Bracken's Brown Beauty' drops fewer leaves. Magnolias are surface rooters; do not underplant.

Mahonia
(ma-HO-nee-a)
OREGON GRAPE

Mahonia bealei

Hardiness: *Zones 5-10*

Plant type: *evergreen shrub or ground cover*

Height: *10 inches to 12 feet*

Interest: *flowers, fragrance, fruit*

Soil: *moist, well-drained, acid, fertile*

Light: *full to dappled shade*

Mahonia's lemon-yellow flowers in earliest spring can perfume a shady garden. The grapelike berries, maturing in summer, are covered with a blue bloom and are relished by birds. Stiff and formal in habit, mahonia has leathery, hollylike, compound leaves that are blue-green in summer and purplish in winter.

Selected species and varieties: *M. aquifolium* (mountain grape, holly barberry)—slightly fragrant flowers borne in terminal clusters 2 to 3 inches long and wide on upright stems on a 3- to 9-foot-tall shrub; Zones 5-8. *M. bealei* (leatherleaf mahonia)—very fragrant flowers 6 to 12 inches wide and 3 to 6 inches long from late winter to early spring, and berries that turn from robin's-egg blue to blueblack on a 10- to 12-foot-tall shrub; hardy to Zone 7. *M. repens* (creeping mahonia)—spreading mat of stiff stems to 10 inches high, with deep yellow flowers in 1- to 3-inch-long racemes.

Growing conditions and maintenance: Mahonia needs a deep, loamy soil in a site protected from wind. Dry soils or too much sun will yellow leaves. Keep well watered, and mulch to retain moisture.

Malus
(MAY-lus)
APPLE

Malus 'Red Jade'

Hardiness: *Zones 5-8*

Plant type: *tree*

Height: *15 to 25 feet*

Interest: *flowers, fruit, fragrance, form*

Soil: *moist, well-drained, acid to nearly neutral*

Light: *full sun*

In spring, scented blossoms 1 to 2 inches wide cloak the entire length of the tree's branches, followed by small fruit that may linger into fall if birds allow. Although many crab apples flower and fruit heavily in alternate years, the types listed here are all annual bearers.

Selected species and varieties: *M. floribunda* (Japanese flowering crab apple, showy crab apple, purple chokeberry)—arching, rounded habit 15 to 25 feet tall and wide, with clusters of pink to red buds opening white, followed by red or yellow fruit; hardy to Zone 5. *M.* 'Prairifire'—red buds opening to rosy red flowers, reddish new foliage, and maroon fruits, to 20 feet tall and rounded, very disease resistant. *M.* 'Red Jade'—weeping form 15 feet tall, with pendulous branches bearing deep pink buds that open to profuse white blooms, and red fruit.

Growing conditions and maintenance: Although easy to grow in average soil, crab apples do best in heavy loam. Any pruning should be done before summer, when buds are formed for the next year. Crab apples are susceptible to a number of diseases, including fire blight.

Miscanthus
(mis-KAN-thus)
EULALIA

Miscanthus sinensis 'Zebrinus'

Hardiness: *Zones 5-9*

Plant type: *ornamental grass*

Height: *5 to 8 feet*

Interest: *form, foliage, flowers*

Soil: *moist, well-drained*

Light: *full sun*

These tall, fine-textured grasses with their long, narrow, arching leaves and feathery fan-shaped plumes of fall flowers make striking specimens or screens. The clump-forming foliage turns golden tan to buff in winter.

Selected species and varieties: *M. sinensis* (Japanese silver grass, Chinese silver grass)—upright clump 6 to 8 feet tall to 3 feet wide or more, consisting of leaves 3 to 4 feet long and ⅜ inch wide, with pale pink to reddish flower clusters 8 inches long blooming in fall and lasting nearly all winter; 'Gracillimus' (maiden grass) produces narrower leaves than the species with a white midvein, 5 to 8 feet tall; 'Morning Light', light green leaves with silvery white margins and midrib; 'Zebrinus' (zebra grass), yellow bands across the leaves, and pinkish brown flower clusters.

Growing conditions and maintenance: Eulalia grows well in any ordinary garden soil. Too-rich soil may cause stems to fall over. Although eulalia tolerates light shade, it grows best in full sun. Cut clump to within 2 to 6 inches of the ground in late winter.

Myrica
(mi-RYE-ka)
BAYBERRY

Myrica pensylvanica

Hardiness: *Zones 2-9*

Plant type: *shrub or tree*

Height: *5 to 20 feet*

Interest: *foliage, fruit, fragrance, bark*

Soil: *well-drained*

Light: *partial shade to full sun*

Bayberry (also called wax myrtle) forms a dense, upright mound whose leaves are aromatic when crushed. Small gray berries, whose waxy coating is used in candlemaking, cover the stems of the female plant from fall into winter. Useful in shrub borders and masses, it can also be clipped into a hedge. The southern species can be used as a screen or trained into a tree to expose the attractive bark. A male plant is needed to set berries.

Selected species and varieties: *M. cerifera* (southern bayberry, candleberry, waxberry)—shrub or small tree to 20 feet tall, with evergreen leaves up to 3 inches long and ¾ inch wide; Zones 7-9. *M. pensylvanica* (northern bayberry, swamp candleberry)—deciduous to semi-evergreen, usually 5 to 10 feet tall and wide, with leathery leaves to 4 inches long and up to 1½ inches wide, and clusters of grayish white berries ⅛ inch wide; Zones 3-8.

Growing conditions and maintenance: Native to coastal dunes, bayberry grows well in poor, dry, sandy soils but seems adaptable to almost any other condition except high alkalinity. Northern bayberry can be grown in Zone 2 with protection.

Nandina
(nan-DEE-na)
HEAVENLY BAMBOO

Nandina domestica

Hardiness: *Zones 6-9*

Plant type: *evergreen shrub*

Height: *2 to 8 feet*

Interest: *foliage, fruit, flowers, form*

Soil: *moist, fertile*

Light: *full shade to full sun*

Nandina's fine-textured bluish green foliage, emerging pink or coppery and often turning red to reddish purple in fall and winter, splays out from bamboo-like canes. In late spring or early summer, panicles of creamy flowers appear, followed by spectacular clusters of red berries that persist through winter. Nandina is suited for foundations or borders, in masses, or as a specimen.

Selected species and varieties: *N. domestica* (sacred bamboo)—erect habit, 6 to 8 feet tall, with compound leaves having sharply tapered leaflets, each 1½ to 4 inches long and half as wide, 8- to 15-inch-long clusters of tiny white flowers with yellow anthers, and heavy panicles of ⅓-inch berries; 'Harbour Dwarf' grows to 2 or 3 feet, forming a graceful mound.

Growing conditions and maintenance: Although nandina grows best in acid loam, it tolerates a wide range of other soils and withstands drought. Winter sun helps redden foliage. Plant in groups to improve berrying. If left unpruned, it becomes leggy; remove old canes or cut canes to various lengths to create a dense plant. Canes cannot be forced to branch.

Pennisetum
(pen-i-SEE-tum)
FOUNTAIN GRASS

Pennisetum alopecuroides 'Hameln'

Hardiness: *Zones 5-10*

Plant type: *perennial*

Height: *2 to 4 feet*

Interest: *form, foliage*

Soil: *well-drained, fertile*

Light: *full sun*

Fountain grass forms a spray of arching leaves with bottle-brush flower heads borne on thin, arching stems in summer and fall. Stunning in masses, fountain grass graces borders, rock gardens, water features, and fall-blooming perennial beds. It is also useful as an accent plant.

Selected species and varieties: *P. alopecuroides* (Chinese fountain grass, swamp foxtail grass)—clumps of light green foliage 3 to 4 feet high, with nodding, reddish brown flowers 6 inches long; 'Hameln' grows to 2 feet; 'National Arboretum', to 2 feet with a dark brown inflorescence; Zones 7-9. *P. setaceum* (annual fountain grass)—2 to 3 feet tall, with narrow leaves and pinkish spikes 1 foot long, Zones 8-10; 'Rubrum' (purple-leaved fountain grass) has rose-colored foliage and rosy to dark red spikes.

Growing conditions and maintenance: Set plants 2 feet apart. In spring, cut to within 6 inches of the ground before new growth begins. Divide every 5 to 10 years to prevent the center from falling open. *P. setaceum* self-sows readily; it is often grown as an annual in climates where it is not hardy.

Phellodendron
(fell-o-DEN-dron)
CORK TREE

Phellodendron amurense

Hardiness: *Zones 3-8*

Plant type: *tree*

Height: *30 to 45 feet*

Interest: *bark*

Soil: *adaptable*

Light: *full sun*

Cork tree is valued for the heavily ridged and furrowed gray-brown bark, resembling cork, that cloaks the few wide-spreading horizontal main branches on old trees. Inconspicuous yellowish green flowers bloom in late spring, followed by small clusters of black berries in late fall on female trees. Both flowers and fruit have a turpentine-like odor when they are bruised. Lustrous green compound leaves, like those of black walnut, cast a light shade and sometimes turn yellow in fall, lingering on the tree only briefly.

Selected species and varieties: *P. amurense* (Amur cork tree)—30 to 45 feet tall with equal or greater spread, with orange-yellow stems bearing glossy dark green leaflets to 4 inches long, and corky bark developing in old age. *P. chinense* (Chinese cork tree)—grows 30 feet tall, with dark yellow-green leaflets to 5 inches long on red-brown stems; hardy to Zone 5.

Growing conditions and maintenance: Cork tree tolerates drought, pollution, and a wide variety of soil types. It is easily transplanted and is usually pest free. Prune in winter.

Picea
(PYE-see-a)
SPRUCE

Picea abies 'Nidiformis'

Hardiness: *Zones 2-7*

Plant type: *tree or shrub*

Height: *3 to 60 feet or more*

Interest: *foliage, form*

Soil: *moist, well-drained, acid*

Light: *full sun to partial shade*

These needled evergreens form towering pyramids useful as windbreaks, screens, or single specimens. Smaller forms are good as accents or in groups.

Selected species and varieties: *P. abies* (Norway spruce)—a fast-growing pyramid with drooping branches, 40 to 60 feet tall (can reach 150 feet) and 25 to 30 feet wide, its medium green foliage maturing to dark green, bearing 4- to 6-inch cylindrical cones and often losing its form in old age; 'Nidiformis' (bird's-nest spruce) is a 3- to 6-foot-tall spreading mound. *P. glauca* (white spruce)—a tree aging to a narrow, dense spire 40 to 60 feet tall by 10 to 20 feet wide, with ascending branches, Zones 2-6; 'Conica' (dwarf Alberta spruce) is a neat, very slow growing (to 10 feet in 25 years) cone-shaped plant with light green foliage.

Growing conditions and maintenance: Spruces prefer moist, acid, deep loam but tolerate other soils with adequate moisture, especially in the first few years. They prefer sunny sites in cold climates. White spruce withstands heat and drought better than many other species.

Pieris
(PYE-er-is)
PIERIS

Pieris japonica 'Variegata'

Hardiness: *Zones 5-8*

Plant type: *evergreen shrub*

Height: *6 to 12 feet*

Interest: *foliage, flowers, buds*

Soil: *moist, well-drained, slightly acid*

Light: *full sun to light shade*

Clustered chains of greenish to red buds decorate this mounding shrub from late summer to the following spring, when they open into white or pink urn-shaped flowers. New foliage, tinged with reddish bronze, unfurls and retains that hue for weeks before turning a lustrous dark green. Japanese pieris makes a beautiful four-season specimen, and also works well in foundations and borders. Caution: Pieris buds and flowers are poisonous.

Selected species and varieties: *P. japonica* (Japanese pieris, lily-of-the-valley bush)—upright shrub 6 to 8 feet wide, with spreading branches bearing rosettes of shiny leaves and slightly fragrant 3- to 6-inch-long flower clusters; 'Compacta' grows densely to a height of 6 feet, with small leaves and prolific bloom; 'Crispa' has wavy leaves; 'Variegata' has leaves with creamy to silver margins.

Growing conditions and maintenance: Japanese pieris grows best in well-drained soil well supplemented with leaf mold or peat moss. Protect from strong winds. If protection is provided, it can be grown in Zone 4. Provide light shade where summers are hot.

Pinus
(PYE-nus)
PINE

Pinus strobus

Hardiness: *Zones 2-10*

Plant type: *evergreen tree*

Height: *6 to 90 feet*

Interest: *foliage, form, fruit*

Soil: *wet to dry*

Light: *full sun*

This diverse genus of needle-leaved evergreen conifers includes picturesque specimen and accent plants, towering screens, and lovely single shade trees.

Selected species and varieties: *P. arisata* (bristlecone pine)—a very slow grower, some examples of which are, at over 4,000 years old, the oldest living things on earth, reaching 8 to 20 feet tall with bluish white to dark green needles; Zones 4-7. *P. contorta* var. *contorta* (shore pine)—a 25- to 30-foot-tall tree with twisted trunk and branches; hardy to Zone 7. *P. densiflora* 'Umbraculifera' (Japanese umbrella pine)—upright-spreading, with umbrella-like crown to 9 feet tall or more, with exfoliating orange bark and bright to dark green needles; Zones 3-7. *P. edulis* [also classified as *P. cembroides* var. *edulis*] (pinyon, nut pine)—slow growing, 10 to 20 feet tall, with horizontal branches and an often flat crown, and dark green needles; hardy to Zone 5. *P. eldarica* (Afghanistan pine)—fast growing, 30 to 80 feet tall, with dark green needles to 6 inches long; hardy to Zone 7. *P. mugo* (mountain pine, mugo pine)—a broad pyramid to 20 feet tall or

a low, broad, bushy shrub, with usually medium green foliage; Zones 2-7. *P. nigra* (Austrian pine)—pyramidal shape broadening over time to a flat top with heavy, spreading branches, 50 to 60 feet tall by 20 to 40 foot wide, with dark green needles; Zones 4-7. *P. palustris* (longleaf pine, southern yellow pine, pitch pine)—a sparsely branched tree 55 to 90 feet tall, bearing needles to 9 inches long on mature trees and 10-inch cones; Zones 7-10. *P. strobus* (white pine)—a low-branched tree growing 50 to 80 feet tall and half as wide, pyramidal when young but becoming broad crowned with age, producing a dense growth of bluish green needles; Zones 3-8. *P. thunbergiana* (Japanese black pine)—an irregular pyramid usually 20 to 40 feet tall, with sometimes

Pinus thunbergiana

drooping, wide-spreading branches bearing dark green, crowded, twisted needles 2½ to 7 inches long and 1½- to 2½-inch cones; Zones 5-7.

Growing conditions and maintenance: Bristlecone pine does well in poor, dry soils but suffers in drying winds or pollution. Shore pine grows naturally in boggy areas. Japanese umbrella pine prefers well-drained, slightly acid soil. Afghanistan pine and pinyon thrive in desert conditions; the former also tolerates salt spray. Mountain pine needs moist, deep loam. Austrian pine tolerates alkaline soils, moderate drought, salt, and urban pollution but grows best where moisture is assured. White pine grows best in moist loams but is also found on dry, shallow soils and wet bogs; it is intolerant of air pollutants, salt, and highly alkaline soil. Japanese black pine thrives in moist loams but is tolerant of sand and salt.

Pistacia
(pis-TAY-shee-a)
PISTACHIO

Pistacia chinensis

Hardiness: *Zones 6-9*

Plant type: *tree*

Height: *30 to 35 feet*

Interest: *foliage, fruit*

Soil: *adaptable*

Light: *full sun*

One of the best deciduous trees for fall foliage in the South, Chinese pistache has lustrous dark green compound leaves that turn a brilliant orange to orange-red even in semidesert conditions. Tiny inedible fruits begin red and mature to robin's-egg blue. Chinese pistache is usually the rootstock onto which the pistachio-nut tree is grafted. In the tree's native China, young shoots are eaten as a vegetable.

Selected species and varieties: *P. chinensis* (Chinese pistache)—30 to 35 feet high with equal spread, rather awkward in youth, eventually oval to rounded, bearing 10 to 12 leaflets 2 to 4 inches long per leaf, and inconspicuous male and female flowers on separate trees.

Growing conditions and maintenance: Chinese pistache grows best in moist, well-drained soil, where it may achieve 2 to 3 feet per year, but it tolerates other soil types and drought. Young trees develop multiple leaders and may not have straight trunks; stake trees early. Once corrective pruning is done, Chinese pistache usually needs little other special attention and is disease and insect free.

Pittosporum
(pit-o-SPO-rum)
PITTOSPORUM

Pittosporum tobira

Hardiness: *Zones 8-10*

Plant type: *evergreen shrub*

Height: *10 to 12 feet*

Interest: *foliage, fragrance, form*

Soil: *well-drained*

Light: *full sun to full shade*

A dense, impenetrable evergreen shrub whose insignificant flowers carry the scent of orange blossoms, Japanese pittosporum is used in foundation beds, drifts, barriers, hedges, and windbreaks. The round-tipped leaves are borne in rosettes at the ends of branches, lending a soft, clean appearance to the slow-growing, symmetrical mound. A variegated form works well as a bright accent. Japanese pittosporums may be left unsheared or pruned into formal shapes.

Selected species and varieties: *P. tobira* (Japanese pittosporum, mock orange)— 10 to 12 feet high and nearly twice as wide, with leathery dark green leaves 1½ to 4 inches long and up to 1½ inches wide, and tiny, five-petaled creamy white flowers in 2- to 3-inch clusters in spring, turning yellow with age and eventually becoming green to brown pods that split to expose orange seeds in fall.

Growing conditions and maintenance: Japanese pittosporums tolerate soil from dry and sandy to moist clay, requiring only that the soil be well drained. They withstand salt spray and thrive in hot, humid climates and exposed locations.

Populus
(POP-yew-lus)
POPLAR, ASPEN

Populus tremuloides

Hardiness: *Zones 1-7*

Plant type: *tree*

Height: *40 to 90 feet*

Interest: *form, foliage, bark*

Soil: *adaptable*

Light: *full sun*

Quaking aspen is a fast-growing slender deciduous tree whose lustrous dark green leaves, turning yellow in the fall, quiver with the slightest breeze. The bark is smooth, creamy to greenish white, becoming dark and furrowed on old trees. Quaking aspens are best planted in groups rather than as single specimens. Invasive root systems also make them good for erosion control.

Selected species and varieties: *P. tremuloides* (quaking aspen, trembling aspen, quiverleaf)—slender and pyramidal in youth, developing a slightly more rounded crown with age, usually high branched and spreading 20 to 30 feet, with pointed, roundish, finely serrated leaves 1½ to 3 inches long and wide that turn medium yellow in fall.

Growing conditions and maintenance: The most widely distributed tree in North America, quaking aspen grows in almost any site except soggy soils. Best growth occurs, however, in moist, deep, well-drained soil. The wood is weak and easily broken by storms. Quaking aspens usually live less than 50 years. They tolerate drought, salt spray, and urban pollution.

Potentilla
(po-ten-TILL-a)
CINQUEFOIL

Potentilla nepalensis 'Miss Wilmott'

Hardiness: *Zones 2-7*

Plant type: *shrub or perennial*

Height: *1 to 4 feet*

Interest: *flowers, foliage*

Soil: *adaptable*

Light: *full sun to partial shade*

Cinquefoils offer long-blooming flowers and small compound leaves. Bush cinquefoil can be used as a low hedge, edging, or facer plant for a mixed border. Nepal cinquefoil is ideal for rock gardens or as a ground cover on slopes.

Selected species and varieties: *P. fruticosa* (bush cinquefoil, shrubby cinquefoil, widdy)—very bushy, rounded deciduous shrub 1 to 4 feet high and 2 to 4 feet wide, with bright yellow flowers 1 inch wide from early summer till frost; 'Klondike' is a compact form, 2 feet high, with 1½-inch deep yellow flowers. *P. nepalensis* (Nepal cinquefoil)—a sprawling perennial, 18 inches tall, with weak stems bearing serrated leaves in a star-shaped pattern, and 1-inch-wide cup-shaped flowers in a range of colors from late spring to summer, hardy to Zone 5; 'Miss Wilmott' grows to 1 foot high and has cherry pink flowers.

Growing conditions and maintenance: Cinquefoils grow almost anywhere but perform best in moist, well-drained soil. Both species prefer full sun; bush cinquefoil tolerates partial shade. Remove a third of the oldest stems in late winter.

Prunus
(PROO-nus)
CHERRY, APRICOT

Prunus subhirtella var. pendula

Hardiness: *Zones 4-10*

Plant type: *shrub or tree*

Height: *3 to 50 feet*

Interest: *flowers, foliage, fruit*

Soil: *moist, well-drained*

Light: *full sun to partial shade*

This huge genus ranges from shrubs and small to mid-size deciduous trees valued for their spring flowers to robust broad-leaved evergreens used for screens, foundation plants, and hedges. None of the species listed here have edible fruits.

Selected species and varieties: *P. caroliniana* (Carolina cherry laurel, mock orange)—an evergreen oval-pyramidal shrub or tree, 20 to 30 feet high and 15 to 25 feet wide, with lustrous dark green, sharply tapered, sometimes spiny leaves 2 to 3 inches long and 1 inch wide hiding black fruits, and heavily scented white flower clusters to 3 inches long in early spring, Zones 7-10; 'Bright 'n' Tight' has smooth-edged leaves smaller than the species on a tightly branched pyramid growing to 20 feet tall. *P. laurocerasus* (common cherry laurel, English laurel)—lustrous medium to dark green leaves 2 to 6 inches long and a third as wide, slightly toothed and borne on green stems tightly branched on a broad 10- to 18-foot-tall evergreen shrub that produces heavily fragrant flowers in racemes 2 to 5 inches long, and purple to black fruit masked by the leaves, hardy

to Zone 6; 'Otto Luyken' is a compact form 3 to 4 feet tall and 6 to 8 feet wide that blooms profusely and has dark green leaves 4 inches long and 1 inch wide; 'Schipkaensis' has shorter, slightly narrower, smooth-edged leaves, to 5 feet high; hardy to Zone 5. *P. lusitanica* (Portugal laurel, Portuguese cherry laurel)—fragrant white clusters 6 to 10 inches long in late spring and dark purple cone-shaped fruits on a bushy shrub or tree 10 to 20 feet high with evergreen leaves 2½ to 5 inches long; Zones 7-9. *P. mume* (Japanese flowering apricot)—pale rose flowers in winter, after which shiny green leaves and yellowish fruit appear on a tree to 20 feet; Zones 6-9 (to

Prunus x yedoensis

Zone 10 in California). *P. subhirtella* var. *pendula* (weeping Higan cherry)—pink single flowers appear before the leaves on graceful, weeping branches on a 20- to 40-foot tree, followed by black fruit; Zones 4-9. *P. x yedoensis* (Japanese flowering cherry)—40- to 50-foot tree that bears pink or white flowers in spring before or as the leaves appear, black fruit, Zones 5-8; 'Akebono' has pink double flowers on a tree 25 feet high and wide.

Growing conditions and maintenance: As a rule, plant flowering fruit trees in full sun in well-worked loam; add sand to loosen heavy clay. Prune cherries only when necessary, removing crossed or ungainly branches. Laurels can thrive in full sun to partial shade in soil enriched with organic matter, usually enduring drought once established. In warmer climates, provide afternoon shade for Carolina cherry laurel, even in winter. Common cherry laurel is tolerant of wind and salt spray. Laurels take pruning well.

Punica
(PEW-ni-ka)
PUNICA

Punica granatum

Hardiness: *Zones 8-10*

Plant type: *shrub or small tree*

Height: *12 to 20 feet*

Interest: *flowers, fruit*

Soil: *moist, well-drained*

Light: *full sun to partial shade*

Small, carnation-like flowers with crumpled petals in red, orange, pink, white, or yellow adorn this multistemmed rounded deciduous shrub from early summer and sometimes into fall. Juicy yellow edible fruits up to 3 inches across, sporting thick, leathery skins, develop a reddish flush and are ready to be picked by early to midfall. Use pomegranates in shrub borders and groups, or grow in containers for a handsome small patio specimen.

Selected species and varieties: *P. granatum* (pomegranate)—12 to 20 feet high, with equal or less spread, bearing lustrous dark green leaves 1 to 3 inches long and 1 inch or less wide that unfurl bronzy and turn yellow in fall, and producing red flowers 1 inch wide; 'Legrellei' has double flowers with salmon pink petals variegated with white.

Growing conditions and maintenance: Easily cultivated, pomegranate makes its best growth in rich, moist loam but is adaptable to a range of other soils as long as they are well drained. Prune after flowering.

Pyrus
(PYE-rus)
PEAR

Pyrus calleryana 'Chanticleer'

Hardiness: *Zones 5-8*

Plant type: *tree*

Height: *to 40 feet*

Interest: *flowers, foliage*

Soil: *well-drained*

Light: *full sun*

Callery pears are showy trees that burst with white flowers in early spring. Their lustrous dark green leaves form a dense, symmetrical canopy until midfall, when they turn reddish purple and finally drop. Because the foliage appears early and remains late, Callery pear makes a good aerial privacy screen in urban gardens. Small fruit is inedible to humans but is enjoyed by birds in winter.

Selected species and varieties: *P. calleryana* 'Chanticleer' (Callery pear)—grows 35 feet high to 16 feet wide in 15 years, with a pyramidal crown narrower than some other cultivars in this species, bearing ⅓-inch-wide flowers in profuse 3-inch clusters and oval-rounded leaves to 3½ inches long.

Growing conditions and maintenance: Callery pears adjust to almost any well-drained soil and tolerate drought and pollution. Prune in late winter while still dormant. They tend to lose their tight form after 20 years or so, due to many branches arising close together on the trunk; 'Chanticleer' has stronger crotches than other cultivars and shows good resistance to fire blight.

Quercus
(KWER-kus)
OAK

Quercus ilex

Hardiness: *Zones 2-9*

Plant type: *tree*

Height: *40 to 100 feet or more*

Interest: *form, foliage*

Soil: *light to heavy, well-drained*

Light: *full sun*

Deciduous or evergreen trees that can provide the dominant structure and framework for the landscape, oaks have a central main trunk and usually stout horizontal branches supporting a broad canopy of dark green foliage. The leaves of deciduous forms often remain into winter. Small flowers form in spring, followed by acorns in late summer to fall.

Selected species and varieties: *Q. ilex* (holly oak, holm oak, evergreen oak)—reaching 40 to 70 feet high and wide, with leathery evergreen leaves, sometimes toothed and usually 1½ to 3 inches long, deep green above and yellowish to gray below; hardy to Zone 5. *Q. macrocarpa* (bur oak, mossy-cup oak)—spreading crown of heavy branches, usually 70 to 80 feet tall and at least as wide but has been known to top 100 feet, with 4- to 10-inch-long leaves, lobed near the stem, dark green above and whitish below, showing greenish yellow to yellow-brown fall color, and acorns, usually fringed, up to 1½ inches long; Zones 2-8. *Q. phellos* (willow oak)—narrow, slightly wavy, willowlike leaves up to 5½ inches long, turning yellow, yellow-brown, and reddish in fall, on an oval crown 40 to 60 feet high and two-thirds as wide; Zones 5-9. *Q. robur* (English oak, truffle oak, common oak, pedunculate oak)—a short trunk leads to a broad, fairly open crown, 40 to 60 feet tall with equal spread under average landscape conditions (but can reach 100 feet tall), with 2- to 5-inch-long rounded-lobed leaves that are dark green above and pale blue-green below, showing no

Quercus robur

fall color, and oblong acorns; Zones 4-8. *Q. shumardii* (Shumard's oak, Shumard red oak)—grows 40 to 60 feet tall and wide, pyramidal when young but maturing to a spreading crown, with russet-red to red fall color on deeply lobed and sharply pointed leaves 4 to 6 inches long and 3 to 4 inches wide; Zones 5-9. *Q. suber* (cork oak)—trunk and main limbs clad in thick, corky bark on an evergreen tree 60 feet high and equally wide, bearing coarsely toothed 3-inch lobeless leaves that are dark green above, fuzzy gray below; Zones 7-9.

Growing conditions and maintenance: Oaks grow best in moist, deep soil, but most species fare well in a wide range of soil types as long as there is no hardpan present. Although oaks tolerate partial shade, they grow best, and stay healthier, in full sun. Holly oak can withstand inland drought and salt spray, but may become shrubby in exposed, seaside locations. Shumard oak tolerates either wet or dry sites. A good oak for desert conditions, cork oak needs well-drained soil and is drought resistant once established; its leaves yellow in alkaline soil. Do not compact or change the elevation of soil within the oak's root zone, which usually extends far beyond the canopy's reach.

Raphiolepis
(raf-i-O-le-pis)
HAWTHORN

Raphiolepis indica

Hardiness: *Zones 9-10*

Plant type: *shrub*

Height: *3 to 5 feet*

Interest: *foliage, flowers*

Soil: *moist, well-drained, slightly acid to neutral*

Light: *full sun*

Indian hawthorn is a dense, glossy-leaved evergreen shrub that produces loose, showy clusters of white or pink flowers in early spring. Purplish to blue-black berries, visible only at close range, ripen in fall and linger though winter. This slow-growing, sturdy shrub is often used in low hedges and borders or as background for a flower bed. It also makes a good container plant for the patio.

Selected species and varieties: *R. indica* (Indian hawthorn)—a 3- to 5-foot-wide dense mound of 2- to 3-inch-long dark green lance-shaped leaves with toothy margins clustered at the ends of branches, sometimes turning a dull purplish green in winter, and ½-inch-wide fragrant white flowers blushed with pink toward the center and red stamens; 'White Enchantress' is a dwarf form with single white flowers.

Growing conditions and maintenance: Indian hawthorn may get leggy in light shade, and it flowers best in full sun. Encourage dense growth by pinching off the tips. Once established, it withstands drought. Tolerant of salt, it grows well at the seashore.

Rhododendron
(roh-doh-DEN-dron)
RHODODENDRON

Rhododendron schlippenbachii

Hardiness: *Zones 4-8*

Plant type: *shrub*

Height: *2 to 12 feet*

Interest: *flowers, foliage*

Soil: *moist, well-drained, acid, fertile*

Light: *partial to bright full shade*

Over 900 species of rhododendrons and azaleas are included in the genus *Rhododendron*. Most rhododendrons are evergreen, have bell-shaped flowers, and often have scaly leaves. Most azaleas are deciduous, have funnel-shaped flowers, and have leaves that are never scaly. Both are effective in borders, groupings, and naturalistic shady gardens.

Selected species and varieties: *R. catawbiense* (Catawba rhododendron, mountain rosebay, purple laurel)—lilac-purple, sometimes purplish rose, flowers in mid-spring, 6 to 10 feet tall and not as wide; Zones 4-8. *R.* 'Gibraltar'—an upright deciduous shrub 8 to 12 feet tall and almost as wide with medium green leaves that turn orangish in fall and extra large, orange ruffled flowers. *R.* hybrids—'Blue Diamond' grows to 3 feet, with lavender-blue flowers, hardy to Zone 7; 'Bow Bells' has bright pink flowers, rounded leaves, and bronzy new growth to 4 feet, hardy to Zone 6; 'Cilpinense' grows to 2½ feet with light pink flowers fading to white, its buds reliably hardy only in Zone 8; 'Moonstone' grows to 2 feet, with pale pink flowers turning creamy yellow, reliably hardy to Zone 7; 'Ramapo' has blue-green new foliage and violet-blue flowers, 2 to 4 feet tall, to Zone 5; 'Scarlet Wonder', 2 feet tall, with bright red flowers and shiny, quilted foliage, to Zone 6. *R. mucronulatum* (Korean rhododendron)—a deciduous shrub of rounded, open habit, 4 to 8 feet tall and wide, with rosy purple flowers in late winter, followed by 1- to 4-inch-long medium green leaves that are aromatic when crushed and turn yellow to bronzy red in fall. *R.*

Rhododendron 'P.J.M.'

'P.J.M.'—3 to 6 feet tall and wide, with lavender-pink flowers borne profusely in early to midspring and dark green evergreen leaves 1 to 2½ inches long turning plum in fall and winter. *R. schlippenbachii* (royal azalea)—a rounded deciduous shrub 6 to 8 feet tall and wide bearing fragrant, pale to rosy pink flowers 2 to 3 inches wide as new leaves unfurl bronze, later turning dark green before changing to yellow, orange, or red in fall.

Growing conditions and maintenance: Make sure that soil is well drained, and add peat moss or leaf mold liberally. Set plant so that the top of the rootball is an inch or two above the surface of the soil. Mulch to conserve moisture and to keep roots cool. Water deeply in dry periods, particularly before the onset of winter. Evergreen types should be protected from hot afternoon sun and winter winds. Morning sun enhances bloom without stressing the plant. Foundation plantings run the risk of failing because lime leaching from structural cement sweetens the soil; in these cases, increase soil acidity with aluminum sulfate. Unlike other members of this genus, royal azalea does well in near neutral soils.

Rosa
(RO-za)
ROSE

Rosa 'Betty Prior'

Hardiness: *Zones 2-10*

Plant type: *shrub or vine*

Height: *1½ to 20 feet*

Interest: *flowers, fragrance*

Soil: *well-drained, organic*

Light: *full sun*

Beloved for the timeless quality they lend to the garden, roses have single, double, or very double flowers, often fragrant, on thorny stems. Colorful fruit (hips) may appear in fall. Mass them for a hedge or border, let them ramble over a slope, or train them against a trellis or fence. Some varieties offer good fall foliage.

Selected species and varieties: *R.* 'Betty Prior'—5-foot upright floribunda, with semiglossy green leaves and clusters of 3-inch-wide five-petaled flowers with a spicy fragrance that are red in cool weather and medium pink in warm weather, yellow stamens that turn brown, blooming in early summer with several repeats to fall. *R.* 'Cécile Brunner'—1½-inch light pink double flowers in late spring with several recurrent blooms until frost on a 2- to 4-foot-tall bush; a climbing form shares the same name. *R. glauca* [also listed under *R. rubrifolia*] (redleaf rose)—almost thornless bush 6 to 8 feet tall and wide, with glaucous foliage that is gray-green in shade, coppery mauve in sun, borne on purple-red stems that produce clusters of pink single flowers with white centers and yellow stamens in late

spring to early summer, and brownish red hips that persist into fall; Zones 2-8. *R.* 'New Dawn'—climbing rose 12 to 20 feet tall or loose, sprawling bush, with fragrant semidouble blush pink flowers 3 to 4 inches wide that open to show stamens, repeating until fall, and dark green glossy foliage on thorny canes. *R. rugosa* (rugosa rose, Japanese rose)—fragrant open flowers with yellow stamens bloom all summer on arching canes on a vigorous bush 4 to 6 feet tall and wide, followed by red hips in fall, Zones 2-8; 'Albo-plena', 4 feet tall, has fragrant white double flowers 4 inches wide and orange-red hips; 'Frau Dagmar Hartopp' grows 3 feet tall and 4 feet wide, with crinkled rich green foliage turning yellow to orange in fall, and fragrant silvery pink petals around yellow stamens, repeat bloomer; 'Hansa', 5 feet tall and 4 feet wide and very free

Rosa rugosa 'Frau Dagmar Hartopp'

flowering, with deep red-purple double flowers 3 inches wide with clovelike fragrance in early summer, orange-red hips, and yellow to orange fall foliage; ssp. *rubra*—large crimson-purple flowers. *R.* 'The Fairy'—sprawling, sometimes trailing, polyantha rose, 1½ to 3 feet tall and wider, with clusters of light pink double flowers, 1- to 1½ inches wide, blooming recurrently, and tiny dark green leaves. *R.* 'White Pet' [also called 'Little White Pet'] —large clusters of small, scented, very double white flowers in summer on a bushy, compact plant 2 feet tall and wide.

Growing conditions and maintenance: Roses grow best in moist, slightly acid soil and prefer good air circulation. Mulch to conserve moisture, suppress weeds, and protect roots in winter. Rugosa roses adapt to sand and salt.

Rosmarinus
(rose-ma-RY-nus)
ROSEMARY

Rosmarinus officinalis

Hardiness: *Zones 7-10*

Plant type: *evergreen shrub*

Height: *2 to 6 feet or more*

Interest: *foliage, fragrance, flowers*

Soil: *moist to dry, well-drained*

Light: *full sun to partial shade*

Rosemary is a culinary herb and sachet ingredient that can also spice up the shrub border. Its gray-green needlelike foliage, aromatic when bruised, and its loose, irregular habit contrast well with dark green plants of formal shapes. Tiny blue flowers are borne in the leaf axils from fall to spring. Shrub varieties can be pruned into hedges. Trailing forms work well as ground covers, in rock gardens, and in window boxes.

Selected species and varieties: *R. officinalis*—a dense shrub with many erect stems, usually growing 2 to 4 feet tall and wide in free form, but topping 6 feet if conditions are favorable, and bearing closely spaced leathery leaves and ½-inch light blue flowers; 'Lockwood de Forest' grows 2 feet high with a 3- to 8-foot spread and has trailing stems with lighter green leaves and bluer flowers than the species.

Growing conditions and maintenance: Rosemary needs at least 4 hours of midday sun but grows best in full sun. It is intolerant of wet soils but performs well in seaside gardens.

Rudbeckia
(rood-BEK-ee-a)
CONEFLOWER

Rudbeckia fulgida 'Goldsturm'

Hardiness: *Zones 3-10*

Plant type: *perennial*

Height: *1½ to 5 feet*

Interest: *flowers*

Soil: *moist, well-drained, slightly acid*

Light: *full sun to light shade*

Coneflowers, with blossoms consisting of yellow raylike petals around a raised center of another color, produce abundant bloom over a long season. They are a cheerful and reliable addition to any sunny perennial border and are excellent for cutting. Because coneflowers self-sow freely to form large colonies, they are also good for naturalizing.

Selected species and varieties: *R. fulgida* var. *sullivantii* 'Goldsturm' (orange coneflower)—deep yellow rays around cone-shaped brownish black centers from midsummer into fall on a compact, bushy plant 18 to 30 inches tall with dark green foliage; Zones 3-9. *R. nitida* 'Herbstsonne' ('Autumn Sun')—a very dense, 4- to 5-foot clump, with leathery, divided leaves and drooping yellow rays around a greenish disk, blooming nonstop from mid- to late summer; hardy to Zone 4.

Growing conditions and maintenance: Coneflowers thrive in heat and produce more flowers in full sun. Amend soil with peat moss, leaf mold, or finished compost. Stake the taller forms early to prevent wind damage.

Sapindus
(SAP-in-dus)
SOAPBERRY

Sapindus drummondii

Hardiness: *Zones 5-9*

Plant type: *tree*

Height: *25 to 50 feet*

Interest: *flowers, foliage, fruit, bark*

Soil: *dry to adaptable*

Light: *full sun to light shade*

Panicles of yellowish white flowers 6 to 10 inches long bloom in late spring on this graceful deciduous shade tree. The strong-wooded, rounded crown bears medium green compound leaves that turn gold in fall. Small yellow-orange berries, supposedly used by American Indians to make soap, emerge in fall and persist through winter, finally turning black. Scaly bark flakes off to expose gray, orange-brown, and reddish brown tissue.

Selected species and varieties: *S. drummondii* (western soapberry, wild China tree)—either single stemmed or low branched, 25 to 50 feet tall with an equal spread, producing 8 to 18 tapered, slightly curved leaflets, each 1½ to 3½ inches long, per 10- to 15-inch leaf, glossy above and fuzzy below, and sometimes abundant crops of ½-inch berries.

Growing conditions and maintenance: Soapberry is tolerant of most soils but is especially at home in the poor, dry soils of its native Southwest. It is also tolerant of urban pollution and is insect and disease resistant. Easy to cultivate, soapberry needs little special attention and usually hangs on to its branches in storms.

Sedum
(SEE-dum)
STONECROP

Sedum x 'Autumn Joy'

Hardiness: *Zones 3-10*

Plant type: *succulent perennial*

Height: *8 to 24 inches*

Interest: *foliage, flowers, form*

Soil: *well-drained*

Light: *full sun to light shade*

Stonecrops form neat, bushy globes of thick, fleshy foliage covered with clusters of tiny star-shaped flowers. The broccoli-like blooms draw hummingbirds and butterflies and often remain attractive into winter. Stonecrops are useful in rock gardens, borders, and edgings.

Selected species and varieties: *S.* x 'Autumn Joy'—gray-green foliage to 2 feet tall, with pink flower buds in midsummer opening rusty red in fall and changing to golden brown in winter. *S. kamtschaticum* (orange stonecrop)—orange-yellow flowers in midsummer on compact 8-inch plants; Zones 3-8. *S.* x 'Ruby Glow'—8 inches tall with gray-blue leaves tinged with dark red and pinkish red flowers in late summer and fall; hardy to Zone 4. *S. spectabile* (live-forever, showy sedum)—large heads of bright pink, red, and white fall flowers, 1½ feet tall; 'Brilliant' has raspberry pink flowers. *S.* x 'Vera Jameson'—12 inches tall, with coppery purple foliage and pink fall flowers.

Growing conditions and maintenance: Sedum tolerates almost any well-drained soil, even poor and dry. Propagate by division or by rooting leaf or stem cuttings.

Spiraea
(spy-REE-a)
BRIDAL WREATH

Spiraea x bumalda 'Anthony Waterer'

Hardiness: *Zones 3-8*

Plant type: *shrub*

Height: *2 to 8 feet*

Interest: *flowers, foliage*

Soil: *well-drained*

Light: *full sun to partial shade*

Rugged and hardy deciduous shrubs, spireas produce showy clusters of dainty flowers in spring or summer.

Selected species and varieties: *S.* x *bumalda* (Bumald spirea)—a flat-topped shrub, 2 to 3 feet tall and 3 to 5 feet wide, with 4- to 6-inch white to deep pink clusters in summer, and leaves that are pinkish when young, aging to blue-green and turning subdued bronzy red or purplish in fall; 'Anthony Waterer' is 3 to 4 feet tall and 4 to 5 feet wide, with brownish red new foliage and pink flowers; 'Gold Flame' has reddish orange new leaves that turn yellow-green in summer and bright red-orange in fall, with pinkish blooms. *S. japonica* 'Little Princess' (Japanese spirea)—pink flowers and blue-green leaves tinted red in fall on a 30-inch plant; hardy to Zone 4. *S.* x *vanhouttei* (Vanhoutte spirea)—vase- or fountain-shaped 6 to 8 feet tall by 10 to 12 feet wide, with 1- to 2-inch white clusters in spring; hardy to Zone 4.

Growing conditions and maintenance: Spireas are easy to grow in any garden soil. Prune summer bloomers in late winter, spring bloomers after flowering.

Stewartia
(stew-AR-tee-a)
STEWARTIA

Stewartia pseudocamellia

Hardiness: *Zones 5-9*

Plant type: *shrub or tree*

Height: *10 to 40 feet*

Interest: *flowers, foliage, bark*

Soil: *moist, well-drained, acid, organic*

Light: *partial shade to full sun*

Stewartia has camellia-like summer flowers and colorful fall foliage. A fine specimen tree, Japanese stewartia has exfoliating bark in cream, rusty red, and gray.

Selected species and varieties: *S. ovata* (mountain stewartia, mountain camellia)—creamy white flowers 2½ to 3 inches wide and oval leaves 2 to 5 inches long that turn orange to red in fall on spreading branches of a bushy shrub or small tree 10 to 15 feet tall and wide, with bark not as showy as that of Japanese stewartia. *S. pseudocamellia* (Japanese stewartia)—20 to 40 feet tall with open, spreading branches, producing white 2- to 2½-inch flowers with white filaments and orange anthers amid 1½- to 3½-inch leaves that turn vibrant yellow, red, and reddish purple in fall; Zones 5-7.

Growing conditions and maintenance: Stewartia is difficult to transplant and should be put into the ground as a 4- to 5-foot-tall balled-and-burlapped plant and not moved again. Dig a large hole and amend the soil liberally with peat moss, leaf mold, or compost. In warmer climates, provide some afternoon shade. Stewartias rarely need pruning.

Styrax
(STY-racks)
SNOWBELL, STORAX

Styrax japonicus

Hardiness: *Zones 5-8*

Plant type: *tree*

Height: *20 to 30 feet*

Interest: *flowers, bark*

Soil: *moist, well-drained, acid, organic*

Light: *full sun to partial shade*

The delicate white bell-like flowers that dangle from Japanese snowbell's wide-spreading branches are most visible from below, making this deciduous tree an ideal candidate to shade a patio or garden bench or to plant on slopes above walkways. The smooth, dark gray bark with interwoven orangish fissures is attractive in winter.

Selected species and varieties: *S. japonicus* (Japanese snowbell)—a dainty, low-branched tree whose crown is broader than its height, bearing medium to dark green pointed-oval leaves 1 to 3½ inches long along the upper part of the branches, and loose pendulous clusters of three to six slightly fragrant ¾-inch white flowers with prominent yellow stamens below the branches in late spring to early summer, and foliage that remains in place long enough to be killed by frost.

Growing conditions and maintenance: Provide partial shade in Zones 7 and 8, and shelter from winter winds and low areas in colder climates. Amend soil with generous amounts of leaf mold or peat moss. Prune in winter. Japanese snowbell is a remarkably pest-free plant.

Syringa
(si-RING-ga)
LILAC

Syringa reticulata

Hardiness: *Zones 3-8*

Plant type: *tree or shrub*

Height: *3 to 30 feet*

Interest: *flowers, fragrance*

Soil: *moist, well-drained*

Light: *full sun*

Deciduous staples of gardens past, lilacs produce fat, highly scented flower clusters after their dark green pointed-oval leaves have appeared.

Selected species and varieties: *S. patula* [formerly classified as *S. velutina*] 'Miss Kim' (Manchurian lilac)—fragrant 4- to 6-inch-long icy blue bloom clusters open from purple buds in late spring to early summer on a 3- to 6-foot-tall shrub. *S. reticulata* [formerly classified as *S. amurensis* var. *japonica*] (Japanese tree lilac)—20 to 30 feet tall, with branches spread stiffly 15 to 25 feet before becoming more arching and graceful with age, with an oval to round crown and creamy white, privet-scented terminal flower clusters 6 to 12 inches long and wide for 2 weeks in early summer, and reddish brown cherrylike bark; Zones 3-7.

Growing conditions and maintenance: Lilacs grow best in loose, slightly acid loam, but they adjust to both acid or slightly alkaline soil. Prune after flowering and remove crowded branches; lilacs need good air circulation. Japanese tree lilac is unusually pest free and resistant to mildew.

Taxodium
(taks-ODE-ee-um)
CYPRESS

Taxodium distichum

Hardiness: *Zones 4-9*

Plant type: *tree*

Height: *50 to 70 feet or more*

Interest: *form, foliage, bark*

Soil: *moist, sandy, acid*

Light: *full sun*

These stately deciduous conifers have sage green needlelike foliage that turns bright orange-brown in fall and is shed. In swampy areas or along the edge of a lake, the shaggy reddish brown main trunk is flanked by narrow root projections that reach out of the water in knee-like bends to collect oxygen for the tree. Inconspicuous flowers bloom in spring, and fragrant green to purple cones 1 inch across mature to brown. Use common bald cypress as a dramatic fine-textured vertical accent in the garden, or plant in groups along the edge of a pond.

Selected species and varieties: *T. distichum* (common bald cypress, swamp cypress, tidewater red cypress)—new foliage opens bright yellow-green in graceful sprays amid short, ascending branches on a slender pyramid 50 to 70 feet high or more by 20 to 30 feet wide.

Growing conditions and maintenance: Although common bald cypress makes its best growth in moist to wet deep, sandy loams, it is surprisingly tolerant of dry soil and low fertility. It is also very resistant to strong winds, and is seldom seriously bothered by disease or insects.

Taxus
(TAKS-us)
YEW

Taxus x media 'Hicksii'

Hardiness: *Zones 4-7*

Plant type: *shrub or tree*

Height: *2 to 60 feet*

Interest: *foliage, form, fruit*

Soil: *well-drained*

Light: *light shade to full sun*

The dense, very dark green needled foliage of yews provides a consistent year-round anchor to the landscape. Female plants produce bright red berries if a male is nearby. (Caution: The berries are poisonous.) Smaller forms make superb foundation plants or entrance shrubs, or they may be clipped into hedges.

Selected species and varieties: *T. baccata* (English yew, common yew)—a dense shrub or tree 30 to 60 feet high and 15 to 25 feet wide with a variable habit, often used as a screen or hedge, Zones 6-7; 'Repandens' (spreading English Yew)—2 to 4 feet high and 12 to 15 feet wide, with drooping branch tips; hardy to Zone 5. *T.* x *media* (Anglojap yew)—extremely variable form 3 to 20 feet high, either a pyramidal tree or a spreading shrub, often with a central trunk, Zones 4-7; 'Hicksii' develops a columnar form to 20 feet tall in 15 to 20 years, narrow when young and becoming broader with age.

Growing conditions and maintenance: Yews adapt to almost any soil as along as it is well drained but prefer slightly acid, sandy loam. They usually need no pruning but tolerate severe shearing.

Ternstroemia
(tern-STRO-mee-a)
TERNSTROEMIA

Ternstroemia gymnanthera

Hardiness: *Zones 7-10*

Plant type: *evergreen shrub*

Height: *to 20 feet*

Interest: *foliage, flowers, fruit*

Soil: *moist, well-drained, organic*

Light: *full to partial shade*

Leathery leaves that open brownish red and mature to rich, glossy green clothe gracefully arching branches. In early summer, small clusters of fragrant creamy white flowers put on a modest display. Small red berries turn black and last through winter. Primarily grown for its foliage, ternstroemia works well as a foundation plant or hedge; it can also be trained into a small tree.

Selected species and varieties: *T. gymnanthera* [sometimes confused with *Cleyera japonica*] (Japanese ternstroemia)—6 to 15 feet tall and wide, with elliptic to oblong 2- to 6-inch-long leaves often arranged in whorls on the ends of branches and ½-inch flowers produced in clusters on the previous year's growth, with bloom and berries occurring only on mature plants.

Growing conditions and maintenance: Although Japanese ternstroemia grows best in rich, slightly acid soil that stays moist, it tolerates occasional drought. Good drainage is essential. Given suitable conditions, the species is usually problem free. Prune after flowering. Propagate by stem cuttings.

Ulmus
(UL-mus)
ELM

Ulmus parvifolia

Hardiness: *Zones 4-9*

Plant type: *tree*

Height: *40 to 70 feet*

Interest: *bark, form, foliage*

Soil: *moist, well-drained*

Light: *full sun*

Exfoliating, mottled gray, green, orange, or brown bark is this graceful, durable shade tree's most outstanding feature. Lacebark elm has a spreading, rounded crown of medium fine, lustrous dark green foliage that holds late into fall, when it turns yellow to reddish purple.

Selected species and varieties: *U. parvifolia* (lacebark elm, Chinese elm, evergreen elm)—40 to 50 feet high and wide in most situations, usually with a forked trunk and drooping branches, bearing leathery, saw-toothed elliptical leaves ¾ to 2½ inches long and inconspicuous flower clusters hidden by the foliage in late summer to early fall, followed by ⅓-inch-wide winged fruits.

Growing conditions and maintenance: Lacebark elm grows best in moist, well-drained loams but adapts well to poor, dry soils, both acid and alkaline. Soil should be deep to accommodate the extensive root system. Growth averages 1½ feet per year. Prune to remove weak, narrow crotches. Although it is not immune to Dutch elm disease, it shows considerable resistance.

Viburnum
(vy-BUR-num)
ARROWWOOD

Viburnum carlesii

Hardiness: *Zones 4-9*

Plant type: *shrub*

Height: *3 to 12 feet*

Interest: *flowers, fruit, foliage*

Soil: *moist, well-drained*

Light: *full sun to partial shade*

The mostly deciduous, highly ornamental viburnums listed here offer snowy clouds of flowers in spring and often colorful berries that may persist well into winter. Others are valued for their fragrance, reddish fall foliage, or branching patterns. Viburnums are useful in shrub borders, as screens, or as specimens.

Selected species and varieties: *V. carlesii* (Koreanspice viburnum)—pink buds open to white, domelike, enchantingly fragrant flower clusters 2 to 3 inches wide on a rounded, dense shrub 4 to 8 feet tall and wide, followed by ineffective black fruit in late summer; Zones 4-8. *V. davidii* (David viburnum)—turquoise blue fruits on an evergreen mound 3 to 5 feet high that also produces dull white flower clusters 2 to 3 inches wide; Zones 8-9. *V. dilatatum* (linden viburnum)— 8 to 10 feet tall and 6 to 8 feet wide, bearing flat, creamy white clusters to 5 inches wide in late spring, bright red or scarlet berries that ripen in fall and persist into winter, and semilustrous dark green leaves 2 to 5 inches long, sometimes turning russet-red in fall, Zones 5-7; 'Catskill' is a dwarf form 5 to 6 feet

tall and 8 feet wide with dark green leaves that turn yellow, orange, and red in fall, and dark red fruit clusters that ripen in late summer and linger until midwinter. *V. plicatum* var. *tomentosum* (doublefile viburnum)—layered, tierlike, horizontal branches on a plant 8 to 10 feet tall and wide, with flat, pure white flower clusters 2 to 4 inches wide on 2-inch stems consisting of fertile non-showy flowers rimmed by a ring of showy sterile flowers, followed by red berries that turn black in summer amid coarsely toothed, prominently veined leaves 2 to 4 inches long that turn reddish purple in fall, Zones 5-8; 'Mariesii' has larger sterile flowers and slightly longer flower stems; 'Shasta' grows 6 feet tall and 10 to 12 feet

Viburnum setigerum

wide, with 4- to 6-inch wide-spreading flower clusters that obscure the leaves. *V. setigerum* (tea viburnum)—a multi-stemmed shrub 8 to 12 feet tall and 6 to 8 feet wide, with 3- to 6-inch-long blue-green leaves, once used to make tea, and unremarkable 1- to 2-inch white flower clusters but with a profuse crop of bright red berries in fall; Zones 5-7.

Growing conditions and maintenance: Viburnums grow best in slightly acid loam but tolerate slightly alkaline soils. Amend the soil with peat moss or leaf mold to increase moisture retention, and add sand if soil is poorly drained. Allow enough lateral room for the plant to fully develop; prune if necessary after flowering.

Vitex
(VY-tex)
VITEX

Vitex agnus-castus

Hardiness: *Zones 6-9*

Plant type: *shrub or tree*

Height: *to 20 feet*

Interest: *flowers, fragrance*

Soil: *moist, well-drained, neutral*

Light: *full sun*

A vase-shaped shrub or small tree with an airy, open habit and leaves that are aromatic when bruised, chaste tree produces fragrant lilac or pale violet flowers in foot-long mounded clusters of 3- to 6-inch spikes on new wood. Let chaste tree provide late-summer color for the shrub border, or prune high to create a specimen.

Selected species and varieties: *V. agnus-castus* (chaste tree, hemp tree, sage tree, Indian-spice, wild pepper, monk's pepper tree)—multistemmed, 8 to 10 feet tall, and reaching to 20 feet in the southern part of its range, with deciduous compound leaves composed of leaflets arranged in maple-leaf fashion, gray-green above and fuzzy gray below, showing no fall color, and showy flower panicles from midsummer to fall; 'Rosea' has pink flowers.

Growing conditions and maintenance: Chaste tree is marginally hardy in Zone 6, where it is usually killed to the ground in winter but revives in spring. Fast growing, it can often achieve 5 or 6 feet in the next season. Too much fertilizer creates paler flowers. Chaste tree has no significant pests.

Wisteria
(wis-TEE-ree-a)
WISTERIA

Wisteria sinensis

Hardiness: *Zones 4-9*

Plant type: *woody vine*

Height: *30 feet*

Interest: *flowers*

Soil: *moist, well-drained*

Light: *full sun*

Panicles of lavender flowers drip from this vigorous, twining vine. Lovely near patios and porches, where its bright green foliage provides dense shade for the rest of the growing season, wisteria needs a sturdy support, since the vines can eventually crush wood. It can also be trained into a tree form. Velvety green pods turn brown and persist into winter.

Selected species and varieties: *W. floribunda* (Japanese wisteria)—twines clockwise, bearing small, slightly fragrant, violet or violet-blue flowers in clusters 9 to 20 inches long in early to midspring just before the leaves emerge. *W. sinensis* (Chinese wisteria)—twines counterclockwise and produces blue-violet flowers, not as fragrant as those of Japanese wisteria, borne in dense, 6- to 12-inch-long clusters in mid- to late spring; cultivars include white, dark purple, double, and more fragrant varieties; Zones 5-8.

Growing conditions and maintenance: Amend soil to create a deep, well-drained loam, and add lime if soil is very acid. Prune roots before planting. Feed with superphosphate fertilizers; too much nitrogen creates excessive foliage.

Yucca
(YUK-a)
YUCCA

Yucca filamentosa 'Bright Edge'

Hardiness: *Zones 4-9*

Plant type: *shrub*

Height: *2 to 12 feet*

Interest: *foliage, flowers, form*

Soil: *light, well-drained*

Light: *full sun*

Yucca's rosette of stiff, lance-shaped evergreen leaves accents rock gardens and entranceway designs. In early to midsummer, 3- to 12-foot-tall stalks bear erect panicles of waxy, drooping, creamy or yellowish white flowers that emit a lemony fragrance in the evening. Yuccas are best planted in small groups, since individual plants may not bloom every year.

Selected species and varieties: *Y. filamentosa* (Adam's-needle, needle palm, spoon-leaf yucca)—a 2- to 3-foot clump, with succulent leathery leaves to 30 inches long and 1 to 2 inches wide, having long, curly threads along the margins and sharp spines at the tips, and puffy, hanging flowers 1 to 2 inches long; 'Bright Edge' has gold leaf margins; 'Golden Sword' leaves have yellow centers and green margins.

Growing conditions and maintenance: Yucca grows best in fast-draining soils. It easily tolerates drought and is seldom bothered by insects or disease.

Zelkova
(zel-KOH-va)
ZELKOVA

Zelkova serrata

Hardiness: *Zones 5-8*

Plant type: *tree*

Height: *50 to 80 feet*

Interest: *foliage, form, bark*

Soil: *moist, well-drained*

Light: *full sun*

Japanese zelkova is an elmlike deciduous tree resistant to Dutch elm disease. Vase shaped and often multistemmed, it frequently develops attractive exfoliating bark as it ages. Sharply toothed dark green leaves turn yellow or russet in fall.

Selected species and varieties: *Z. serrata* (Japanese zelkova, saw-leaf zelkova)—50 to 80 feet high and wide, with ascending branches bearing 2- to 5-inch-long pointed oval leaves, somewhat rough with prominent veins, the smaller ones located on upper branches, insignificant male and female flowers in spring, and bark that is smooth, gray, and beechlike in youth, eventually flaking to expose patches of orange; 'Green Vase' is a vigorous, extremely fast-growing tree 60 to 70 feet tall with arching branches bearing orange-brown to bronze-red fall foliage.

Growing conditions and maintenance: Japanese zelkova grows best in deep, moist, fertile soil and adjusts to either alkalinity or acidity. Mulch to conserve moisture when the tree is young and to prevent mower damage. Once established, the tree tolerates wind, drought, and pollution.

Acknowledgments and Picture Credits

The editors wish to thank the following for their valuable assistance in the preparation of this volume:

Loy Andrews, Bar Harbor, Maine; Richard Dubé, Environmental Information and Design, Inc., Gorham, Maine; John Elsley, Director of Horticulture, Wayside Gardens, Hodges, South Carolina; Elise Felton, Manset, Maine; Karen Kettlety, Mount Desert, Maine; Peter J. Murray, Hidden Lane Landscaping, Oakton, Virginia.

The sources for the illustrations that appear in this book are listed below. Credits from left to right are separated by semicolons; credits from top to bottom are separated by dashes.

Cover: Roger Foley/designed by Karen Burroughs and Gary Hayre, Ashton, Md. Back cover insets: © Robert Holmes—art by George Bell—Robert Walch/designed by Andrew Hartnagle and Wayne Stork, Doylestown, Pa. End papers: Virginia Weiler/designed by Cathy and Peter Wallenborn, Asheville, N.C. 2, 3: Bernard Fallon/designed by Mel Light. 4: Catherine Davis; courtesy Nan Booth Simpson, photo Ron Green. 6, 7: Roger Foley/designed by Oehme, van Sweden and Associates, Inc. 8, 9: © Robert Perron. 10, 11: Jerry Pavia. 12: Bernard Fallon/designed by Sandy Kennedy/Kennedy Landscape Design Associates, Woodland Hills, Calif. 13: Leonard G. Phillips. 14, 15: © Michael P. Gadomski/Bruce Coleman Inc.; © Karen Bussolini; Gay Bumgarner. 16: Jerry Pavia, courtesy Diane and Jon Spieler, garden designed by Johnathan Plant, Los Angeles, Calif. 17: © Carole Ottesen. 18, 19: Mary-Gray Hunter/designed by William T. Smith, Landscape Architect, ASLA, Atlanta, Ga. 20, 21: © R. Todd Davis; Virginia Weiler/designed by Alan Kronhaus/Kim Hawks, Niche Gardens, Chapel Hill, N.C. 22: Bernard Fallon/designed by Barry Campion. 23: Jerry Pavia; art by Andrew Lewis/ARCOBALENO. 24: Art by Andrew Lewis/ARCOBALENO. 25: Leonard G. Phillips/designed by Joe Saury. 26: Jerry Pavia. 27: Dency Kane/designed by Robert Levenson and Kathe Tanous, East Hampton, N.Y. 28, 29: Lynne Karlin/designed by Beth Straus. 30, 31: Robert Walch/designed by Carter van Dyke, Landscape Architect, ASLA; art by Andrew Lewis/ARCOBALENO. 32: Jerry Pavia/designed by Linda Chisari. 33: Bernard Fallon/designed by Laura Cooper. 34: Art by Andrew Lewis/ARCOBALENO. 36, 37: Dency Kane/designed by Ellen Penick. 39: Roger Foley—Roger Foley/art by Andrew Lewis/ARCOBALENO. 40, 41: Robert Walch/designed by Andrew Hartnagle and Wayne Stork, Doylestown, Pa. 42, 43: Jerry Pavia. 44, 45: Lynne Karlin/designed by Beth Straus. 46, 47: Dency Kane/designed by Shiro Nakane with Julie Moir Messervy. 48, 49: © Charles Mann. 50: Robert Walch/designed by Andrew Hartnagle and Wayne Stork, Doylestown, Pa. (2). 51: Jerry Pavia (2). 52: Lynne Karlin/designed by Beth Straus (2). 53: Dency Kane/designed by Shiro Nakane with Julie Moir Messervy (2)—© Charles Mann (2). 54, 55: © Robert Holmes. 56: Jerry Pavia. 57: © Robert Holmes. 58: Art by George Bell. 59: Art by Stephen R. Wagner—Bernard Fallon/designed by Chris Rosmini. 60, 61: Jerry Pavia. 62, 63: Dency Kane/designed by Robert Levenson and Kathe Tanous, East Hampton, N.Y.—art by Andrew Lewis/ARCOBALENO. 64: Art by George Bell. 65: Leonard G. Phillips—art by George Bell. 66: © Walter Chandoha. 67: Bernard Fallon/designed by Laura Cooper. 68, 69: Jerry Pavia; art by Stephen R. Wagner. 70: Jerry Pavia/designed by Sydney Baumgartner. 71: © Anita Sabarese. 72: Jerry Pavia. 75: Virginia Weiler/designed by Peter Gentling. 76: Art by Sharron O'Neil. 77: Art by Andrew Lewis/ARCOBALENO. 78, 79: Roger Foley/designed by Karen Burroughs and Gary Hayre, Ashton, Md. 80: Roger Foley. 81: Leonard G. Phillips/designed by Donna L. Hearn and Howard A. Wynne. 83: Jerry Pavia. 84: Robert Walch/designed by Andrew Hartnagle and Wayne Stork, Doylestown, Pa. 86, 87: Roger Foley/designed by Oehme, van Sweden and Associates, Inc. 88: © Walter Chandoha. 89: Roger Foley. 91: © Charles Mann. 92, 93: © Karen Bussolini—art by Andrew Lewis/ARCOBALENO. 94: Dency Kane/designed by Robert Levenson and Kathe Tanous, East Hampton, N.Y. 95: Art by Andrew Lewis/ARCOBALENO. 100: Art by Lorraine Mosley Epstein—art by Sharron O'Neil. 101: Art by Lorraine Mosley Epstein—art by Sharron O'Neil—art by Lorraine Mosley Epstein. 102: Art by Lorraine Mosley Epstein. 103: Art by Lorraine Mosley Epstein—art by Fred Holz—art by Sharron O'Neil. 108: Map by John Drummond, Time-Life Books. 110: Richard Shiell; Jerry Pavia. 111: Jerry Pavia. 112: Richard Shiell (2); Jerry Pavia. 113: Jerry Pavia. 114: Michael Dirr; © Alan and Linda Detrick; © Hal H. Harrison/Grant Heilman Photography, Lititz, Pa. 115: Jerry Pavia (2); Thomas E. Eltzroth. 116: © Saxon Holt; Jerry Pavia; Richard Shiell. 117: Dency Kane; Richard Shiell (2). 118: © Jane Grushow/Grant Heilman Photography, Lititz, Pa.; Dency Kane; © Jim Strawser/Grant Heilman Photography, Lititz, Pa. 119, 120: Jerry Pavia. 121: Thomas E. Eltzroth; Jerry Pavia (2). 122: Dency Kane; Richard Shiell; Michael Dirr. 123: Richard Shiell; Dency Kane; Jerry Pavia. 124: Michael Dirr; Jerry Pavia (2). 125: Michael Dirr; Jerry Pavia (2). 126: Dency Kane; Richard Shiell; Jerry Pavia. 127: Jerry Pavia (2); Joanne Pavia. 128: Jerry Pavia (2); Joanne Pavia. 129: Dency Kane; Jerry Pavia (2). 130: Dency Kane; Deni Bown, Oxford Scientific Films, Long Hanborough, Oxfordshire; Jerry Pavia. 131: Thomas E. Eltzroth; Jerry Pavia; Thomas E. Eltzroth. 132: Jerry Pavia; © R. Todd Davis; Joanne Pavia. 133: Jerry Pavia; Richard Shiell; © R. Todd Davis. 134: Jerry Pavia (2); © R. Todd Davis. 135: C. Colston Burrell; Jerry Pavia (2). 136: Jerry Pavia; © Lefever/Grushow/Grant Heilman Photography, Lititz, Pa.; Jerry Pavia. 137: Dency Kane; © R. Todd Davis; Jerry Pavia. 138: Richard Shiell; Jerry Pavia (2). 139: Richard Shiell (2); © Grant Heilman/Grant Heilman Photography, Lititz, Pa. 140: Jerry Pavia. 141: Richard Shiell; Jerry Pavia (2). 142: Jerry Pavia (2); Dency Kane. 143: Jerry Pavia (2); Dency Kane. 144: Richard Shiell; © R. Todd Davis; Michael Dirr. 145: Jerry Pavia; © Alan and Linda Detrick; Joanne Pavia. 146: C. Colston Burrell; Jerry Pavia (2). 147: Jerry Pavia; Thomas E. Eltzroth (2). 148: Jerry Pavia; Dency Kane; © Jane Grushow/Grant Heilman Photography, Lititz, Pa. 149: Richard Shiell; © R. Todd Davis; © Runk/Schoenberger/Grant Heilman Photography, Lititz, Pa.

Bibliography

BOOKS:

All about Landscaping. San Ramon, Calif.: Ortho Books, 1988.

Better Homes and Gardens® Step-by-Step Landscaping. Des Moines: Meredith® Books, 1991.

Boisset, Caroline. *Vertical Gardening.* New York: Weidenfeld & Nicolson, 1988.

Breskend, Jean Spiro. *Backyard Design.* Boston: Little, Brown, 1991.

Brookes, John. *The Book of Garden Design.* New York: Macmillan, 1991.

Carr, Anna. *Rodale's Color Handbook of Garden Insects.* Emmaus, Pa.: Rodale Press, 1979.

Church, Thomas D. *Gardens Are for People.* New York: Reinhold Publishing, 1995.

Clausen, Ruth Rogers, and Nicolas H. Ekstrom. *Perennials for American Gardens.* New York: Random House, 1989.

Cox, Jeff. *Landscaping with Nature.* Emmaus, Pa.: Rodale Press, 1991.

Creative Home Landscaping. San Francisco: Ortho Books, 1987.

Crowe, Sylvia. *Garden Design* (3d ed.). Wappingers' Falls, N.Y.: Garden Art Press, 1994.

Dirr, Michael A. *Manual of Woody Landscape Plants* (4th ed., rev.). Champaign, Ill.: Stipes Publishing, 1990.

Douglas, William Lake. *Hillside Gardening.* Stamford, Conn.: Longmeadow Press, 1993.

Ellefson, Connie Lockhart, Thomas L. Stephens, and Doug Welsh. *Xeriscape Gardening.* New York: Macmillan, 1992.

Erler, Catriona Tudor:
  The Garden Problem Solver. New York: Simon & Schuster, 1994.
  Trees and Shrubs. (Better Homes and Gardens® Step-by-Step Successful Gardening series). Des Moines: Meredith® Books, 1995.

Erler, Catriona Tudor, and Derek Fell. *550 Home Landscaping Ideas.* New York: Simon & Schuster, 1991.

Ferguson, Nicola. *Right Plant, Right Place.* New York: Simon & Schuster, 1984.

Flemer, William, III. *Trees in Color.* New York: Grosset & Dunlap, 1965.

Frey, Susan Rademacher, and Barbara W. Ellis. *Outdoor Living Spaces.* Emmaus, Pa.: Rodale Press, 1992.

Grant, John A., and Carol L. Grant. *Trees and Shrubs for Pacific Northwest Gardens* (2d ed., rev.). Portland, Ore.: Timber Press, 1990.

Hill, Lewis. *Pruning Simplified* (Garden Way Publishing). Pownal, Vt.: Storey Communications, 1986.

Ingels, Jack E. *Landscaping: Principles and Practices* (4th ed.). Albany, N.Y.: Delmar Publishers, 1992.

Jelitto, Leo, and Wilhelm Schacht. *Hardy Herbaceous Perennials* (Vol. 2, 3d ed., rev.). Translated by Michael E. Epp. Portland, Ore.: Timber Press, 1990.

Johnson, Warren T., and Howard H. Lyon. *Insects That Feed on Trees and Shrubs* (2d ed., rev.). Ithaca, N.Y.: Cornell University Press, 1994.

Landscape Plans. Ramon, Calif.: Ortho Books, 1989.

Landscaping Illustrated (Sunset Books). Menlo Park, Calif.: Lane Publishing, 1984.

Leighton, Phebe, and Calvin Simonds. *The New American Landscape Gardener.* Emmaus, Pa.: Rodale Press, 1987.

Lerner, Joel. *Home Landscaping Ideas.* Los Angeles: Price Stern Sloan, 1988.

Lisney, Adrian, and Ken Fieldhouse. *Landscape Design Guide:*
  Soft Landscape (Vol. 1). Brookfield, Vt.: Gower Publishing, 1990.
  Hard Landscape (Vol. 2). Brookfield, Vt.: Gower, 1990.

Loewer, Peter. *The New Small Garden.* Mechanicsburg, Pa.: Stackpole Books, 1994.

Macunovich, Janet. *Easy Garden Design* (Garden Way Publishing). Pownal, Vt.: Storey Communications, 1993.

Messervy, Julie Moir. *The Inward Garden.* Boston: Little, Brown, 1995.

The Ortho Home Gardener's Problem Solver. San Ramon, Calif.: Ortho Books, 1993.

Pleasant, Barbara:
  The Gardener's Bug Book. Pownal, Vt.: Storey Communications, 1995.
  The Gardener's Guide to Plant Diseases. Pownal, Vt.: Storey Communications, 1995.

Reid, Grant W. *From Concept to Form in Landscape Design.* New York: Van Nostrand Reinhold, 1993.

Robinson, Nick. *The Planting Design Handbook.* Brookfield, Vt.: Gower Publishing, 1992.

Rose, Graham. *The Small Garden Planner.* New York: Simon & Schuster, 1987.

Smith, Ken. *Home Landscaping in the Northeast and Midwest.* Tucson, Ariz.: HPBooks, 1985.

Springer, Lauren. *The Undaunted Garden.* Golden, Colo.: Fulcrum Publishing, 1994.

Stevens, David. *The Outdoor Room: Garden Design for Living.* New York: Random House, 1994.

Stiles, David, and Jeanie Stiles. *Garden Projects You Can Build.* Shelburne, Vt.: Chapters Publishing, 1995.

Still, Steven M. *Manual of Herbaceous Ornamental Plants* (4th ed.). Champaign, Ill.: Stipes Publishing, 1994.

Strong, Roy. *Creating Formal Gardens.* Boston: Little, Brown, 1989.

Thomas, Graham Stuart. *Ornamental Shrubs, Climbers, and Bamboos.* Portland, Ore.: Timber Press, 1992.

Western Garden Book (Sunset Books). Menlo Park, Calif.: Sunset Publishing, 1995.

Williams, Robin. *Garden Design.* Pleasantville, N.Y.: Reader's Digest Association, 1995.

Wyman, Donald. *Wyman's Gardening Encyclopedia* (2d ed.). New York: Macmillan, 1986.

Yang, Linda. *The City Gardener's Handbook.* New York: Random House, 1990.

Zucker, Isabel. *Flowering Shrubs and Small Trees.* Revised and expanded by Derek Fell. New York: Grove Weidenfeld, 1990.

PERIODICALS:

Braun-Kenisberg, Lisa. "Landscaping by Computer." *Washington Home* (*Washington Post* magazine), April 7, 1994.

"Design with a Camera." *Garden Gate.* April/May 1995.

Dubé, Richard L. "Natural Inspirations." *American Horticulturist,* December 1994.

Helliwell, Rodney. "The Patterns of Nature." *Landscape Design,* May 1993.

"How to Prune Everything." *Woman's Day Gardening and Outdoor Living Ideas,* Vol. 5, no. 1, 1995.

Raver, Anne. "Step One for a Rustic Trellis: Find Some Woods." *New York Times,* July 9, 1995.

Sorvig, Kim. "The Light Stuff." *American Nurseryman,* July 15, 1995.

Steadman, Todd A. "Site Analysis." *Garden Gate,* n.d.

OTHER SOURCES:

"American Cottage Gardens." *Plants and Gardens, Brooklyn Botanic Record.* Brooklyn, N.Y.: Brooklyn Botanic Garden, 1990.

U

Ulmus: 27, *chart* 107, *chart* 109, *147. See also* Elm
United States: hardiness zones, *map* 108
Utilities: 32, 35

V

Varnish tree: 27, *132. See also Koelreuteria*
Vegetables: *44-45, 52*
Venetian sumac: *chart* 109, *119. See also Cotinus*
Verbascum: 51
Verbena: 87
Veronica: 87
Verticillium wilt: *chart* 103
Viburnum: 85, 94, *chart* 109, *148; carlesii, 148; davidii, chart* 106, 148; *dilatatum,* 83, 148; *plicatum, chart* 105, 148; *setigerum, 148; tinus,* 61
Vinca: 66. See also Periwinkle
Vines: 80, 85, 99
Virgilia: 118. See also Cladrastis
Virginia bluebells: 90
Virginia creeper: 85
Virgin's-bower: *chart* 109, *118. See also Clematis*
Vitex: chart 105, *chart* 109, *148*
Vitis: 69. *See also* Grape

W

Walks: *See* Paths
Wallflower: *42-43,* 51
Walls: *6-7, 10-11,* 13, 14, *18-19, 60-61, 63-64, 81. See also* Fences
Water gardens: *15, 46-47, 53, 71, 72, 73, 74. See also* Streams
Water lily: 15, *72,* 73
Waxberry: *136. See also Myrica*
Wax myrtle: *chart* 109, *136. See also Myrica*
Whitewood: *chart* 109, *133. See also Liriodendron*
Widdy: 140. *See also Potentilla fruticosa*
Wig tree: *chart* 109, *119. See also Cotinus*
Wild China tree: *chart* 109, *144. See also Sapindus*
Wild ginger: *80*

Wild lilac: *116. See also Ceanothus*
Wild orange: *chart* 109, 140. *See also Prunus caroliniana*
Wild pepper: *chart* 109, *148. See also Vitex*
Wild sweet William: *88*
Willow: *chart* 82, 83-84
Wind: 35
Windbreaks: 85
Windflower: 90
Winter begonia: *chart* 109, 114. *See also Bergenia*
Winterberry: *chart* 109, 129
Winter creeper: 63, 85, 87. *See also Euonymus fortunei*
Wintergreen: 87
Wisteria: 10, 18, 20, 69, 85, *chart* 102, *149; floribunda,* 20, *chart* 105, 149; *sinensis,* 50, *149*
Witch alder: 83
Witch hazel: 94, *chart* 109, *126. See also Hamamelis*
Wolfberry: 53
Wormwood: *chart* 109, *112. See also Artemisia*

Y

Yarrow: *50,* 86. *See also Achillea*
Yaupon: 20, *chart* 109, 130. *See also Ilex vomitoria*
Yellowwood: 27, *chart* 109, *118. See also Cladrastis*
Yew: 20, *84, chart* 109, *147. See also Taxus*
Yucca: 6-7, 19, 90, 91, 99, *chart* 109, *149*
Yucca *(Hesperaloe): 91*

Z

Zebra grass: *chart* 109, *136*
Zelkova: 27, *chart* 107, *149*
Zinnia: 66, 88, 93

Other Publications:
THE NEW HOME REPAIR AND IMPROVEMENT
JOURNEY THROUGH THE MIND AND BODY
WEIGHT WATCHERS® SMART CHOICE RECIPE COLLECTION
TRUE CRIME
THE AMERICAN INDIANS
THE ART OF WOODWORKING
LOST CIVILIZATIONS
ECHOES OF GLORY
THE NEW FACE OF WAR
HOW THINGS WORK
WINGS OF WAR
CREATIVE EVERYDAY COOKING
COLLECTOR'S LIBRARY OF THE UNKNOWN
CLASSICS OF WORLD WAR II
TIME-LIFE LIBRARY OF CURIOUS AND UNUSUAL FACTS
AMERICAN COUNTRY
VOYAGE THROUGH THE UNIVERSE
THE THIRD REICH
MYSTERIES OF THE UNKNOWN
TIME FRAME
FIX IT YOURSELF
FITNESS, HEALTH & NUTRITION
SUCCESSFUL PARENTING
HEALTHY HOME COOKING
UNDERSTANDING COMPUTERS
LIBRARY OF NATIONS
THE ENCHANTED WORLD
THE KODAK LIBRARY OF CREATIVE PHOTOGRAPHY
GREAT MEALS IN MINUTES
THE CIVIL WAR
PLANET EARTH
COLLECTOR'S LIBRARY OF THE CIVIL WAR
THE EPIC OF FLIGHT
THE GOOD COOK
WORLD WAR II
THE OLD WEST

For information on and a full description of any of the
Time-Life Books series listed above, please call
1-800-621-7026 or write:
Reader Information
Time-Life Customer Service
P.O. Box C-32068
Richmond, Virginia 23261-2068